Psychoanalytic Theory and Social Work Practice

Treatment Approaches in the Human Services

FRANCIS J. TURNER, EDITOR

FORTHCOMING

Psychoanalytic Theory and Social Work Practice

Herbert S. Strean

THE FREE PRESS
A Division of Macmillan Publishing Co., Inc.
NEW YORK
Collier Macmillan Publishers
LONDON

The Free Press
A Division of Macmillan Publishing Co., Inc.
866 Third Avenue, New York, N.Y. 10022

Collier Macmillan Canada, Ltd.

Library of Congress Catalog Card Number: 79-4281

Printed in the United States of America

printing number

1 2 3 4 5 6 7 8 9 10

Library of Congress Cataloging in Publication Data

Strean, Herbert S
    Psychoanalytic theory and social work practice.

    (Treatment approaches in the human services)
    1. Social service. 2. Psychoanalysis.
I. Title. II. Series.
HV41.S825   1979   361'.001'9   79-4281
ISBN 0-02-932220-0

To Reuben Fine, Ph.D.

*in gratitude for his courage, creativity,
and human kindness*

Contents

Foreword

"Treatment Approaches in the Human Services" is the first series of professional texts to be prepared under the general auspices of social work. It is understandable that the editor and authors of this endeavor should be enthusiastic about its quality and prospects. But it is equally understandable that our enthusiasm is tempered with caution and prudence. There is a presumptuousness in attempting to be on the leading edge of thinking and aspiring to break new ground, and our professional experience urges us to be restrained.

The first suggestion for this series came from the editorial staff of the Free Press in the spring of 1975. At that time, the early responses to *Social Work Treatment** were available. It was clear from the responses that, useful as that book appeared to be, there was a wish and a need for more detail on each of the various thought systems covered, especially as regards their direct practice implications. These comments led to a proposal from the Free Press that a series be developed that would expand the content of the individual chapters of *Social Work Treatment* into full-length books with the objective of providing a richer and fuller exposition of each system. This idea is still germane to the series, but with the emergence of new thought systems and theories it has moved beyond the notion of expanding the chapters in the original collection. New thinking in the helping profes-

*Francis J. Turner, ed., *Social Work Treatment* (New York: Free Press, 1974).

sions, the diversity of new demands, and the complexity of these demands have increased beyond the expectations of even the harbingers of the knowledge explosion of the early 1970s. No profession can or should stand still, and thus no professional literature can be static. It is our hope that this series will stay continuously current as it takes account of new ideas emerging from practice.

By design, this series has a strong orientation to social work. But it is not designed for social workers alone; it is also intended to be useful to our colleagues in other professions. The point has frequently been made that much of the conceptual base of social work practice has been borrowed and that social work has made few original contributions to other professions. That is no longer true. A principal assumption of this series is that social work must now accept the responsibility for making available to other professions its rich accumulation of theoretical concepts and therapeutic strategies.

The responsibility to share does not presume that professions with a healing and human-development commitment are moving to some commonality of identity and structure. In the next decade, we are probably going to see clearer rather than more obscure professional identities and more rather than less precise professional boundaries, derived not from different knowledge bases but from differential use of shared knowledge. If this prediction is valid, it follows that each profession must develop increased and enriched ways of making available to other professions its own expanding knowledge of the human condition.

Although the books in this series are written from the viewpoint of the clinician, they will be useful for the student-professional, the senior scholar, and the teacher of professionals as well. On the principle that no dynamic profession can tolerate division among its practitioners, theory builders, and teachers, each book is intended to be a bridging resource between practice and theory development. In directing this series to colleagues whose principal targets of practice are individuals, families, and groups, we take the other essential fields of practice as given.

Thus the community-development, social-action, policy, research, and service-delivery roles of the helping professions are not specifically addressed in these books.

One of the risks of living and practicing in an environment characterized by pluralism in professions, practice styles, and theoretical orientations is that one may easily become doctrinaire in defending a particular perspective. Useful and important as is ongoing debate that leads to clarification of similarities and differences, overlaps and gaps in thought systems and theories, the authors of these books have been asked to minimize this function. That is, they are to analyze the conceptual base of their particular topic, identify its theoretical origins, and explain and describe its operationalization in practice, but avoid polemics in behalf of "their" system. Inevitably, some material of this type is needed for comparisons, but the aim is to make the books explicative rather than argumentative.

Although the series has a clear focus and explicit objectives, there is also a strong commitment that it be marked with a quality of development and evolution. It is hoped that we shall be responsive to changes in psychotherapeutic practice and to the needs of colleagues in practice and thus be ready to alter the format of subsequent books as may be necessary.

In a similar way, the ultimate number of books in the series has been left open. Viewing current practice in the late 1970s, it is possible to identify a large number of influential thought systems that need to be addressed. We can only presume that additional perspectives will emerge in the future. These will be addressed as the series continues, as will new developments or reformulations of existing practice perspectives.

The practice of psychotherapy and the wide spectrum of activities that it encompasses is a risky and uncertain endeavor. Clearly, we are just beginning a new era of human knowledge and improved clinical approaches and methods. At one time we were concerned because we knew so little; now we are concerned to use fully the rich progress that has been made in research, practice, and conceptualization. This series is dedicated to that task in the humble hope that it will contribute to man's concern for his fellows.

A compelling argument could be made that Dr. Herbert Strean's book on psychoanalytic theory might be considered as the touchstone for this series. I state this because of the impact of Freudian-based thinking on social work practice over the last six decades, an impact that has not been restricted to social work only but has touched all helping professions. Expecially in North America social workers have long been identified with psychoanalytic thinking. As early as the 1920's practitioners and educators were drawing heavily on this school of thought as a basis for a diagnostic understanding of clients.

Unlike other thought systems influencing contemporary psychotherapy, the psychoanalytic school of thought has few if any practitioners today that are neutral about its effect. Indeed, it is quite feasible to develop an approach to classifying therapists by examining the perspective of their viewpoint, positive or negative, toward psychoanalysis. The importance of this school is still the base for ongoing dispute, but it is interesting to observe that even the most vocal of the anti-analysis group has incorporated many of the analytic insights and concepts about human behavior into its viewpoint.

Because it is yet fashionable to be anti-Freudian, Dr. Strean will undoubtedly be challenged for the strong position he takes concerning the importance of this school for current social work practice. But in spite of this critical trend, it is also clear that the psychoanalytic school is not on the wane. In fact, now that the anti-Freudian fad is diminishing in intensity, a new appreciation of its rich insights into human behavior, the subtle role of the unconscious in client functioning, and the therapeutically critical function of transference are taking place.

Dr. Strean suggests that because of the impact of the many newer therapies there are fewer adherents to this school of thought than in any other time in social work's history. This may be so, although I question it! But whether so or not, in either case the importance of this perspective of the human condition remains.

In his first chapter, Dr. Strean describes in a clear and succinct manner the various shifts and developments, the highs and lows that have marked the spectrum of influence of this school on practice. The low point was reached in the 1970s when psychoanalysis became the "scapegoat for the profession." He then proceeds to argue that, as a principal theme, much of the criticism of this thought system is related to an incomplete mastery of the theory and a correlative misapplication of the basic concepts.

This book should serve as an important text in reducing some of this misunderstanding by skillfully demonstrating the essential relevance of a correct perception of psychoanalytic thinking to current practice. It is also an important book because of its unfashionable yet forthright and valuable insistence on the necessity for making a psychoanalytic understanding of man the basis for psychotherapeutic practice in social work.

FRANCIS J. TURNER

Preface

This book arises out of an effort to make psychoanalysis intelligible to the social work student and to the social work practitioner. Although virtually every social worker has been exposed to facets of Freud's discoveries, there has been no systematic attempt in social work to bring together his major propositions on personality functioning and therapy and to demonstrate their applicability to social work practice. This book is an attempt to fill this void.

While most social workers would agree that the practitioner needs to know more than psychoanalytic theory to be effective as a therapist—he also needs to master dimensions of system theory, role theory, and ego psychology, to name but a few of the resources the worker should have—this book takes the position that certain psychoanalytic concepts should be part of every social worker's professional armamentarium. Regardless of the unit of treatment (individual, dyad, family, or group) and regardless of the setting in which he practices, every social worker should understand the unconscious meaning of the client's problems and behavior, be sensitive to how the client's history is recapitulated in the present, note how the client copes with anxiety and how he defends himself from inner and outer danger. Furthermore, the social work practitioner should be aware of how the client unconsciously experiences the therapist (transference) and how, on his part, he subjectively experiences the client (countertransference). In the ensuing pages, my aim is to demonstrate how these and other psychoanalytic concepts can be integrated into all social work methods and all fields of practice.

It is assumed that the reader has some familiarity with Freudian theory and that he has at least skimmed such books as Freud's *Collected Papers,* Brenner's *Elementary Textbook of Psychoanalysis,* Anna Freud's *Ego and the Mechanisms of Defense,* and Fenichel's *Psychoanalytic Theory of Neuroses.* Although every psychoanalytic concept used in this book is defined and illustrated by a case example, some familiarity with this literature will be helpful.

I am very grateful to Dr. Francis Turner, dean of the Wilfrid Laurier School of Social Work and editor of the series of which this book is a part, for his encouragement and constructive criticism. I would also like to thank Mrs. Gladys Topkis, senior editor at the Free Press, for her helpful suggestions. Finally, thanks are due to my wife, Marcia, and our sons, Richard and Billy, for their forebearance and understanding during the writing of this book.

HERBERT S. STREAN

Chapter 1

Social Work and Psychoanalysis: An Overview

In the middle of his career Sigmund Freud, the founder of psychoanalysis, pointed out that as a theory of the mental unconscious, psychoanalysis could become "indispensable to all of the sciences which are concerned with the evolution of human civilization and its major institutions." The hypothesis that there were unconscious mental processes, he felt certain, "paves the way to a decisive new orientation in the world and in science." Freud never claimed that psychoanalysis provided a complete theory of the human being, but "only expected that what it offered should be applied to supplement and correct knowledge" acquired by other means (Freud, 1953a).

Psychoanalysis as a theory of personality, a form of psychotherapy, and a methodological procedure in research has been applied in sociology, psychology, politics, history, and many other disciplines. More and more, psychoanalysis is becoming a home for all of the social sciences (Fine, 1975).

But applying the insights of psychoanalysis to another discipline involves several problems. Psychoanalysts and other professionals as well sometimes fail to recognize that it takes many years of rigorous training and personal analysis to master the

1

theory and practice of psychoanalysis so that it can be used expertly and confidently. Even when one elects to become a psychoanalyst, there are resistances to resolve and obstacles to overcome. Freud pointed out that anyone who is familiar with the nature of neurosis "will not be astonished to hear that even a man who is very well able to carry out analysis upon others can behave like any other mortal and be capable of producing resistances as soon as he himself becomes the object of analytic investigation" (Freud, 1949).

When the non-analyst attempts to incorporate parts of psychoanalysis into his occupational armamentarium he can also experience violent "resistances." Notions such as the Oedipal conflict or the castration complex can induce anxiety, and certain treatment concepts (e.g., the therapist's passivity) can appear very frustrating to a practitioner who likes to be an active conversant with his clients. Furthermore, introducing psychoanalysis to the non-analyst is more difficult to do today than it has been in any other era, with the possible exception of the early 1900s. As a variety of symptom-oriented therapies have been instituted—sex therapy, couple therapy, behavior modification, transactional analysis, and other therapies that have not been thoroughly evaluated (Greenhill, 1976)—psychoanalysis has become less attractive and in some cases has been totally repudiated. Former Freudian believers are now busy looking for less time-consuming, less expensive, healing techniques and some claim that they have succeeded. Proponents of primal therapy have "discovered" what Freud called "catharsis" eighty years ago. Behaviorists, while touting "conditioning," apparently have ignored such important dimensions of therapy as "working through" and "synthesis." Sensitivity and encounter movement enthusiasts would have us believe that "confrontation" never existed until they came on the scene. Advocates of many of these therapies seem to feel that instant character, like instant coffee, can be marketed through moral suasion and physical exhaustion (Shapiro, 1976).

Social workers have been very much influenced by these newer therapies. Whereas from the 1920s to the 1950s social work practice and education drew their major theoretical sustenance from Freudian psychology, today many have rejected psychoanalysis (Fischer, 1975; Briar and Miller, 1971). There are fewer Freudian adherents in social work today than at any other time since the profession's formal inception, and the new therapies are one of the major reasons for the declining popularity of psychoanalysis in social work practice and education.

In order to understand the rise and fall of Freudianism in social work, it will be helpful to review the history of social work's relationship to psychoanalysis.

The First Encounter

When social work emerged as a profession in United States, Canada, and England at the turn of the twentieth century, its major goal was to "elevate the poor" (Richmond, 1917). Although avowing in theory that a "compassionate" attitude was necessary, the social workers who dealt with the poor often took a harsh stance toward them (Hellenbrand, 1972). One of the pioneers in social work, Josephine Shaw, is quoted as saying: "The necessary relief should be surrounded by circumstances that shall not only repel everyone not in extremity from accepting it but . . . discipline and education should be inseparably associated with any system of public relief" (Pumphrey, 1956). Social workers frequently viewed the relationship between the "friendly visitor" and the client as that of benefactor to inferior. The visitor was to have "uncompromising insistence" on desirable changes to be effected.

Mary Richmond, who wrote the first textbook on social work (*Social Diagnosis,* 1917), tried to infuse warmth and sensitivity as well as an orderly and scientific perspective into agency practice. She emphasized that each case should be individualized and advocated a sympathetic relationship between the friendly visitor and client. Her book was a sociological attempt to locate the causes of the client's plight in an understanding of the transactions between the client and his or her reference groups. Much of the social worker's activity at that time involved intervention in the client's environment. The worker's direct work with clients consisted primarily of advice and moral suasion.

The friendly visitor of the 1920s soon recognized that manipulating the environment of a client or giving advice rarely altered a shaky self-image, a punitive conscience, or self-destructive behavior. The social worker needed a theory that not only would provide some understanding of the social forces contributing to the client's maladjustment but would also consider such crucial intervening variables as the client's motives, affects, anxieties, coping capacities, defenses, conscience, and personal history. Psychoanalysis was the answer, and its founder believed that with certain modifications the classical analytic treatment model could be applied to social work's modal client, the poor man or woman:

> One may reasonably expect that at some time or other the conscience of the community will awake and admonish it that the poor man has just as much right to help for his mind as he now has for the surgeon's means for saving his life. . . . Possibly we may often be able to achieve something if we combine aid to the mind with material support. (Freud, 1950)

Freud's theory refocused the social worker's lens from poverty to the person who is poor, from social problems like desertion and alcoholism to the individuals who are beset with them. Psychoanalytic theory helped transform a one-dimensional moralistic approach to human beings in trouble into a nonjudgmental psychosocial process. Incorporating the notion of the unconscious into diagnostic and therapeutic plans encouraged social workers to be less self-righteous with their clients. Recognizing that unconscious forces stimulated maladaptive behavior, they could take a more realistic view of the human being and be more compassionate as he or she struggled with inner and outer forces. Barely two years had passed since the publication of Richmond's *Social Diagnosis* when it was clearly determined by rediagnosing her cases that at least 50 percent of them presented psychological problems (Hellenbrand, 1972).

The social worker of the late 1920s also looked to Freudian psychology for other purposes. In contrast to some of the concepts that were in vogue at the time—Adlerian psychology, Gestalt theory, and behaviorism—psychoanalysis could demonstrate how the client's past experience was a major contributor to present malfunctioning. Most social workers since the 1920s have made use of the client's history as they assess personal and interpersonal pathology and plan intervention. They have realized that the same kind of attachments to parents and significant others that were experienced in the past are constantly sought in the present, even if these attachments bring disappointing consequences.

Psychoanalytic theory cast light on the relationship between the social worker and client as the earlier managerial, "no nonsense" practitioner was replaced by an empathetic, permissive worker whose role was to help clients achieve greater understanding and mastery of their difficulties. By the late 1920s social workers' use of psychoanalytic theory was helping them make more comprehensive diagnostic assessments. The theory forced them to realize that not only poverty but individuals' prohibitive superegos, weak ego functions, and unresolved infantile wishes were major etiological factors in their psychosocial problems. Psychoanalytic theory helped social workers to recognize how individual suffering can gratify unconscious wishes, such as the need for punishment or masochistic fantasies.

By the 1930s, Freudian psychoanalysis was being utilized by most social workers. Though its insights were often startling and frightening, it had a humanizing effect on much of social work practice.

The Relationship Between Psychoanalysis and Social Work Grows

One of the effects of the Depression was to bring social workers clients from many walks of life, including many who were not unlike the social workers themselves in background and aspirations. Work with these clients helped practitioners to appreciate the universality of such phenomena as injured narcissism, anxiety, defensiveness over sex and aggression, unconscious guilt, and interpersonal conflict. During the 1930s and 1940s, social workers turned to Freudian psychoanalysis for therapeutic procedures to help clients resolve some of these problems.

A psychoanalytic notion that was extremely helpful in treatment was the notion of "transference": a client's tendency to ascribe to a social worker character traits and attitudes that had been held by significant others in his or her past. As social workers began to comprehend why clients' love, hatred, or ambivalence toward them was a distorted expression of certain problems and immature wishes, they could understand, and help clients to understand, how they distorted their perceptions of others.

Psychoanalysis enabled social workers to better understand why some clients improved quickly while others did not change or even regressed. The concept of "resistance"—the individual's means of coping with anxiety by refusing to understand himself or change the status quo—helped social workers to appreciate how difficult it is to make alterations in one's personal and interpersonal life. "Resistance" helped the social worker understand why advice was frequently not taken, interpretations not heard, and environmental assistance repudiated. Psychoanalysis also provided procedures for helping clients resolve their resistances to change: They were encouraged to abreact important memories and feelings, including forbidden sexual and aggressive wishes.

Another therapeutic insight adopted by social workers from psychoanalysis during the 1940s was the notion of the "corrective emotional experience." Sensitizing themselves to a client's perceptions of significant others—particularly those that interfered with self-image, self-esteem, and interpersonal functioning—social workers attempted to conduct themselves in interviews in a manner that enabled a client to have a new experience with an authority figure. For those clients who were deprived of limits in their pasts, the social worker provided limits and structure in the treatment. For those clients who had experienced punitive attitudes and behavior from parents, the social worker was benign, friendly, and permissive.

Writing in the 1940s, Garrett (1940) pointed out that Freudian theory changed Richmond's social diagnosis and social treatment into a psychosocial diagnosis and psychosocial treatment. The social worker, by adapting Freudian theory to practice, could now individualize each person-situation contellation, recognizing not only that external phenomena like unemployment and illness cause stress but that each individual reacts to crises in an idiosyncratic way. Furthermore, Freudian psychoanalysis helped the social worker realize that each individual, with a unique past and unique strengths and weaknesses, determines in many ways what happens to him or her in day-to-day functioning. By the 1940s many of the therapeutic procedures of psychoanalysis such as clarification, confrontation, and interpretation were being used to assist clients in understanding themselves and achieving better mastery of their lives.

Freud also had a radical effect on social work education. Starting in the mid-1930s and continuing until the late 1950s, courses in dynamic psychology, largely based on Freudian concepts, began to be required of all social work students. Students were involved emotionally in the learning process, and self-awareness was considered a crucial dimension in learning. Freudian theory was frequently utilized to resolve problems between student and fieldwork instructor by subjecting transference and countertransference reactions to mutual examination. During the 1930s and 1940s, class and fieldwork were more concerned with stimulating emotional sensitivity in students than with developing their intellectual and critical capacities. Sometimes fieldwork instructors and classroom teachers confused instruction with personal therapy.

Social Workers Become More Discriminating in Using Psychoanalysis

During the 1930s and 1940s, social workers applied to practice those dimensions of psychoanalytic theory that were primarily concerned with libidinal and aggressive drives. Many of them were not sensitized to the notion that making a client aware of his drives could induce anxiety. Defenses such as denial, projection, and repression were needed by the client to ward off the inevitable discomfort when a forbidden impulse reached consciousness. Consequently, many errors in practice occurred because workers did not always appreciate the protective function of defenses.

By the 1950s social workers had learned that the client's defenses often had to be supported and his or her resistances to change respected. As workers focused more on the client's ego functions, particularly the defenses, it became clear that passivity, permissiveness, and therapeutic neutrality were not always helpful, but could be hurtful to some clients. Sometimes it was appropriate to reinforce and support certain behaviors, and at other times it was important to advise the client not to act in a self-destructive manner. Utilizing some of the work of Erik Erikson (1950), who focused on interactional and transactional processes that transpire between the individual and significant others, social workers brought the "social" back to their profession. Erikson's work emphasized that individuals can never be separated from their social milieu when they are diagnostically assessed and treatment is planned for and with them.

In contrast to the earlier overemphasis on internal and instinctual conflicts, in the 1950s social workers began to view the human being as an open system that interacted with many surrounding systems. As a result of refocusing on the client's environment, social workers became interested in wider units of diagnostic and therapeutic attention such as dyads, families, and small groups. They began to think about how people develop in the "average expectable environment" (Hartmann, 1961), how interpersonal relationships evolve, what is the "good enough mother" (Winnicott, 1965), and how the social context can define, exacerbate, or lessen conflict (Stein and Cloward, 1958).

During the 1950s the concept of ego-supportive therapy became quite popular in social work practice (Bandler, 1963).

Rather than constantly making a client aware of conflicts, the social worker began to plan systematically to reinforce workable ego capacities. As the social worker was turning more to the client's ego functioning and ego defects (Turner, 1963), teaching in social work also became more "ego-centered" (Bandler, 1963).

Thus the social worker began to understand that many marital relationships are established to escape anxiety and that the marital partner or the children may serve the purpose of saving the individual from neurotic or psychotic breakdown; or the family as a whole may serve as a bastion against strains and uphold the weak ego of one of its members (Hamilton, 1958). The social worker in the 1950s also learned how to recognize certain differentials in clinical diagnoses—such as psychoneuroses, psychoses, and character disorders—and in treatment methods appropriate for adults and children. In relating to psychotic clients the social worker learned how to support certain functions of the ego by understanding the meaning of hallucinations and delusions (Federn, 1952).

It has been suggested (Hamilton, 1958) that the experience of this period enabled social workers to rediscover those inner resources of the personality to which social work had always been attuned. They integrated the notion that capacity for social functioning continues to develop of its own accord if one can succeed in bringing a troubled person back into social reality to take an active part in it.

Social Work and Psychoanalysis Become Alienated

During the 1960s and into the late 1970s, many factors coalesced to cause social work to move away from psychoanalysis.

As workers concentrated more on the client's ego, particularly its relationship with external reality, their focus on diagnostic and therapeutic attention was considerably altered. More and more they became interested not just in the internal functioning of the individual but in the interactive processes of parent-child and marital dyads, family units, small groups, and communities. As workers became involved with helping clients feel more competent and comfortable in their various roles—as, for example, the interaction of a marital couple was explored rather than just the motives that accounted for the spouses' behavior—the importance of the unconscious receded into the background. Feeling that the client's social context was an extremely important ingredient in determining how and why he or she functioned in a certain way, social workers paid less attention to the diagnosis and treatment of individuals and more to the diagnosis and treatment of dyads, families, and groups. Rather than using the insights of psychoanalysis as theoretical underpinning, they felt that the interactions and transactions of the client could best be understood by applying system theory, role theory, communication theory, and learning theory to their work.

The knowledge explosion of the 1960s stimulated more schools of social work to inaugurate doctoral programs and encouraged many students, practitioners, and academicians to experiment with new social science perspectives that could illuminate dimensions of the client's life that had been explored by psychoanalysis in only a limited way. For example, problems of social stratification, role conflicts, and the agency as a social system were notions that psychoanalysis could only partially explain.

The wider culture of the 1920s had emphasized introspection and self-sufficiency. Consequently, psychoanalytic theory was compatible with the major ethos of the time. However, the 1960s was a time when looking outward was a dominant theme, and social workers refocused their lens on such issues as the War on Poverty, the community mental health movement, the domestic Peace Corps, and Vietnam. Psychoanalysis, with its focus on fantasies, dreams, childhood history, defenses, and anxiety, did not appear to provide much help for the social worker whose goal was to curb poverty in a community, reduce apathy in a suburb where he wanted to start a community health center, or meet the economic, social, and psychological needs of a whole tenement of welfare clients. The social sciences seemed much more pertinent.

As social problems like racism and civil injustice emerged as crucial to the profession in the 1960s and 1970s, social planning became much more prestigious within social work, and clinicians were less valued. Many clinicians started their own professional organizations because they felt that national social work organizations were not paying sufficient attention to their interests; others left social work and went into allied professions. With the status of the clinician devalued, psychoanalysis lost a great deal of its attractiveness to many social workers.

During this period psychoanalysis served as a scapegoat for the profession. Most of the maladies that were charged to social work were blamed on its close affiliation with psychoanalysis. It was alleged that social work's tie to psychoanalysis for four decades had stifled social reform, leading the profession away from addressing social problems with concern and competence (Borenzweig, 1971). Many authors argued that social work's "disengagement from the poor" and its preference for middle-class clients were results of the profession's preoccupation with the human being's internal life and its preference for the verbal techniques of psychoanalysis (Riessman, Cohen, and Pearl, 1964; Miller, 1961). Research that pointed to the ineffectiveness of social work intervention ascribed the failure to social work's tie to psychoanalysis (Fischer, 1976; Briar and Miller, 1971). It was claimed that families were not helped (Ackerman, 1958), children were insensitively placed in institutions and foster homes (Mahoney and Mahoney, 1974), and environmental factors were overlooked in assessing clients' problems (Pincus and Minahan, 1971)—all because social work utilized psychoanalysis as theoretical underpinning for its diagnostic and therapeutic efforts.

The 1960s and 1970s have been described as years when people were very much interested in instant gratification. Swinging, switching, and other forms of sexual gratification influenced the therapeutic community. Sensitivity groups that championed touching and other forms of sexual foreplay, nude encounter groups, and group therapy that prescribed sexual relations among its members all came into vogue, and many social workers endorsed these behaviors and forms of therapy. Obviously psychoanalysis, which prescribes frustration tolerance, introspection, and self-understanding, was the antithesis of what was culturally in style—instant gratification, looking outward, and manipulating others to gain personal satisfaction.

A therapeutic modality that competed very successfully with psychoanalysis was behavior modification. This therapy, in contrast to psychoanalysis, emphasizes behavioral manipulation rather than self-understanding and symptom relief rather than the importance of feelings, thoughts, fantasies, human aspirations, and human relationships. It became one of the most popular orientations among social work practitioners, educators, and students. Many of the tenets of behavior modification appear in task-oriented casework, crisis intervention, and marital and sexual counseling.

Unresolved Problems in Applying Psychoanalysis to Social Work

One of the major difficulties for social workers in applying psychoanalytic theory (or any theory) to their profession has been a vagueness as to just what social work is. Social work has been called an art by some and a science by others. A few writers have perceived it as a semiprofession, while others are adamant in the view that it is a full-fledged profession. A few social work scholars have contended that social work should serve the "normal" as well as the disadvantaged (Kahn, 1973), while others have argued that social work should be concerned exclusively with those who are in distress (Witmer, 1942).

While perhaps the majority of social workers have a perspective on the human being and his or her social environment as a field of interacting forces, and see the focus of their professional activities as the person-in-his-situation (Hamilton, 1958; Hollis, 1972), there is a rich diversity of opinions about how people should be helped. In casework there is the "psychosocial" school (Hollis, 1972), which synthesizes contributions from system theory and ego psychology as well as certain dimensions of psychoanalysis: an understanding of certain aspects of the unconscious, including transference and resistance, and the influence of the client's history on current functioning. In rather sharp contrast to the psychosocial perspective is the behavior-modification orientation (Thomas, 1971), which virtually repudiates the notion that the human being has an internal life. The "problem solving" approach in casework combines aspects of ego psychology, role theory, and learning theory, but also tends to negate the unconscious dynamics of the client in its interventive work.

In group work also, some workers assume a therapeutic stance that incorporates aspects of internal mechanisms (Vitner, 1965), while others focus almost exclusively on the here-and-now conscious behavior of clients (Tropp, 1968).

For those social workers who have attempted to integrate psychoanalysis into their practices, at least two major problems still have not been resolved. One is the failure to differentiate the psychoanalytic view of the personality from its treatment model. It is one thing to have a theoretical understanding of the insights of Freud and his followers; it is another thing to apply these insights in diagnosing and treating a client on welfare, a juvenile delinquent, or a patient in a general or mental hospital. Social workers have used notions like fixation, repression, and identification with the aggressor quite profitably, but they have not attempted to rigorously extrapolate from the classical treatment model of psychoanalysis what is and is not applicable to social work practice.

Can one really expect an economically and socially impoverished client whose ego functions are tenuous to "free associate"? Is it not close to preposterous to ask a rebellious juvenile delinquent who is referred for help involuntarily and full of distrust to immediately confide in the social worker?

Psychoanalysts have long recognized that most of their patients when they first appear are very ready to experience their problems as induced by a boss, spouse, or parent. It takes hard work to resolve resistances against looking at fantasies, infantile wishes, and maladaptive defenses. If this is a challenge for an analyst, it is an onerous task for a social worker whose modal client not only heavily resists introspection, but is also realistically handicapped by an impoverished neighborhood, a dilapidated house, overcrowded schools, and sadistic bureaucrats. Where social work has gone wrong with these clients and where psychoanalysis has led them astray is in thinking that the same procedures for treating a middle-class client with a full stomach, an "observing ego," and high motivation can be used in treating a very disturbed individual who is unmotivated and hungry. Fenichel (1945) has presented the example of a patient who was in psychoanalytic treatment five times a week and in every session reported a dream in which he was drinking milk. The analyst found that interpretations of the wish for a mother, and a wish to be fed and nurtured, fell on deaf ears. It was only after the patient was helped to state that he could not afford to eat because all his money was going to the analyst—and only after steps were taken so that he could eat—that progress took place.

To involve many of social work's clients in a therapeutic relationship, it is necessary to first use what the psychoanalyst Kurt Eissler (1965) has called "parameters." For certain clients the first therapeutic requirement is to get them a home, a bed, or food. For certain marital and parent-child problems that can be characterized as symbiotic, the worker must permit the dyad to see the therapist together for a while, since being alone with the therapist activates too much anxiety and the clients flee from treatment.

Many clients in social work come from subcultures in which an office, a waiting room, a desk, scheduled appointments, and verbal introspection are alien. Consequently, it is sometimes necessary to see them in their homes, where they are the host and the worker is the guest. The storefront, the park, or the street may be better milieus than any office.

Psychoanalysis and the Scientific Method

Academicians within social work frequently attack psychoanalysis by raising the issue of the absence of statistical controls and experimentation. As Alexander (1960) has said, psychoanalysis is "a field devoted to the understanding of the most individual features of every person, a field in which differences are in the focus of interest, and a field which shuns the statistical handling of human beings." Even during Freud's pre-psychoanalytic work, the rare fact—even the singular fact—always commanded respect, and impelled as much scientific thinking as the conspicuous statistical sample based on impressive numbers. It has been difficult for social workers to find a middle way between the frequently advocated narrowness of statistical sophistication and the apparent vagueness of psychoanalysis, which accumulates data by introspection and empathy.

In applying psychoanalysis to any field, whether it be social work, political science, or history, one must remember that one is dealing with distinct and separate disciplines. For example, the social worker who is concerned with a social occurrence such as an economic depression must move back and forth between his macroscopic and microscopic lenses. An economic depression is of course independent of a theory of personality. Yet the way in which people respond to such an event is a human problem and to that extent is relevant to psychoanalytic theory (Roazen, 1968).

In order for psychoanalysis to have a positive impact on social work practice, the social worker must be helped to extract from its theoretical, diagnostic, and therapeutic repertoire what is practical and expedient. Continuing experimentation will be required to see what works best and certain ideas that at first seem sound will undoubtedly be deemphasized later as they have in the past.

David Riesman (1958) has said: "Science thrives on sins of omission." And Paul Roazen (1968) states: "The truest test of character is not the mistakes one makes, but what one can do with them." Mistakes have been made in applying psychoanalysis to social work, but we can learn from them.

Plan of the Book

The major goal of this book is to help the social work practitioner and student apply those concepts from psychoanalysis that are most pertinent to his work.

Chapter 2 presents the psychoanalytic view of the personality and discusses how psychoanalysis explains the etiology of neuroses, psychoses, and character disorders.

Chapter 3 reviews and explains the major psychoanalytic treatment concepts such as free association, dream analysis, transference, countertransference, and resistance.

Chapters 4 and 5 demonstrate how certain concepts from psychoanalysis can be applied to the assessment and intervention processes in social work.

In the final chapter, we review some of the research results from psychoanalysis and discuss how certain psychoanalytic procedures can be utilized in social work research.

Chapter 2

The Human Personality

In contrast to other theories of the personality, which explain only fragments of the human being (e.g., learning theory, Rogerian theory, existential theory), Freudian psychoanalysis postulates the principle of *psychic determinism*. This principle holds that in mental functioning nothing happens by chance. Everything a person feels, thinks, fantasies, dreams, and does has a psychological motive. How individuals earn a living, whom they choose to marry, what kind of love they give and receive, how they interact with their children, their friends, and their colleagues, and how much pleasure they extract from work and interpersonal relationships are all motivated by inner *unconscious* forces (Freud, 1939).

Although external factors are always impinging on the human organism, the notions of "psychic determinism" and "the unconscious" help the student of human psychology recognize that the behaviors of individuals, dyads, groups, and organizations not only are reactions to situational variables like family, friends, and neighborhood, but also are shaped by idiosyncratic hopes, wishes, fears, defenses, and ethical imperatives. When a patient complains about an unloving spouse or a provocative child, the analyst's major concerns are to determine what kind of unconscious gratification the patient receives from complaining, and more important, what *inner* forces are responsible for the tempestuous marital or parent-child relationship. Similarly, when an individual expresses fear of or anger toward a boss, the analyst is interested not only in what kind of a person the boss is but also in what gratification the patient receives from this unpleasant relationship.

The psychoanalytic orientation toward the human personality contends that everybody writes a good part of his or her own script and arranges many of his or her own triumphs and failures, disappointments and blissful moments. If a patient is happy or sad, sadistic or masochistic, aggressive or compliant, the psychoanalytically oriented practitioner is interested not just in what the world is doing to the patient, but in how the patient in many ways is arranging to receive such treatment. Thus, when the notions of psychic determinism and the unconscious are used in assessing human behavior, the diagnostician may learn that the husband who constantly complains his wife is asexual wants her to be that way; the parent who is overwhelmed by a child's aggression is provoking it; and the employee who constantly feels rejected by his employer feels that he is unworthy of love from a parental figure.

In presenting his psychoanalytic orientation, Freud saw the human personality from five distinct but intermeshing points of view: the structural, the topographic, the genetic, the dynamic, and the economic (Freud, 1938, 1939). These points of view when combined are called "the metapsychological approach," and all of them are needed to fully comprehend the functioning of the human personality.

The Structural Point of View

According to Freud, the human psyche is comprised of *id, ego,* and *superego*. The id, the most primitive part of the mind and totally unconscious, is the repository of the drives and is concerned with their gratification. The ego, which develops out of experience and reason, is the executive of the personality; it mediates between the inner world of id drives and of superego commands and the demands of the external world. Some of the functions of the ego are judgment, reality testing, frustration tolerance, and relating to others; the ego also erects defenses against anxiety. By assessing a client's ego strengths and weaknesses the therapist can determine how well he or she is adapting, because the more severe the client's disturbances, the less operative are the ego functions and vice versa.

The superego is the judge or censor of the mind, and is essentially the product of interpersonal experiences. It is divided into two parts, the conscience and the ego ideal. The conscience is that part of the superego which forbids and admonishes "Thou shalt not!" while the ego ideal is the storehouse of values, ethical imperatives, and morals. It commands the person in the form of "Thou shalt!"

It is important to keep in mind that the id, ego, and superego never function in isolation, but work interdependently. Therapists sometimes overlook the fact that a patient or client with a punitive and exacting superego may also have strong id wishes, usually of a murderous nature, that cause great anxiety. Rather than constantly live with unbearable anxiety, the individual with unacceptable wishes arranges for the superego to constantly admonish, "Thou shalt not enjoy pleasure!" By staying away from potentially pleasureful situations, the individual does not have to face the murderous and sadistic fantasies that are in conflict with the superego's commands.

An example of the cooperative activity of id, ego, and superego can be seen in waking up in the morning. When the alarm clock goes off, many of us would like to continue to sleep (id wish). However, the superego states, "You must go to work. You are considered bad if you don't!" If we are particularly resentful about getting up and going to work and feel a great deal of contempt toward the boss, these feelings may induce the superego to be very punitive. How the matter gets finally resolved is up to the mediating, judging ego. The ego can renounce the wish to sleep (defense mechanism of repression) and submit to the superego's injunction; we will then get up and go to work. Or the ego may temporarily renounce the superego's pressure and the reality of work and go back to sleep. To appease the superego, we may dream that we are busily at work and the boss is lauding our efforts. However, whether we go to work resentfully or go back to sleep but feel guilty about it, the component parts of the psychic structure are busily at work.

Anybody working with human beings on a therapeutic basis should understand how the id, ego, and superego function. For example, the person seeking help who consistently fails at work or in love relationships usually has unresolved and infantile id wishes for which he is busily punishing himself. These id wishes have to be discussed during therapy so that the patient can see for himself, in the company of a nonpunitive helper, just how and why he is arranging to fail. Problems that individuals bring to therapists—such as parent-child conflict, marital disturbance, family pathology, crime, alcohol or drug addiction, and even poverty—must be appraised in terms of particular id wishes, superego mandates, and ego functions.

Beth, an intelligent seventeen-year-old high school student was referred for professional help because she was failing many of her courses, was feeling very depressed, and was unable to enjoy relationships with her peers.

As Beth was helped to talk about herself in therapy, it became clear to both patient and therapist how Beth was in many ways arranging for her own misery. Beth had strong competitive fantasies about most of her peers, which took the form of her always wanting to be "the one and only"; in addition, she had secret wishes that her peers would die. Her murderous wishes created strong anxiety because they were in conflict with her punitive superego. To Beth, success was experienced as unconsciously gratifying her murderous wishes; consequently, her ego capitulated to the voice of her superego and she punished herself by failing at school.

As psychoanalysts observed their patients with greater precision—adults and children—they began to conceptualize the ego not only as a mediator but as a psychic structure that had autonomy and power of its own (A. Freud, 1937; Erikson, 1950; Hartmann, 1951). Further psychoanalytic research revealed that the ego's power arises primarily from the development of "secondary processes": locomotion, cognition, memory, perception, and rational thought and action.

Once the ego was considered as more than a mediator—by the late 1940s and early 1950s—psychoanalysts became much more interested in their patients' strengths as well as their neurotic difficulties. In their diagnostic assessments psychoanalysts now try to determine what gives the patient mature pleasure, what parts of the psyche are *not* involved in conflict, and which dimensions of the personality do *not* need to be modified. The psychoanalyst asks, for example, "Have the ego's defenses been over-developed?" "Is the patient's social situation such that these defenses are necessary adaptations to the environment—for example, a decrepit ghetto?"

THE EGO AND DEFENSES

One of the most important ego functions to which the psychoanalyst gives much attention, is how the patient defends against anxiety. When an impulse such as a sexual wish or an aggressive desire is activated, and the person feels that further acknowledgment of the impulse will conflict with ethical mandates or other superego commands, he or she erects defenses against experiencing the impulses.

Whenever the ego senses that acting on an impulse or even just feeling it will create danger, the ego produces anxiety. The anxiety serves as a *signal* of the impending danger and is able to offer opposition to the emergence of unacceptable impulses. Such opposition is referred to as *defense*, or as the defensive operation of the ego (Brenner, 1955).

A defense mechanism that Freud recognized early in his career is *repression*. Repressive activity bars the id impulse that creates anxiety from consciousness so that in the individual's conscious life the forbidden id wish does not exist. The repressed impulse, e.g., sexual or aggressive desire, constantly seeks discharge, while the ego tries to maintain the repression by a constant expenditure of psychic energy. As is true of any defense mechanism, repression is an unconscious process. One is never consciously of repressing something.

Reaction formation is a mechanism whereby one of a pair of ambivalent attitudes is rendered unconscious by overemphasis on the other. For example, an individual may find himself feeling uncomfortable with certain hateful feelings; therefore he overemphasizes his love. Adolescents use reaction formation a great deal. Feeling uncomfortable with loving feelings, they overemphasize their hatred; because they often experience anxiety when they feel dependent, afraid, or cooperative, they go overboard to appear independent, self-confident, and defiant. Whenever the therapist notes an attitude which is unusually strong, she or he should be alert to the possibility that what is being overemphasized is a defense against its opposite. For example, the vice crusader, though explicitly deploring pornography, is unconsciously enamored of it. If he didn't get a great deal of satisfaction from reading pornographic books and magazines, he would not arrange to do so for several hours each day. Similarly, we might expect a devoted pacifist, antivivisectionist, or vegetarian to have unconscious hostile fantasies that are dangerous to the ego and arouse anxiety.

Mr. Cameron constantly deplored his son's watching boxing and wrestling on television. He engaged in long sermons, pointing out to the boy that fighting was a sadistic, murderous enterprise that ruined the character of the spectator and was a detriment to society. When Mr. Cameron discussed with a therapist how upset he was by his son's interest in "blood sports," the sadistic impulse against which he was defending through reaction formation emerged in the following statement: "Anybody who dares to watch boxing or wrestling ought to be shot!"

Isolation is a defense used to protect the individual against the danger he would feel if he experienced certain emotions in association with certain thoughts. To ward off anxiety he isolates feelings from thoughts, or vice versa. Thus, in order not to feel the full impact of anger a person might experience the angry thoughts consciously but not permit himself to feel the intensity of his rage; or he might feel the physiological accompaniments of rage, such as rapid heartbeat or sweating, but not have many angry ideas at his conscious disposal. Another example of isolation is when an individual suffers trauma such as the sudden death of a loved one and describes the details of the crisis without expressing affect.

Another important defense machanism is *denial*. When something in the external world is experienced as unwanted and unpleasant, its existence is denied. A young boy may look in the mirror, note for a moment his small size, dislike what he sees, deny it, and then fantasy that he is Superman or Batman. In this way he can relieve himself of the discomfort and anxiety that are activated when he notes his smallness.

In *projection* the individual attributes his own unacceptable wishes or impulses to some other person. When one feels hostile toward a competitor it is easy to project violent and sadistic impulses onto him. In projection the individual is saying, "It is not I who have the thought or wish. It is the other who does!"

When the individual feels certain emotions toward another but finds these emotions unacceptable, he may use the defense mechanism of *turning against the self*. Rather than feeling rage toward another person—particularly one who is valued, loved, or feared—the individual abuses and demeans himself.

If adaptation is difficult or reality presents a danger, one may use the defense mechanism of *regression,* the return to a less mature form of functioning. A child of three or four who has difficulty coping with anger about the arrival of a baby brother or sister may regress by soiling and urinating in bed, even though he or she has been toilet-trained for some time.

Undoing is an action whose purpose is to disprove the harm the individual unconsciously imagines may be caused if he were consciously to feel certain or aggressive wishes. Brenner (1955) presents an example of undoing in his description of a child whose hostile wishes toward a younger sibling created great anxiety. The child developed a strong conscious desire to rescue sick or injured animals and nurse them back to health. In this way he could undo the harm he thought he would inflict on his sibling.

In all defense mechanisms there is always an attempt to repudiate an impulse (A. Freud, 1937). To the id's "yes," the ego defends itself and says "no," to avoid the danger of the forbidden impulse coming to consciousness. The ego can and does use as a defense anything available to it that will lessen the danger arising from the demands of an unwanted instinctual drive (Brenner, 1955).

The mechanisms discussed above are only a few of the defensive processes in which individuals engage. An isolated conflict between one particular drive and one particular opposing anxiety rarely occurs. More frequently there are complex interactions among many drives and many anxieties. A defensive struggle is rarely brought to a successful conclusion by one particular defensive activity. Defenses may be more or less successful, they may work under certain circumstances or be insufficient under others (Fine, 1973).

Seemingly irrational, provocative behavior that appears disruptive to interpersonal relationships can often be understood and related to with empathy if the observer is aware that all human beings defend themselves from ideas, thoughts, and feelings that arouse anxiety.

Mrs. Diamond, a teacher in a public school, was fighting the idea that the children should be given milk and cookies at recess. She averred, "Children should not be indulged and spoiled—they should be educated. If you give them milk and cookies every day, you'll give them no reason to work hard." Virtually all of Mrs. Diamond's remarks demeaned the children, and she became very hostile whenever she used words like "fed," "given to," and "pleasure."

After Mrs. Diamond's colleagues saw that arguing with her was of no avail, they decided to listen to her more carefully. What emerged was that Mrs. Diamond was *projecting* her own unacceptable appetite onto the children and criticizing them for impulses in herself that provoked danger for her. This seemed to be verified when she said, "I'd love someone to take care of me, feed me, and indulge me, but if it ever happened I'd feel very humiliated."

An individual who bitterly accuses somebody else of "hunger" or "perversity" is probably projecting unacceptable wishes of his or her own onto another. Similarly, when repression, reaction formation, or regression is viewed as a protective maneuver that individuals summon when they are in danger, behavior that at first appears puzzling begins to become more understandable.

SPECIFYING EGO AND SUPEREGO FUNCTIONS

Now that psychoanalysts have focused more attention on the ego's functions (such as judgment, reality testing, frustration tolerance, impulse control, and various defenses), they no longer generalize about "ego strength" and "ego weakness." They now specify the functions to which they are referring. The analyst making diagnostic assessments is now interested in answering questions like the following: "Does the ego have sufficient energy to control instincts and selectively discharge tension?" "Is the ego dominated by aggressive impulses or by a punitive superego so that judgment and reality testing cannot operate well?" "Is the ego making a poor choice of defense mechanisms (e.g., constant denial and projection) so that further interpersonal problems are created?" (Stamm, 1959).

Part of every good psychosocial assessment is a determination of the level and quality of the patient's superego functioning. For example, if patients are very strict with themselves and others, an understanding of their superego development and functioning will help in determining the strength or weakness of such ego functions as self-image and interpersonal relationships. Similarly, when patients are destructive, manipulative, and damaging to others, an understanding of the development and functioning of the superego will guide the analyst in diagnostic assessments and formulation of treatment plans.

The Topographic Point of View

The topographical approach refers to the *conscious, preconscious,* and *unconscious* states of mind. The conscious is that part of our mental activities of which we are fully aware at any time; the preconscious refers to thoughts and feelings that can be brought into consciousness fairly easily; the unconscious refers to thoughts, feelings, and desires of which we are not aware but which powerfully influence all of our behavior. The unconscious not only consists of drives, defenses, and superego mandates but also contains memories of events and attitudes that have been repressed (Freud, 1938, 1939). It is only when unconscious wishes are discharged in fantasies, dreams, or neurotic symptoms that the unconscious becomes known. Otherwise it acts silently and completely beyond the awareness of the observer.

One of the chief characteristics of the unconscious is the *primary process,* a type of mental functioning radically different from rational thinking. The primary process is best observed in dreams, which are frequently illogical or primitive, and do not adhere to the laws of reality. One of the devices of the primary process is *condensation:* one idea standing for many, much as symbols do in works of art. Another is *displacement:* the shifting of ideas to a different area, so that, for example, in a dream one may revile an old friend from the past while really being angry at someone in the present.

A third device of the primary process is *symbolization,* which allows for representation of unconscious material in conscious life because it conceals the true meaning of what is represented. For example, a cigar may symbolize a penis, and a purse a vagina.

Contrasted to the primary process is the *secondary process,* which governs conscious thinking. It is rational, logical, and obeys all the rules of reality.

As has been indicated earlier in this chapter, one of the basic tenets of psychoanalysis is that the unconscious is always operative in all behavior, adaptive and maladaptive. This perspective leads the diagnostician to ask why the student who fails unconsciously wants to fail, or why the patient who complains that he or she is unmarried unconsciously desires that status. If a marital pair tells a psychoanalytically oriented therapist that they would like to communicate better but always find themselves bickering, the therapist begins to look for the sadistic and masochistic gratification that each member of the dyad is unconsciously receiving.

Mr. and Mrs. Davis reported to their therapist that although both of them tried very hard to communicate lovingly, they could not and instead found themselves constantly demeaning each other. The Davises were unaware of the unconscious struggle in which they were engaged: Each was trying to dominate the other. Both of them were much more competitive than either realized, and neither could tolerate strength and competence in the other.

The topographic point of view states that to understand and help a patient, whether an individual or a group of individuals, the unconscious meaning of the patient's behavior should be well understood. The psychoanalytically oriented practitioner always wants to know the unconscious purpose of painful symptomology. For example, "What unconscious protection and unconscious gratification does this patient get from his sexual impotence?" Similarly, he recognizes that the tempestuous battles of a married couple, alienation or divisiveness in a family or a group, and dissension in an organization or a community all have unconscious meaning that must be understood before therapeutic assistance can be given. Because unconscious wishes, defenses, and memories strongly influence interpersonal behavior as well as the individual patient's self-image and self-esteem, the unconscious is an indispensable concept in diagnosis and treatment.

The Genetic-Developmental Point of View

Each individual's past participates in and shapes his or her present functioning. During the first five or six years of life the child experiences a series of dynamically differentiated stages that are of extreme importance for the formation of personality. In the oral stage (from birth to about age eighteen months) the mouth is the principal focus of dynamic activity; in the anal phase (from approximately age eighteen months to three years) the child turns his or her interests to elimination functions; in the phallic stage (ages three to six) he or she forms the rudiments of sexual identity; in latency (ages seven to eleven) erotic and libidinal interests are quiescent; and at puberty there is a recrudescence of biological drives, particularly of the Oedipal interests that emerged during the phallic phase. Ambivalence toward parents and other authority figures is also characteristic of puberty and adolescence (Freud, 1939).

According to Freudian theory, children are *polymorphous perverse;* that is, they can derive pleasure from any bodily activity. From the age of three to five, the child engages in extensive sexual exploration and tries to find out where babies come from. Frequently children believe that babies are conceived by eating and are born through the rectum; often they regard sexual intercourse as an act of sadism. Sex never remains a subject of indifference for any child, and even if he or she is uninformed about sexual matters there will be fantasies about them.

A central concept in Freudian theory is the Oedipal complex, which occurs in the phallic period of development. The familial arrangements a child experiences in most societies create in him or her a wish to replace the parent of the same sex and to have sexual contact with the parent of the opposite sex. As a consequence of the Oedipal conflict, the male experiences castration anxiety, the female penis envy. The boy anticipates castration as retaliation for his murderous wishes toward Father; the girl envies the penis because as a part of Father, whom she treasures, it appears to be a valuable piece of property, and also because all children want to own everything they see that is not theirs (e.g., most boys fantasy themselves at one time or another as having breasts and giving birth to a baby).

Although Freud believed that penis envy is a biological fact of life, most writers today believe that it is a cultural phenomenon. Fine (1973, p. 13) has noted:

> In view of the attack levied upon this concept by the Women's Liberation Movement, it should be emphasized that penis envy is essentially a clinical observation about what women feel, not a derogation of women. Psychoanalysis believes very strongly in the liberation of women, and should be looked upon as one of the major movements in that direction.

Both the Oedipal complex and penis envy can be seen as inevitable psychological occurrences if one keeps in mind that all children have omnipotent fantasies—i.e., they want what they want when they want it. Consequently girls envy boys, boys envy girls, and both would like to enjoy the privileges and prerogatives of their parents (Freud, 1937).

Erik Erikson (1950) greatly expanded Freud's theory of genetic stages of instinctual development by placing development in a social and cultural matrix, emphasizing the tasks of ego mastery presented by each stage of maturation. He defined eight nuclear conflicts, or developmental crises—trust vs. mistrust, autonomy vs. shame and doubt, initiative vs. guilt, industry vs. inferiority, identity vs. role diffusion, intimacy vs. isolation, generativity vs. stagnation, and integrity vs. despair—that correspond to Freud's stages of orality, anality, genitality, latency, puberty, and so on.

According to Erikson, not only does the human being unfold according to predetermined biological phases, but human maturation cannot be viewed apart from the social context in which it transpires. For example, the infant's functioning during the oral phase cannot be assessed without taking into consideration its transactions with its mother. If the infant and mother mutually gratify each other in many basic ways—e.g., during feeding and playing—the child will learn to ''trust'' rather than ''distrust'' the environment. Similarly, the child who is helped to forgo certain pleasures and take on some frustration during toilet training in the anal phase will develop a sense of ''autonomy'' rather than feel ''shame and doubt.'' If parents help the child to feel comfortable with his or her sexual interests and impulses, the child will be more apt to participate creatively and constructively in interpersonal relationships, and to be ''industrious'' rather than feel ''inferior.''

Central to the genetic-developmental point of view are two important concepts, *regression* and *fixation*. When an individual experiences a great deal of anxiety in coping with a particular psychosocial task, he may attempt to diminish the anxiety by returning to less mature modes of psychosocial functioning. For example, a five-year-old who has difficulty accepting certain sexual wishes may cope with the problem by returning to thumbsucking, even though he gave it up when he was two or three years old. An adult who has guilt about his sexual wishes may cope with his anxiety by getting drunk frequently. Regression implies that the individual has successfully mastered certain psychosocial tasks but he or she returns to previous, less mature gratifications when certain demands induce anxiety. In diagnosing a patient who has regressed to older modes of gratification, the psychoanalyst will ask: ''What triggered the client's regression?'' ''At what level of psychosocial functioning is the patient now operating?'' ''What is occurring in the present that is reminiscent of the past?''

The term ''fixation'' is used to describe certain individuals who have never matured beyond a certain point of psychosocial development and are unable, in many ways, to mature further. Individuals may be fixated at any level of development: oral, anal, phallic-Oedipal, and so on. As part of the diagnostic assessment, the analyst has to determine where the patient is fixated. Has he ever learned to trust? Has he ever established sufficient autonomy? Has he ever mastered the maturational task of learning how to relate intimately with another human being? (Wood, 1970)

It is not always easy to determine whether a particular symptom or interpersonal difficulty is a manifestation of regression or fixation. In order to be sure, the therapist has to take into consideration the many dimensions of the patient's current functioning, history, and transference reactions.

After the therapist had about twenty interviews with Mr. Easton, an inpatient at a Veterans Administration mental hospital, he was able to determine that his alcoholism was part of his oral fixation. Mr. Easton had a long history of social isolation; was extremely mistrustful, often to the point of paranoia; wanted very little to do with the therapist; and for many interviews refused to talk to him.

Mr. Easton's mother had died when he was only six months old, and his father sent him from one foster home to the other. Feeling angry and abandoned, Mr. Easton relied on alcohol for gratification rather than on people.

Mr. Forest, on the other hand, who also suffered from alcoholism, was not fixated at the oral stage. He regressed to alcoholism because conflicts at a higher stage of development were too overwhelming for him.

After Mr. Forest became a sales manager in a firm that he had been with for many years, he became depressed. Interviews with his therapist revealed that Mr. Forest experienced his job promotion as an Oedipal victory and became very guilty. Not wanting to surpass his father because he felt like a murderer for doing so, he became very submissive to men as a defense against his aggression. However, Mr. Forest's submissive feelings toward other men also created anxiety for him; therefore he regressed further, and drank alcohol to alleviate his tension.

The determination of where the patient's struggle is—i.e., at what level of maturational development—has extremely important implications for treatment. If the patient is fixated at an oral level of development, he will probably need a therapeutic experience that will enable him to express his oral aggression and mistrust of maternal figures, including the therapist, so that he can then move up the psychosexual ladder, with the therapist serving as maturational agent. However, if the patient's alcoholism is a regression that serves to protect him against Oedipal anxiety, the therapeutic task will be to help him feel more comfortable with his phallic aggression in and out of the therapy.

Not only does the therapist seek to establish what stage of development the patient's conflict is at; perhaps more important, it is necessary to know how significant others have responded to the patient's needs at a particular stage of development. A patient suffering from alcoholism and one suffering from drug addiction may both be trying to cope with anxieties emanating from the oral period. However, in one case the client may have been underfed, and in the other instance overfed and overindulged. If the patient has been overfed he will need an experience in therapy where he can learn to take on some frustration, develop controls, and defer gratification—i.e., be weaned. If, on the other hand, he was insufficiently nourished, the therapist will attempt to create an atmosphere in the therapy so that the patient can express his aggressive desires and oral hunger and eventually come to regard them as more acceptable.

Knowledge of the patient's maturational deficits not only helps the clinician understand maladaptive behavior with more certainty but provides guides for treatment. Is the homosexual patient defending against an Oedipal conflict? Is he identifying with an oral mother, so that by "feeding" his sexual partner he is vicariously ministering to his own oral hunger? Is the gambler storing up "gold" in his fantasies—i.e., does he have an anal problem?—or is he omnipotently striving to be an emperor, a conflict that evolves from the early oral phase when the baby wants to be a narcissistic king? Is the addict pricking himself in a phallic manner or is he feeding himself in an oral manner? Is he sniffing, and enjoying the anal smells?

In some cases the psychoanalyst recognizes that the patient's symptoms emanate from more than one maturational dysfunction; i.e., they are "overdetermined." Gambling may express both oral and anal fantasies; homosexuality may derive from oral and phallic conflicts; and addictions may be in the service of phallic, anal, and/or oral fantasies.

The Dynamic Point of View

The dynamic point of view refers to Freud's instinct theory, which is concerned with the libidinal and aggressive drives. Nature and nurture are two variables that are always present in the development of the human being; the drives or instincts represent the "nature" factor (Rapaport, 1951). An instinct has four characteristics: a source, an aim, an object, and an impetus. The source is a bodily condition or need, such as hunger, sex, or aggression. The aim is always to release tension and receive pleasure. The object includes both the object on which the drive is focused—e.g., food—and all the activities necessary to secure it, such as going to the refrigerator, ingesting, and masticating. The impetus of an instinct is its strength, which is determined by the force or intensity of the underlying need—e.g., hunger, sexual need, aggressive wish—and a need varies in quantity in different individuals or in the same individual at different times.

In making a diagnostic evaluation, the psychoanalyst first wants to ascertain if the patient's instincts are being gratified. Is he getting enough food and enjoying it? If not, why not? Is he realistically being deprived and/or is he arranging to feel deprived? Does gratifying the hunger instinct create anxiety for the patient, and is that why he does not want to eat too much? Similar questions may be asked of the patient regarding his sexual life and his elimination habits. The answers to these questions help pinpoint conflict, plan intervention, gauge the patient's motivation, and determine his capacity for a working relationship with the therapist.

The Economic Point of View

The economic point of view stresses the quantitative factor in mental functioning. According to this principle, all behavior is regulated by the need to dispose of psychological energy. Energy is discharged by forming *cathexes*—i.e., something or somebody is *cathected* if it is emotionally significant to a person.

Freud felt that energy is needed to fuel the psychic structure, and he saw this energy coming from the sexual drive. Later Hartmann (1964) concluded that the ego works with "deaggressivized" and "desexualized" energy, which he called "neutral" energy. The energy concept is among the most controversial in the field, and many theoreticians contend that it can be dispensed with entirely (Fine, 1973).

Although the dynamic, genetic, topographic, structural, and economic points of view comprise all of the dimensions necessary for a complete psychoanalytic understanding of the human being, Freud and other psychoanalysts have elaborated on the metapsychological approach by offering further notions of interpersonal relationships, culture, and values.

Interpersonal Relationships, Culture, and Values

According to psychoanalytic theory, how an individual relates to others is essentially based on how he experienced himself vis-à-vis family members. The vicissitudes of interpersonal relationships depend very heavily on *transferences* from the individual's family structure. Although the concept of transference is largely used in connection with psychotherapy, it is a universal characteristic of human beings. The kinds of experience that offered gratification in the family tend to be pursued, while those that frustrated the individual tend to be avoided. Most relationships in adult life reflect the kinds of gratifications and frustrations that a person experienced within the nuclear family.

Freud (1933) suggested that the child proceeds from a narcissistic stage, in which he is concerned only with himself, to an anaclitic stage, in which he is dependent upon somebody else, and eventually to a stage of object love. In object love there is a mutuality between one person and another, and this love involves a synthesis of tender and erotic feelings toward the opposite sex. Hartmann (1964) has proposed a movement in relationships from "need-gratifying" ones to those where there is mutuality and "constancy." Fine (1971) has suggested that relationships start off as "attachment" in infancy and move to "admiration" (of the parents), then to "intimacy," and finally to "devotion." All love relationships, according to Fine, have these phases of interpersonal maturation as components.

In his early work, especially in *Totem and Taboo,* Freud (1913b) demonstrated that the same psychological mechanisms were to be found in all cultures. While the same libidinal and aggressive drives exist in all human beings and in all cultures, they are molded in different ways by different societies.

One of the most notable attempts to unify psychoanalysis and the study of culture was made by Kardiner (1939, 1945). He coined the term "basic personality structure" to designate a group of character traits in the typical individual of a particular culture. This concept was a refinement of the older term "national character." Examples of American character traits are "ambitiousness" and "greed."

The question of whether there are any universal values inherent in psychoanalysis has been much debated. Freud did not speak much of values but did take the position that the mature person is one who can love and work. Fine (1971) has attempted to extend Freud's image of love and work and has argued that psychotherapy is the first scientific attempt to make people happy. His "analytic ideal" involves pursuing pleasure, releasing positive emotions, eliminating hatred and other negative emotions, acquiring a meaningful role in the family and a sense of identity in the larger society, engaging in some satisfying form of work, pursuing some form of creative activity, and being able to communicate with other people.

A Psychoanalytic View of Psychopathology

According to Freudian theory, whenever an individual is suffering from a neurotic symptom such as an obsession, a phobia, or a psychosomatic disease, psychic conflict is present. The individual's defenses (e.g., projection, denial), which have been used for protection against ideas, thoughts, or memories that are unbearable and cause anxiety, have broken down. As mentioned earlier in this chapter, anxiety is a warning to the person that some unacceptable drive, thought, or action will reach consciousness (Freud, 1923). If the unacceptable element is too strong or the defense is too weak, anxiety erupts and the person forms a neurotic symptom. The symptom expresses concomitantly the individual's need to express what is forbidden and his dread of that expression. In a phobia—e.g., fear of going out on the streets—two variables are at work: The very situation that the individual fears also excites him. The stimulation that is induced causes anxiety because the excitement emanates from sexual fantasies that are unacceptable. A symptom is often referred to as a "compromise formation" because it is a composite expression of the patient's wishes, anxiety, defenses, and fears.

George, an eighteen-year-old college freshman, reported to his therapist that he was plagued by obsessive thoughts and compulsions. The obsessive thoughts took the form of constantly wanting to blurt out in class "Drop dead, drop dead!" These thoughts created anxiety and interfered with George's concentration. In addition, when he left his dormitory he was compelled to make sure that the door to his room was locked. Even after he had checked it several times, he had to go back to see that it was secure.

As the therapist and George reviewed his history it became quite clear that George was very angry about being away from home for the first time in his life. At home and in his community George was loved by all and felt very important; at college he was one of many and not particularly well known. This situation punctured his narcissism and activated a great deal of anger toward his college peers and the college authorities. However, George's anger and homesickness were unacceptable to him. He repudiated his dependency feelings (through denial) and repressed his anger. Nonetheless, his drives were intense and his defenses were not strong enough to negate them. Consequently, his anger erupted in a neurotic symptom; he developed an obsessive thought: "Drop dead, drop dead!"

Unconsciously George wished that his parents and friends would visit him, perhaps taking him by surprise. Also unconsciously, he wished to leave his door open so that they could walk in and be there when he returned from classes.

As George was able to share with his therapist his fantasies of kissing and hugging his parents and being a young boy again, his symptoms diminished. As he was able to acknowledge his anger and dependency, particularly his wishes to be bathed and fed by Mother and cuddled by Father, he did not need to use as much energy to defend himself and his functioning improved.

Freud never abandoned the idea that the roots of a psychoneurosis lie in a disturbance of the libidinal life of childhood. However, he later recognized that the stories his patients told him of having been sexually seduced in childhood were fantasies rather than real memories, even though the patients themselves believed them to be true. Although this discovery was at first a blow to Freud, he made a step forward by recognizing that sexual interests and activities, far from being limited in childhood to exceptional, traumatic events like seductions, are a normal part of human psychic life from earliest infancy (Brenner, 1955).

In his research on psychoneurosis, Freud compared a symptom to a dream in that both are compromise formations of one or more repressed impulses and those forces of the personality that oppose the entrance of forbidden impulses into conscious thoughts and behavior. Freud was also able to demonstrate that neurotic symptoms, like the elements of a dream, had a meaning; symptoms could be shown to be the disguised and distorted expressions of unconscious fantasies.

By permitting a partial and disguised emergence of an id wish via a psychoneurotic symptom—e.g., George's obsessional "drop dead!"—the ego is able to avoid some of the anxiety it would otherwise develop. By permitting an impulse a fantasied gratification (as in a dream) that is disguised and distorted, the ego can avoid the displeasure of experiencing extreme anxiety. By coping with his unacceptable thoughts through an obsession, Geroge was able to ward off his murderous wishes, his anxiety, and his guilt. This is what is known as the *primary gain* of a neurosis: warding off a dangerous impulse from consciousness and diminishing anxiety and guilt.

Secondary gain refers to the efforts of the ego to exploit the gratifying possibilities of a neurotic symptom. For example, a child may enjoy the overprotection and solicitude he receives when he brings his parents' attention to his school phobia. Similarly, an adult with a psychosomatic problem such as an ulcer may be able to get tender loving care when he complains of acute stomachaches.

It is important to recognize that the difference between the functioning of a "normal" and a neurotic individual is one of degree. All individuals have id impulses, and most people experience sadistic, masochistic, incestuous, or murderous wishes that are not acceptable to them. When defenses, which all individuals use, are not strong enough to cope with id wishes, anxiety erupts and symptoms appear. In the example mentioned above, George's unconscious yearning for his parents may have been stronger than that of his peers, and he probably experienced his dependency as more nearly unbearable than do most college students who are away from home for the first time; but his psychological functioning was not too different from that of others. The similarities between George and his classmates were many; the differences were few.

PSYCHOSES, NEUROSES, CHARACTER DISORDERS, AND OTHER SIGNS OF PATHOLOGY

In trying to understand the meaning of specific forms of maladaptive behavior, the psychoanalytically oriented clinician will utilize the metapsychological approach and assess the client structurally, topographically, economically, genetically and dynamically. The clinician will want to know what drives (sex, aggression, or both) are seeking discharge; what are the client's superego admonitions; what defenses are in operation; what history is being recapitulated in present behavior and emotions; what cultural and interpersonal forces are at play, and so on. Because of the number and complexity of the factors that must be taken into account in diagnosing any patient, the use of labels has many limitations. To call a patient "neurotic" or "psychotic" not only fails to individualize the person but does not tell us very much about the intensity and pervasiveness of his "disease," or the disruptive effects it has on the patient or on his interpersonal relationships. It tells us little about the strength of the individual's ego functions and drives, and virtually nothing about the flexibility of his superego. The label contains little information about the patient's unique conflicts and gives limited clues to the etiology of his stresses.

Because clinical diagnoses like "psychopath" or "character disorder" do not fully describe an individual but tend to stigmatize him, many analytically oriented clinicians have rejected this form of assessment altogether. (Recently the American Psychiatric Association recognized that individuals labeled "homosexual" were stereotyped in many sectors of society and often had many of their civil rights curbed. The APA therefore dropped the clinical label from its diagnostic nomenclature.) However, inasmuch as terms like "schizophrenia," "obsessive-compulsive neurotic," and "oral character disorder" appear frequently in the literature, are utilized quite often in case discussions and supervisory conferences, and sometimes serve as short-cuts in discussion, it is important for the practitioner to be cognizant of the major clinical syndromes. In the discussion to follow we will be examining these syndromes from a metapsychological perspective.

SCHIZOPHRENIA

There is continuing controversy among clinicians about the etiology of schizophrenia. Some contend that the dysfunction is strictly a constitutional and biological phenomenon that should be treated by pharmaceutical agents, while others view it as evolving from faulty interpersonal experiences. While the psychoanalytically oriented practitioner never denies constitutional and biological vulnerabilities, he or she views schizophrenia and the other psychoses and neuroses as primarily maturational problems that derive from negative interpersonal experiences early in life.

There is now abundant literature affirming the notion that the schizophrenic patient has been deprived of normal physical handling and stimulation by a maternal figure during the first year of life (Brenner, 1955). Consequently, many of his ego functions have failed to develop properly, and his capacity to relate to and deal with his external environment is severely impaired—so much so that he may even appear feebleminded (Spitz, 1965). The schizophrenic patient usually suffers from hallucinations and delusions, distorts reality severely, is plagued by strong murderous fantasies that he usually projects onto others, and feels that others are out to persecute him. Because this patient is convinced that most people are his enemies, he withdraws from reality and remains quite seclusive, sometimes talking only to himself. Usually his interests involve things rather than people—e.g., physics, biology, or mechanics—and keep him isolated from others as much as possible (Searles, 1965).

As has already been implied, the schizophrenic is an individual who has been poorly nurtured during the early phases of psychosocial development; consequently, he is distrustful, suspicious, even paranoid. Because he has not been appropriately responded to by a trustworthy person, he is always angry and cautious, feeling that his environment is full of sinister forces.

Like the primarily narcissistic infant, in whom the systems of the mental apparatus are not yet differentiated from each other, the schizophrenic patient is very much preoccupied with himself. Just as the infant has not developed to the point where he can relate to people in a thoughtful, considerate way, so the schizophrenic patient has no emotionally significant contact with people. Furthermore, just as we do not expect the infant to have well-developed ego functions like judgment, reality testing, impulse control, and perception, the person labeled schizophrenic has parted with reality and most of his ego functions have broken down. His ego has returned to its original undifferentiated state and has dissolved almost entirely into the id, which has no real knowledge of people and reality (Fenichel, 1945).

Although the schizophrenic patient experiences strong quantities of murderous rage, he feels unable to discharge it because he is very worried that his hatred will damage those he very much needs—parents or parental figures. Consequently, he represses his murderous wishes but feels like a guilty and unworthy child because his hostility exerts an effect on his self-image. Rage pervades his entire psyche and prevents him from maturing, just as powerful infectious toxins can retard physical development (Josselyn, 1948).

Because the schizophrenic patient has withdrawn his libido (energy) from other people and directed it toward himself, he feels estranged, depersonalized, and preoccupied with body sensations. The regression to or fixation at the infantile narcissistic state accounts for his megalomania; he fantasies that he is somebody very special, such as an emperor or a queen.

Erikson (1950) describes the schizophrenic individual as one who has either lost or never gained a basic sense of trust and therefore has to resort to a narcissistic, paranoid orientation to the world. His thinking falls back from the logical to the prelogical level, and he is consumed by archaic wishes that give rise to hallucinatory and delusional thinking.

Like the baby, who wishes to have a relationship with a mother figure, the schizophrenic adult does not completely abandon his wish for contact with people. He often demonstrates this wish in such infantile thought processes as the conviction that "everyone is looking at me!" The catatonic schizophrenic is an exception: he has given up the search and lies mute for hours or days, often having to be fed intravenously.

Just as the differences between a "normal" individual and a neurotic are a matter of degree, so it can be said that the differences between a schizophrenic individual and a neurotic are also a matter of degree. Furthermore, the precipitating factors in schizophrenia are not essentially different from the precipitating factors in neuroses. Both are almost always activated by a maturational crisis (e.g., puberty, senility) or an environmental one (e.g., divorce, death, job loss). The crisis increases the individual's instinctual tension and floods his ego, and therefore the ego is unable to function properly.

In both neuroses and psychoses (schizophrenia and manic-depressive psychoses), the crisis usually revives and intensifies infantile sexual wishes. According to Fenichel (1945), the Oedipus complex is an essential factor in schizophrenia, and individuals who become schizophrenic usually have strong incestuous fantasies that create overwhelming terror for them. When this occurs they suffer from hallucinations and delusions, because the ego functions of rational thought and judgment have broken down.

In neuroses two steps must be distinguished: (1) repression of an id impulse and (2) its return in a distorted form, as in an obsession or other symptom. In schizophrenia there are two analogous steps: (1) a break with reality and (2) an attempt to regain the lost reality.

An example of a well-functioning human being who regressed to a schizophrenic state is Freud's famous Schreber case (Freud, 1959). Schreber was a distinguished judge, who was highly regarded for his brilliance, logic, and charm. Throughout his life his interpersonal relationships appeared mature and loving. The crisis for Judge Schreber was his "fame." As is true for many individuals, Schreber experienced his celebrated achievements as a murderous victory over his father, whom he loved and hated with great intensity. Unable to cope with the anxiety that emerged from his murderous wishes, he regressed to a homosexual position. However, his homosexual fantasies also aroused terror and anxiety; he regressed further and began to suffer from hallucinations and delusions.

Schreber protected himself from his homosexual tendencies by the use of several defenses. He denied his love for his father by repeating over and over again that he hated him. Then Schreber projected his hatred onto his father and said, "He hates me!" In this way his own hatred became rationalized into "I hate him because he persecutes me."

In *The Ego and the Id* (1923), Freud pointed out that the apparent transformation of love into hate which emerges in delusions of persecution is possible only if there has been strong ambivalence beforehand, as was true in Schreber's case.

MANIC-DEPRESSIVE PSYCHOSES

Insight into the psychological dynamics of schizophrenic phenomena suggests that there is a strong similarity between schizophrenia and manic-depressive psychoses. Both are based on a regression to extreme narcissism and infantilism; and both are characterized by minimal emotional investment in other people, losses of many ego functions, and a departure from reality. However, one of the unique and characteristic features of the individual who has been diagnosed as manic-depressive is his rapid alternation of moods. Within an hour or less he can shift from acute depression to intense joy—as if an extremely helpless, agitated, and depressed infant who had lost his mother (and therefore his whole world) were suddenly transformed into an extremely happy child who had been reunited with the mother.

Just as many writers have contended that the etiology of schizophrenia can be found in the biological, physiological, and constitutional dimensions of the patient's life, many have also taken this position in discussing the etiology of the manic-depressive psychoses. But it is difficult to discount psychological and interpersonal factors when one notes the alternating states of depression and joy in the person diagnosed as manic-depressive. These mood swings seem to mirror a situation in which the baby is alternately abandoned and then loved intensely, only to be abandoned again. Differing from the schizophrenic patient, who seems to have suffered from a great deal of estrangement, the manic-depressive appears to be the product of a very tempestuous, unpredictable environment that offered much pain but also sporadic pleasure. However, as Glover (1949) has pointed out, the exaggerated self-love of the manic-depressive patient during the manic phase is also indicative of pathology because it is often accompanied by a flight of ideas and actions. It is as if the patient is desperately holding onto a joyful state but wondering when his mother's comfort will be withdrawn and his joy destroyed.

In the depressive phase of the manic-depressive psychoses, one can usually see that the patient has suffered decisive narcissistic injuries. He has severe and agitated crying jags and appears like a child who is very disappointed in his parents for not loving him and not strengthening his self-esteem (Fenichel, 1945).

The manic-depressive patient seems to be continually alternating between hunger and satiety. Pleasure is expected after every pain, and pain after every pleasure. The primitive idea is set up that any suffering bestows the privilege of some later compensating joy, and vice versa.

Manic-depressive psychoses and schizophrenia are two clinical entities that fall under the overall category of psychoses. Patients diagnosed as psychotic have few operative ego functions. They have lost their hold on reality, have defective judgment, relate to others on a very infantile basis, show poor frustration tolerance, harbor strong murderous fantasies, and are very distrustful of others.

Borderline and Schizoid States

Individuals who do not manifest a true psychosis but function at a trust-mistrust, or oral, level of development have been variously referred to by a host of labels such as borderline, schizoid, ambulatory schizophrenic, pseudo-neurotic, and schizophrenic. Although these patients frequently suffer from the extreme narcissism, feelings of omnipotence, lack of true object-relatedness, departures from reality, and poor judgment associated with psychosis, they usually have some ego functions that are working well, at least at certain times. Sometimes they can use good judgment on a job but are unrelated in a marriage (or vice versa).

They may be extremely preoccupied with their bodies but manage to function for periods of time in a symptom-free manner. They are similar to the schizophrenic and manic-depressive patients in that huge quantities of aggression pervade their psyches. These individuals are potential psychotics; they have not broken with reality, yet under unfavorable circumstances they may become psychotic (Fenichel, 1945; Glover, 1949).

The borderline person may be psychopathic (function with a limited superego, or conscience) and not really concern himself with the needs of others. At times he deceives others by his pseudo-independence, but in many ways he functions as a little child who handles narcissistic hurts by denial and by a protective increase in his narcissism. Occasionally the patient appears "normal" because he has succeeded in substituting "pseudo contacts" for real relationships (Erikson, 1950).

Kaufman (1958) has pointed out that the "borderline personality" can be characterized as having: (1) many overt depressions; (2) an inability to handle many of the realities of living; (3) a tendency to act out, in delinquency, alcoholism, or drug addiction; (4) psychosomatic reactions such as ulcerative colitis; and (5) paranoid reactions. He has further noted that the borderline personality uses a great deal of magical thinking. If he gets into difficulty he believes that a parental figure will come and rescue him, and take care of him for the rest of his life.

The borderline personality usually has a great deal of difficulty coping with omnipotent fantasies, and vascillates between believing that he can control the world and that some omnipotent person is around who will run his life for him (Knight, 1953). He often believes that if he acts in an aggressive and hostile manner he will be more respected. Very often his hostility and aggression serve as a defense against depression and a yearning for love.

When his therapist visited ten-year-old Howard at camp and brought him a present, Howard attacked her unmercifully. He told her that she was stupid and didn't understand him, that he wished she had not come to visit him, and concluded with "Drop dead, you dope!"

Howard, who had been orphaned at the age of two and had then gone from one foster home to another, had a strong desire to be mothered in a nourishing way. Inasmuch as love was not forthcoming, he became very depressed. To cope with his strong dependency wishes (which were unbearable to him) and his strong depression (which he also fought) he handled interpersonal relations by expressing himself very aggressively and adopting an "I don't care" attitude.

Primitive processes such as magical thinking, feelings of omnipotence, and impulsivity are present in all individuals. However, in the borderline personality these qualities are strong and pervasive (Weinberger, 1958). One borderline patient berated his therapist for not knowing which magazines he liked and not keeping them in the waiting room. Another was furious at her therapist because he did not warn her that her boss was going to be ill on a day when she was supposed to have an important conference with him.

In sum, the borderline personality has a tenuous grasp on reality; is very narcissistic, immature, and reluctant to accept responsibility for his acts; and usually is poorly motivated to change his behavior. Most of the time he is ruled by the pleasure principle. His thoughts are frequently grandiose, he uses denial as a defense a great deal of the time, and he does not easily empathize with the needs of others.

ADDICTIONS

Either because they have not been given appropriate love and attention, or because higher levels of development have created too much anxiety for them to master and they then regress, the drug addict, food addict, heavy smoker, and alcoholic are all trying to satisfy a strong emotional hunger. Once the yearning is satisfied by taking marijuana, heroin, food, tobacco, or alcohol, these individuals feel a temporary sense of security and self-esteem.

Because the addict frequently feels distrustful of people and usually holds them in low esteem, he resorts to the solitary pleasure of the addiction rather than depending on interpersonal relationships for gratification. Taking a needle or food or a pipe into himself is like feeding himself, and he would rather do this than depend on someone else for pleasure; he is convinced that other people are most unreliable.

The drug or food the addict ingests is experienced as equivalent to the warmth and comfort that he craves from a mother or mother figure but must consciously repudiate. (It is interesting in this regard that the leader of a drug group or gang is often referred to as "Mother" by the members.)

Like the manic-depressive patient, the addict lives in alternating states of elation and depression that correspond to the alternation of hunger and satiation in the very young infant. The depression is particularly observable in the alcoholic's or drug addict's "morning after" syndrome. Although the effects of this syndrome are painful, alcohol and drugs, like gambling and other addictions, initially remove inhibitions from consciousness so that frustrations appear less overwhelming. Yet most addicts suffer from acute depression and feel quite persecuted. This is an expression of their guilt for "defying the gods" and experiencing forbidden joy.

Berthelsdorf (1976), in his psychoanalytic work with the drug addict, has called attention to the strength of the patient's omnipotent fantasies; when he is on a "high" the addict feels that he can control the world. Berthelsdorf has also commented on the addict's underlying passive wishes and strong conviction of his own weakness, which he tries to surmount through imbibing drugs. He also has noted how very resentful the addict is, and how addictive behavior is frequently an expression of underlying defiance.

PSYCHOSOMATIC DISEASE

Because the growing organism may be regarded as a system that comprises physiological, psychological, and social subsystems, it follows that any modification in one part will affect another. Most people are aware of physiological accompaniments to various emotions. If one is angry, he may find himself breathing quickly, perspiring, and trembling. Loving feelings are often accompanied by fast hearbeat and other visceral sensations. In the 1950s there was a popular song that expressed the relationship between the emotion of love and its somatic manifestations: "When your heart goes bumpety-bump, it's love, love, love!" Even to the casual observer it is apparent that undischarged quantities of anger can lead to a migraine headache or insomnia; unfulfilled dependency wishes that are unacceptable to the person and cause anxiety can lead to an ulcer; and undischarged aggression and frustrated libidinal yearnings can induce heart conditions. People in everyday language point out: "That was a heartbreaker!" "He gives me a headache!" "I couldn't stomach that!"

There is some controversy about the unconscious meaning of psychosomatic illnesses. Some authors contend that they are merely expressions of dammed-up excitation and tension and do not express a unique set of psychodynamic conflicts (Glover, 1949). Others have concluded that a part of the body is unconsciously selected to express a unique psychological conflict (Fenichel, 1945). By those who subscribe to the view that a particular bodily dysfunction expresses a unique conflict, bronchial asthma, for example, would be seen as an intense longing for a mother, expressed in pathological changes in the breathing function. The asthmatic seizure might be interpreted as a cry for help. Similarly, dermatitis might be viewed as "crying out" through the skin ("He gets under my skin"); colitis might express the wish to withhold defiant feelings; and enuresis might be the symbolic expression of angry feelings.

Ian, a twenty-one-year-old army recruit who was referred to the army post's mental hygiene clinic for enuresis, spoke in his interviews about how "pissed off" his sergeant got him, how "pissed off" he was at the company commander, and how much the army "stops you from saying how 'pissed off' you feel." When Ian was helped to articulate his angry feelings in his sessions with a therapist, who did not censure their expression, his enuresis diminished considerably.

The clinician working with an individual who has a psychosomatic problem cannot fail to note the diminution of symptoms when the patient is given the opportunity to talk about what his "grinding stomach" or "heavy heart" is saying. Somatic distress, at least some of the time, is a reflection of psychic tension that attaches itself to a weak constitutional zone. When the person who complains of a heart pain or stomachache is given a chance to speak about his psychological conflict, the pain tends to lessen considerably (Deutsch, 1953).

It is important to keep in mind that the age and circumstances of the patient are salient factors in determining the exact meaning of the symptom to him. Ian, in the above example, was feeling strong quantities of anger, which he felt he could not express in his barracks or to the army authorities. By carefully listening to his remarks and getting in tune with his circumstances and the way he was coping with them, the therapist could fairly safely conclude that the enuresis was a bodily expression of Ian's anger. However, in the following case enuresis expressed other psychological conflicts.

Fourteen-year-old Jerry was seen in a mental health clinic for depression, free-floating anxiety, poor academic performance, poor interpersonal relationships, and enuresis. One of the important etiological factors in Jerry's acute distress was his extreme guilt about his sexual wishes. As he talked a great deal about "a need to hold back" so much of what he felt, particularly sexual fantasies, it became quite clear that he had a severe masturbatory conflict. He wanted very much to masturbate but felt too inhibited. As Jerry discussed his sexual fantasies with his therapist and felt less guilty about masturbating, his enuresis disappeared.

Apparently Jerry's enuresis was a masturbatory and orgastic equivalent. When he masturbated and felt less guilty about it, he did not need to express sexual tension through enuresis.

Psychosomatic reactions frequently are accommodations made in childhood, and the same somatic reactions can continue into adult life.

Mrs. Klein, an attractive twenty-three-year-old woman, sought psychotherapy because she found herself vomiting quite frequently and her physician could find no organic basis for it. Interviews with a therapist revealed that Mrs. Klein, who was recently married, could not "stomach" many features of her marriage. Among other things, she resented her husband's wish "to have sex on demand" and "working hard all day and then having to take care of the meals while he reads the paper." Mrs. Klein was vomiting up angry feelings, and as she discussed her resentment with the therapist she recalled that she had also vomited when she was five years old and her mother insisted that she eat certain foods she hated.

Like the infant who expresses his tensions by calling attention to his body, the frustrated adult resorts to this infantile form of expression. Hypochondriasis may be viewed as an attempt to have the therapist or somebody else comfort the patient's shaky body and hold it. In hypochondriasis, feelings that the patient has toward parents and significant others that cannot be discharged because of feared retaliation or abandonment are "kept inside" the body.

All psychosomatic disorders can be viewed as manifestations of the patient's need to inhibit certain impulses. Stuttering and stammering may occur if verbal expressions of feelings are experienced by the speaker as attacks on the listener. If the patient feels that seeing is a forbidden act, eye tics can result. In petitmal epilepsy, the patient is usually a narcissistically oriented individual with a primitive ego who suffers from intense murderous wishes. His seizure may be compared to the thrashing, kicking, and screaming of a frustrated infant (Glover, 1949).

James Lynch, in his book *The Broken Heart* (1977), has discussed the medical consequences of loneliness in America. He has pointed out that "unconnected humans"—the divorced, the widowed, the single—die sooner than married people, and that among unmarried Americans heart disease is almost double the rate for the married. In the first six months after bereavement, the risk of death among the widowed may be ten times as high as for the married. Lynch has also noted that both human and animal infants, deprived of both parents and reared in emotionally barren institutionalized settings, fail to thrive—and may be vulnerable, later, to early death. He has also been able to document that sudden and adverse life changes are frequently followed by a sudden onset of illness.

Lynch's studies on cardiovascular disease tend to support the psychoanalytic view of psychosomatic disease, which contends that the mind and body never function in isolation. When feelings are not discharged in normal channels, the equivalents of anger, dependency, and yearnings for love are expressed through dysfunctions of the heart and other parts of the body.

SEXUAL DISORDERS

Because so many patterns of unconventional sexual behavior have gained much acceptance in recent years, many therapists have been reluctant to examine their dynamic meanings. Some clinicians seem to feel that seeking to unravel the unconscious meanings of homosexuality, bisexuality, transvestism, or other forms of nontraditional sexual behavior is evidence of arrogance, intolerance, or lack of empathy.

Psychoanalysis has always taken the position that behavior by itself does not convey very much meaning to the diagnostician. It is much more pertinent, in understanding a person's functioning, to place behavior into a metapsychological context, ascertaining the activity of the id, ego, and superego; the recapitulation of the past in the present; unconscious fantasies; how psychic energy is used; and how the social context affects personal behavior. Therefore, sex practiced outside the bedroom may be considered neurotic or adaptive and healthy; homosexuality practiced in a prison can mean something quite different from homosexuality at a heterosexual golf club. To the psychoanalytically oriented practitioner, the patient's overt sexual behavior is much less crucial than how he experiences himself and his partner while engaging in sex. What fantasies are operative? What defenses are at work? What impulses stimulate anxiety? What is the patient's capacity for empathy? The answers to these questions are more important diagnostically than the behavior itself.

To the psychoanalytically oriented, sex is much more than a bodily experience; in many ways it is an interpersonal transaction. In sex, the individual expresses his deepest feelings and fantasies, defenses, conflicts, body image, self-esteem, capacity for intimacy and empathy—his complete metapsychology is at work. It therefore should come as no surprise that those who cannot easily trust others are not going to be able to enjoy the intimacy inherent in a sexual relationship. The tenderness, movements, and closeness in sex recapitulate the closeness of the early oral, or trust-mistrust, period. Lovers frequently refer to each other in oral terms: "sweetie pie," "cookie," and so on.

Mr. and Mrs. Lewis, a couple in their early thirties, sought therapeutic help because neither of them could enjoy themselves or each other in sex. Both frequently felt nausea, depression, and extreme anxiety when they were confronted by just the idea of sexuality. As their histories unfolded and fantasies were examined, it became clear that both the Lewises had many unresolved infantile wishes that frightened them. Each of them unconsciously wanted to be an infant and be ministered to and nurtured by the other, but each unconsciously ascribed to the other an image of a gigantic, omnipotent parent. In effect, they felt like helpless, weak, and vulnerable babies in the hands of a powerful parent who could devour them. It was not until after their mutual wishes for symbiosis and their cannibalistic fantasies became conscious that they were able to understand better why they felt compelled to avoid a sexual relationship.

Psychoanalysis takes the position that sexual difficulties, if they are to be resolved, require the patient and therapist to get in touch with the patient's feelings and fantasies about himself and his partner—particularly those unconscious feelings and fantasies that distort the meaning of sexual activity. Because sex is not a mechanical, bodily experience but an interpersonal one, it requires an interpersonal experience to modify the patient's difficulties.

As indicated in the case described above, one of the ways patients distort sex is by experiencing it as if they were submitting to an arbitrary parent. They view sex not as mutual pleasure but as "putting out," being exploited by a tyrannical parent. Like children who refuse to defecate or urinate "for" their parents because they see no pleasure in it for themselves, many adults see "nothing in sex for me." In addition, just as the child can view assertiveness and the spontaneous expression of "animal" impulses as "bad," so the adult patient can experience sexual activity as something bad—something his introjected parental voice, or superego, prohibits. Sex, if it is to be culminated successfully, requires the individual to discharge his sexual tensions and enjoy an orgasm. Some patients equate the sexual discharge with anal or urinary discharge, and consequently feel that sex is something "dirty." It is as if they are urinating or defecating on or in their partner, or their partner is defecating on or in them.

Impotence and Frigidity

Many individuals seek out a therapist to resolve problems of impotence and frigidity. Both of these disorders take many forms. The impotent man may be totally unable to have an erection, or he may not be able to sustain one long enough to satisfy himself or his partner. He may ejaculate prematurely or take an unusually long time to do so. Finally, he may be able to have an erection and an ejaculation but derives little or no pleasure from his orgasm. The frigid female may be unable to feel any enjoyable sensations in her vagina and/or from her clitoris; she may be unable to experience an orgasm. In some cases, the woman's fears are so great that penetration by the penis is impossible.

The impotent man frequently equates his sexual partner with his mother and wants to compete aggressively with his father. The incestuous fantasies that become recapitulated in his relationship with his sexual partner and the murderous thoughts that he unconsciously entertains toward a father figure create enormous anxiety. To avoid this unbearable anxiety, he withdraws psychologically from sex. Often the man's Oedipal fantasies are so distasteful that he defends himself by regressing to the fantasy of being a woman—which implies that he will have sex with a man. Conscious recognition of his homosexual wishes is also very anxiety-provoking, so he avoids sex altogether.

Mr. Morton, aged thirty-five, was frequently impotent with his wife. Although he felt quite comfortable with her as a nonsexual partner, he often experienced acute anxiety in the form of headaches, perspiration, and impotence when his wife approached him sexually.

It turned out that when Mr. Morton was a young boy his mother was very seductive with him and frequently avoided his father. Mr. Morton began to feel quite competitive with his father and often entertained fantasies of "wiping him out."

Mr. Morton's Oedipal fantasies posed an enormous problem for him. His wish to defeat his father was in conflict with his strong desire to have his father's love. He attempted to resolve the conflict by submitting to his father in an "inverted Oedipal," or homosexual, manner. In sex with Mrs. Morton he fantasied himself as a woman having sex with a man. By psychologically castrating himself, Mr. Morton could avoid the threat of an Oedipal victory.

It took over a year of therapeutic work with Mr. Morton before he could see that his impotency was an expression of intense sexual and aggressive fantasies and that it served the purpose of protecting him from feeling like a hostile warrior.

The frigid woman may also be unconsciously equating her sexual partner with the parent of the opposite sex and then punishing herself for her rivalry with her mother. Frequently the woman who does not enjoy sex with a man is in competition with him and would like to castrate him. Feeling envious of her partner, she cannot enjoy him.

Miss North, a twenty-four-year-old single woman, found herself constantly involved with married men. Initially she would feel extreme excitement and elation, but this subsided after a few weeks. Then she would become very hostile to her partner and quite unresponsive sexually.

In her work with a male therapist, she recapitulated in the transference her sexual conflicts. It turned out that the men "who turn me on" were always unavailable—i.e., married men like her father. She derived most of her sexual satisfaction from the unconscious fight with her mother rather than from genuinely loving and appreciating her partner. A very important element in her sexual conflict was her anger at her father for not succumbing to her charms; to retaliate, she wanted to hurt and eventually destroy him. She acted out her revengeful feelings toward her father with her sexual partners, and because she felt so much contempt for them she could not enjoy either herself or her partners very much.

As is true of many psychological disorders, impotence and frigidity may be overdetermined; i.e., the patient's oral, anal, and phallic-Oedipal difficulties may all be operative in the symptom, and all of these conflicts will have to be confronted in the patient's therapy.

Homosexuality

In the process of growing up, everyone develops sexual feelings indiscriminately and retains a certain amount of sexual feeling toward one's own sex. In situations where there are no members of the opposite sex, such as in prisons, many individuals who have previously been heterosexual turn toward homosexual relationships. This is what Fenichel (1945) has referred to as "accidental homosexualtiy," and it tends to prove that latently every individual is capable of a homosexual object choice.

There is no doubt that biological factors such as hormonal balance contribute toward a particular sexual predisposition. However, in any discussion of homosexuality it is important to remember that what is termed "masculine" or "feminine" depends more on social and cultural than on biological factors. The roles of "woman" and "man" are based on a host of factors—economic arrangements, status arrangements, arbitrary role requirements, traditional mores, and so on. Inasmuch as so many elements are operative in the etiology of homosexuality, and because it is now considered a legitimate way of life by many individuals, organizations like the American Psychiatric Association are reluctant to study the psychodynamics of homosexual men and women, contending that this is a disservice to them. The psychoanalytically oriented theorist or practitioner takes the position that if a person is understood metapsychologically, he will be enhanced, not demeaned. Whether the patient wishes to be heterosexual, bisexual, or homosexual is his own decision. However, his life may become more enjoyable when he can give up maladaptive defenses, reduce anxiety, and become more tolerant of his instincts. In some cases, men and women who are homosexual or bisexual learn in psychotherapy that their sexual behavior has been used as a defensive operation, much as frigidity and impotency are used, and with lessened anxiety move to full heterosexuality.

Because of the political, ethical, and other social dimensions that impinge on the subject of homosexuality and bisexuality, some crucial psychological questions often become obliterated in a frank discussion of the subject. One question that should be confronted is: When members of both sexes are available to the individual, why does he (or she) choose same-sex partners for sexual gratification?

In Freudian theory, the prime etiological factor in male homosexuality appears to be castration anxiety. The male, usually because of strong incestuous fantasies, would rather submit to Father and be his lover than oppose him and compete with him, as was illustrated in the discussion of Freud's Schreber case. To the homosexual man, the sight of anyone without a penis is so terrifying that he avoids it by rejecting any sexual relationship with a woman (Freud, 1939). Recognition that there are human beings without a penis leads to the conclusion that one might oneself become such a being.

Frequently male homosexuals have an exaggerated love for their mothers, and homosexuality can express itself not only as submitting to Father but also as mothering oneself. The homosexual man gives to his partner as he would have liked to receive from his mother. He may choose as love objects young men or boys, whom he treats with the tenderness he would have desired from his mother (Fenichel, 1945).

Another etiological factor in homosexuality is the question of identification. Children tend to identify more with the parent from whom they have experienced the more impressive frustrations. This explains Freud's finding (1939) that men who are inclined to become homosexuals have had a weak father or no father at all and have been frustrated in crucial areas by their mother. However, boys who have had no mother are also inclined to become homosexual, because the enjoyment of the passive pleasures at the hands of a man instead of a woman creates a disposition toward homosexuality (Glover, 1949).

In female homosexuality, the etiological factors usually emanate from Oedipal conflicts and penis envy. Many women respond to disappointment over their Oedipal wishes by an identification with their father. In their anger toward their father for not loving them the way they would have liked, they incorporate him in fantasy and become him, thus assuming an active masculine relation to women. For a woman, this inverted-Oedipal identification with the parent of the opposite sex wards off Mother's disapproval and possible abandonment. Usually the female homosexual regresses to an early mother-daughter relationship, and the activities of homosexual women consist mainly of the mutual playing of mother and child (Fenichel, 1945).

Frequently the sight of a penis for the homosexual woman creates a fear of impending violation, but more often it mobilizes thoughts and emotions about the difference in appearance between male and female. The female homosexual, in effect, is saying to the man, "I hate you for the pleasures you can have with your penis. I will have nothing to do with it. I will relate to women sexually and do a better job than you can."

The Psychoneuroses

We have already discussed the major factors that contribute to a psychoneurosis. To briefly recapitulate, the patient has sexual and aggressive fantasies that are unacceptable to him and create anxiety. His defenses are not strong enough to bind his anxiety, and symptoms such as obsessions, compulsions, and phobias erupt. A symptom expresses in disguised form a patient's impulses as well as his anxiety.

There are three major psychoneuroses: obsessive-compulsive neurosis, anxiety hysteria, and conversion hysteria.

OBSESSIVE-COMPULSIVE NEUROSIS

The obsessive-compulsive neurotic is tormented by continuous and unwanted thoughts and/or feels compelled to perform certain actions over which he has little or no conscious control. He is in a constant struggle between his strong sadistic wishes to hurt others and a very powerful need to punish himself for these "evil" thoughts. The compulsion or obsession is a compromise between two opposing forces: the id's wish to hurt others and the superego's wish for punishment. The ego compromises by forming the obsessive or compulsive symptom.

Several forms of obsessions and compulsions are well known. The person with a hand-washing compulsion must continually clean away his dirty thoughts; the housewife who must constantly check the gas jets is attempting to cope with her wishes to burn down the house; the obsessive thought "God, strike me dead!" is the response to the death wishes an individual has toward important persons in his life.

The unconscious conflicts in an obsessive-compulsive neurosis deal with problems of love and hate, right and wrong, cleanliness and dirt, orderliness and disorder; because of his demanding superego, the patient suffers from intense guilt. One of the paramount features of the obsessive-compulsive patient is his omnipotence of thought, or magical thinking; he really believes his thoughts can kill (Cameron, 1963).

Afraid of his feelings because he is convinced they will do damage, the obsessive-compulsive patient lacks spontaneity and is frequently sexually impotent or frigid. He must organize his life around the fear that he will "step on a crack and break Mother's back."

Thirty-two-year-old Mr. Oliver suffered from a compulsion to look behind him. Whether he was at home, at work, or on the street, he had to look behind him. When he started treatment he could not give any reasons for his compulsion, but he did mention that when he did not look behind him he felt extreme anxiety and worried that someone might hurt him.

Mr. Oliver's compulsion was an expression of many wishes and fears. Plagued by an omnipotent desire to be an emperor "or someone like Muhammad Ali," he was very contemptuous of most people because they did not "recognize his superiority." Inasmuch as his wish to be omnipotent was so frequently frustrated, he became very angry and he harbored many sadistic wishes toward others. However he felt guilty about these wishes and felt that he should be punished for them.

Constantly looking back kept Mr. Oliver in contact with his enemies so that the battle could be waged unconsciously. The compulsion also placated his superego by putting him on the constant lookout for punishment of his sadistic wishes.

Anxiety Hysteria

The patient suffering from anxiety hysteria experiences pervasive anxiety. Most of the time this anxiety is attached to special objects or situations and is manifested in the form of phobias—fears of the dark, animals, certain foods, airplanes, and so on. The dreaded object or person that must be avoided usually symbolizes exciting situations. For example, darkness can stimulate forbidden sexual wishes and then create anxiety. To avoid feeling anxious, the person avoids dark rooms.

Mrs. Peters sought treatment because she needed to travel by airplane as part of her work but was extremely frightened of flying. She became very anxious on the plane, vomited, and trembled. In treatment she brought out that going up on an airplane reminded her of "getting high" sexually, and she could not feel comfortable with her fantasies of having sex with the pilot and the passengers. As she was able to understand her unconscious wish to rebel against her parents and others by being sexually promiscuous, her phobic reactions became more understandable to her.

The hysterical patient usually suffers from much guilt because he has strong incestuous and aggressive wishes. He frequently fears abandonment, death, and mutilation. He also tends to over-dramatize his emotions—an exhibitionistic trait that is appropriate to the excitement associated with this neurosis. Fearful of losing love, he is eager to please others.

In his history, it can usually be found that the hysterical patient has been totally or almost totally unacknowledged as a developing sexual boy or girl. He or she attempts as an adult to gratify Oedipal desires, but guilt and inhibition usually result. Frequently the patient has been conditioned by seductive experiences, which are kept secret because of guilt over the accompanying sexual excitement (Austin, 1958).

As was mentioned earlier in the chapter, Freud originally thought that the patient suffering from anxiety hysteria was always a victim of a sexual seduction. He later learned that the memory reported was often a fantasy of seduction, which was a defense against the memory of sexual activities practiced by the patient, such as masturbation.

Lucille Austin (1958) has pointed out that the presenting problems of the patient or client with anxiety hysteria may take the form of difficulties in family relationships, in the job situation, or in personal adjustments. The external event that stimulates anxiety signifies a psychosexual danger.

The emotional deprivation that the anxiety hysteric has experienced is of a particular kind (Perry, 1958). It is not that the patient has not been loved, but that his parents could not accept him gracefully with his sexual wishes. The patient, when a child, repressed his (or her) desire to be wholly masculine (or feminine), and the resulting difficulties are usually in the sexual sphere: frigidity, impotence, diffuse anxiety when sexually stimulated, and phobias designed to lessen exposure to sexual relationships.

CONVERSION HYSTERIA

In conversion hysteria, the patient's psychodynamics are quite similar to those of an anxiety hysteric except that symptoms are expressed in a physical form. The physical symptoms give expression to instinctual impulses that previously had been repressed, and the organ of the body that is chosen expresses the patient's specific conflict. In Breuer and Freud's famous case of Anna O. (1936), the patient suffered from paralysis of the arm whenever she was unconsciously reminded of her sexual and aggressive feelings toward her father. At the time her father died, Anna had been sitting with her arm pressed against a chair at the side of his bed, and her paralysis expressed some of her desires for and fears of her father while at his bedside.

The somatic compliance in conversion hysteria is determined in part by unconscious sexual fantasies and a corresponding erogeneity of the afflicted body part—i.e., nongenital zones are "genitalized." Spasms, rhythmical muscular contractions, and sensory disturbances often prove to be simultaneous defenses against and substitutes for masturbatory activities.

In sum, the patient suffering from conversion hysteria is blocking the expression of sexual impulses. The sexuality dammed up inside expresses itself in unsuitable places and at inconvenient times.

CHARACTER DISORDERS

In contrast to the person with symptomatic neuroses (obsessive-compulsive neuroses, anxiety hysteria, and conversion hysteria) the patient with a character disorder does not suffer from symptoms, but expresses his psychological conflicts in such character traits as stinginess, demandingness, and Don Juan behavior. Whereas the neurotic suffers *ego-alien* symptoms, the person with a character disorder induces suffering in others. He sees his character traits as appropriate ways of coping with life, and will always defend them as the "right way." Thus his character traits are *ego-syntonic*.

THE ORAL CHARACTER

The client with an oral character is one who seeks physical or emotional "mergers" with practically everyone he encounters. Although consistently fed and nurtured as a child, he has never been successfully weaned. Consequently, if he cannot control a relationship and get what he wants pronto, he will persist in his demands for long periods of time. This very narcissistic individual knows little autonomy; like the baby, he must symbiotically attach himself to another person in order to feel some sense of identity. Often the product of a mother who could not let her child separate from her, this patient feels empty and depressed when alone. He has to hold onto another person and psychologically "eat him up" in order to feel alive. The oral character devours knowledge, particularly other people's business; in short, he feels a compulsion to take in every physical or psychological gratification that he can.

THE ANAL CHARACTER

Freud (1933) discovered that certain character traits are dominant in persons whose instinctual life is anally oriented. These traits are partly reaction formations against anal-erotic activities and partly sublimations of them. The main traits are orderliness, frugality, and obstinacy. Anal character traits express concomitantly a resistance and an obedience to the demands of the environment.

THE HYSTERICAL CHARACTER

Like all patients with character disorders, the person with a hysterical character does not suffer consciously from anxiety or guilt. Ego-alien symptoms do not exist, and Glover (1949) has pointed out that a true hysterical character often goes undetected because his behavior is seen as an exaggeration of normal behavior.

Hysterical characters are usually over-sanguine and passionate in their social likes and dislikes, and in their sexual and social relations they are quite aggrandizing. Frequently they are babyish in their emotional contacts, and they are subject on occasion to illusions. Their character traits express a conflict between intense fear of sexuality and strong but repressed sexual strivings. The hysterical character tends to sexualize most "nonsexual" relations, and he is usually inclined toward suggestibility, irrational emotional outbreaks, chaotic behavior, and histrionic behavior (Fenichel, 1945).

PSYCHOPATHY

The psychopath or sociopath is an individual who suffers from weakness in his superego functioning. Either because he has not been trained to develop limits and controls, or because his training has been abusive and punitive, he has refused to develop inner controls, or a conscience. The psychopath is an impulsive individual, extremely narcissistic, who is unwilling to curb his aggressive and sexual impulses because he does not feel any obligation to cooperate with an uncooperative world. He is a psychological infant, who is fighting restrictions and training and refusing to surrender. His only real fear is getting caught, and he rarely suffers from pangs of conscience if he has behaved in a socially unacceptable or illegal manner (Cameron, 1963).

Occasionally we see an isolation of guilt feelings in a nonpsychopathic patient. This neurotic individual performs illegal or socially unacceptable acts without any guilt and later experiences exaggerated guilt on some other occasion without being aware of the connection (Fenichel, 1945).

THE PARANOID CHARACTER

The paranoid person is always afraid of hidden persecutors. He is a guilt-ridden individual who is always anticipating punishment. Frequently hating himself and experiencing much shame for sexual and aggressive wishes, the paranoid person is always ready for an assault from his environment, which he experiences as omnipotent and punishing.

In completing our review of clinical diagnoses, we would like to reiterate that diagnostic labels have many limitations: They do not give us a real understanding of the patient's psychic structure or dynamics, or the pressures that come from his environment. Frequently they serve to stigmatize and stereotype the person and hinder the process of individualization.

Chapter 3

The Psychoanalytic Theory of Therapeutic Intervention

The psychoanalytic theory of therapeutic intervention parallels the theory's orientation to personality functioning. Just as the psychoanalytic theory of human behavior contends that the individual's adaptation to life cannot be fully understood unless the meaning of personal id wishes, ego defenses, superego admonitions, and history is exposed, so a patient cannot be substantially helped, psychoanalysis alleges, unless he becomes aware of certain id wishes, faces persistent superego admonitions, and recognizes how he is distorting the present and perceiving it as if it were part of his childhood past. If neurotic and other dysfunctional behavior is to be significantly altered, the patient must become sensitized to how he is *unconsciously* arranging a good part of his own misery. As mentioned in Chapter 2, the patient's symptoms, maladaptive defenses, self-destructive character traits, and conflicted interpersonal relationships receive their major impetus from the dynamic unconscious.

Although other forms of therapeutic intervention such as behavior modification therapy can and do alleviate distress, the major difference between psychoanalytically oriented treatment and other therapies is that intervention which adheres to psychoanalytic principles takes the patient's complete metapsychology into serious consideration. The Freudian orientation to therapy states that treatment which does not relate to the patient's unconscious can achieve only superficial and temporary results.

The aims and goals of psychoanalytic psychotherapy are much more ambitious than those of most other therapies. In contrast to symptom relief or improvement of one or two interpersonal relationships, a psychoanalytically oriented therapist aims to help the patient diminish defensive hatred and become more loving in most, if not all, relationships; derive substantial pleasure and happiness from work and love relationships; communicate with more ease; have a positive self-image that is based on reality; tone down childish demands; and assume a constructive and enjoyable role in the family and in the social order (Fine, 1971).

In this chapter we will review and discuss the major therapeutic procedures and concepts used by Freudian psychoanalysis. Some of these procedures and concepts and the accompanying case illustrations are not applicable to therapy with social work clients, but many of them are. In Chapter 4 and 5 we will discuss those dimensions of psychoanalytic theory that can be utilized in the assessment and treatment of clients of social workers.

Free Association: The Fundamental Rule

To help the patient become aware of how he is unconsciously arranging to distort love and work relationships and thus failing to achieve the happiness and pleasure he consciously desires, the therapist asks him to observe "the fundamental rule" established by Freud (1904): He must say *everything* that comes into his mind—what he feels, thinks, remembers, fantasies, dreams. The rationale for this rule is as follows:

1. As he tells an unintrusive and empathetic listener what comes into his mind, the patient begins to see for himself just how much he is writing his own script, i.e., arranging for his own successes and failures. For example, if the patient finds himself

in a chaotic marriage, in an unrewarding job situation, or in a tense parent-child relationship, by listening to his own associations he slowly becomes aware of his fantasies of doing battle, his desires to seduce, his fears of interacting, and his urges to be mistreated.

2. If the therapist assumes a neutral posture during this process, the patient's self-esteem usually rises and his anxiety lessens. When the therapist neither champions nor repudiates his productions, the patient begins to feel very much like a child who has confessed a misdeed to an understanding and empathetic parent. Like the well-understood child who is not disliked or criticized for what he has reported, the patient begins to like himself more and more.

3. Free association usually induces the patient to regress, and he begins to recall memories and distorted notions from the past that influence his functioning in the present. He begins to see, for example, how the battle with a colleague that is causing his present psychosomatic symptoms may be part of an unresolved problem with a sibling. He may learn that his oversensitivity to his wife's demands is due to his wish that she become the punitive mother of his past.

4. As the patient begins, through free association, to realize some of the factors that account for his behavior and to appreciate that to go on hating himself for what he wishes and fears is self-destructive and counterproductive, he begins to apply this perspective to others. As he becomes less judgmental with relatives, friends, and colleagues, they appreciate him more.

When Mr. Zeller, a man in his early forties, consulted a therapist for help in coping with his teen-age son Joe, at first he made many derogatory remarks about his son. He said that Joe was extremely defiant and questioned everything his father valued. After about four sessions of debasing Joe, Mr. Zeller commented that although he was feeling a little less tense in the relationship because he had "got a lot off my chest," there was "something about Joe's rebelliousness that makes me uptight." When the therapist asked Mr. Zeller to freely associate to the idea of "rebelliousness," this was extremely helpful. He talked about how he had always harbored a great deal of resentment toward his own father and had frequently had fantasies of defying him, but never did. As he reflected on his own wishes to defy his father, Mr. Zeller could then move on to recognize how he was unconsciously encouraging Joe to be rebellious and was getting vicarious pleasure from Joe's provocative behavior. Mr. Zeller could eventually see how he frequently neglected to provide limits and structure for Joe when Joe needed this kind of parental support.

An important but difficult part of doing psychoanalytic psychotherapy is being silent and unintrusive. If the patient is going to free-associate and eventually become aware of latent feelings, thoughts, and memories, the therapist must demonstrate his confidence in the patient's ability to communicate and derive meaning from his associations. When the therapist in effect says "Say what comes to your mind and see what's there! When you do you'll make connections that will help you feel better," the patient eventually identifies with this point of view. As he begins to value his own thoughts and his ability to make sense out of them, he values himself more.

Frequently a patient finds it difficult to free-associate to certain issues in the past and present because he is convinced that the therapist will dislike him for his "bad" behavior. Many patients cast the therapist in the role of their own superego (Freud, 1938; Glover, 1958). Because they are ready to heap abuse on themselves for their real and imagined misdemeanors, they anticipate the same kind of treatment from the therapist.

Mrs. Young, aged thirty, an unemployed woman, found it difficult to discuss her work history. When her therapist asked her what she feared might happen if she did so, she became very agitated and said, "If you knew the truth you'd never help me." In response to the therapist's interpretation that she felt guilty and seemed to anticipate punishment from him, Mrs. Young recalled several incidents of stealing possessions from her co-workers at previous places of employment. When the therapist said nothing in response to these confessions, but simply listened, Mrs. Young asked, "Are you still going to help me?" On the therapist's again pointing out that Mrs. Young expected rejection rather than understanding from him, she was not only able to describe many additional incidents of stealing but also began to see why she stole. Feeling angry and competitive toward co-workers, she wanted to put them in the same psychological position she was in—deprived and wanting.

As Mrs. Young was able to talk more about her stealing without censure from her therapist, she felt less guilty and became more accepting of herself. The more the therapist listened and was nonjudgmental, the more Mrs. Young could be forgiving of herself.

When free association takes place in the presence of a benign superego figure, the atmosphere is such that the therapist appears more and more like a parent to the patient, and therefore he begins to recall incidents from childhood that still influence his everyday behavior.

Mr. Wolfe, aged thirty-five, was seen in therapy for a chronic case of alcoholism. The more he talked about his frustrations in the present and felt free to express himself with his therapist, the more he recalled tempestuous incidents with his mother. When he talked about how he was "spiting my wife by not working and getting drunk," he slowly began to realize how he was keeping himself a little boy with a mother figure. Recalling how he "got even" with his mother by not going to school and raiding candy stores, he could eventually understand some of his defiant behavior as an adult.

As we have already suggested, when the patient is helped to free-associate in the presence of a warm, accepting therapist and sees that this makes him feel better, he begins to recapitulate the therapeutic experience with others.

Mr. Volmer, a twenty-two-year-old single man, came for treatment because of his inability to sustain relationships with women. With his female therapist, he was able to discuss his contempt and hatred for women. His feelings toward women were usually verbalized when he felt frustrated and angry with the therapist. When the therapist did not respond to Mr. Volmer's provocativeness, he was slowly able to recognize that much of his aggression was a defense against sexual and loving feelings, which he feared. As he was more able to get in tune with his loving feelings and express them to the therapist, he felt an increase in his self-esteem. He found himself responding to other people with more empathy and compassion, and after a year of treatment told the therapist, "I seem to do with others what you do with me. If they're angry, I try to understand them rather than get into a fight. This helps all of us get along much better."

Resistance

Although most patients welcome the idea of saying everything that comes into their minds and usually feel better during the early stages of the therapeutic encounter, eventually the therapy becomes painful and creates anxiety. As a patient discovers parts of himself that have been repressed, confronts sexual and aggressive impulses, and recovers embarrassing memories, he begins to feel guilt and shame. Then he may become silent and evasive, or want to quit the therapy altogether. Or in discussing certain incidents from his past or current circumstances, he may become angry at the therapist for not reassuring, praising, or admonishing him.

When the patient stops producing material and ceases to examine himself, we refer to this kind of behavior as *resistance*. Resistance is any action or attitude of the patient's that impedes the course of therapeutic work. Inasmuch as every patient, to some extent, wants unconsciously to preserve the status quo, all therapy must be carried on in the face of some resistance.

What are referred to as defenses in the patient's daily life— e.g., projection, denial, repression—are resistances in therapy. If, for example, a patient has a tendency to project his anger onto his spouse and other individuals, in therapy he will try to avoid examining his own angry thoughts and feelings and will report how his wife, friends, and relatives are hostile to him. From time to time he will also accuse the therapist of being contemptuous toward him.

Resistance is not created by the therapy. The therapeutic situation activates anxiety, and the patient then uses habitual mechanisms to oppose the therapist and the therapy (Greenson, 1967). To a greater or lesser degree resistances are present from the beginning to the end of treatment (Freud, 1912).

Psychoanalytic therapy is characterized by a thorough and systematic examination of resistances. The therapist attempts to uncover how the patient resists, what he is resisting, and why he is doing so. Usually the purpose of resistance is to avoid a painful emotion like guilt or shame, which is frequently aroused by an unacceptable id impulse (Greenson, 1967; A. Freud, 1937; Fenichel, 1945).

In contrast to other forms of therapy—which evade resistances or attempt to overcome them by suggestion, praise, punishment, drugs, shock, or persuasion—psychoanalytically oriented therapy seeks to uncover the cause, purpose, mode, and history of resistances (Knight, 1952; Greenson, 1967). On occasion, the therapist will not try to expose the meaning of the patient's resistance to him because the process might activate too much anxiety. For example, in the case of a very disturbed patient who is projecting his anger onto his wife, the therapist might accept the patient's perception that his wife is angry with him and then examine with the patient what he thinks is bothering the wife. As the patient talks about his wife's anger and sees that the therapist does not condemn the emotion but looks at it as a feeling to be understood, the patient may examine his own anger because he will no longer be as frightened of the therapist's condemnation (Strean, 1978).

Numerous attempts have been made by psychoanalysts to classify resistances. Freud's *Inhibitions, Symptoms, and Anxiety* (1926) presented a metapsychological classification:

1. Repression or other defenses (projection, denial): These defenses are used by the ego to ward off unconscious material that would arouse anxiety. In these instances the patient wards off instinctual impulses (sex and aggression) because these impulses present a danger.

2. Transference resistances: The patient perceives the analyst as if he were a figure of the past; instead of facing unpleasant memories and emotions that he experienced as a child, he ascribes parental qualities to the analyst and then feels that the analyst is provoking, rejecting, or seducing him.
3. Epinosic gain: The patient strives to maintain the gratifications that his illness provides. He avoids work or certain interpersonal relationships and seeks childish indulgences instead.
4. Superego resistance: The patient continues to abuse himself with guilt and self-punishment because of his unacceptable aggressive wishes. This is sometimes referred to as the "negative therapeutic reaction."
5. Id resistance: The patient continues to seek gratification of unrealistic childish wishes, such as a desire to be an omnipotent infant and have all his demands met immediately.

In a paper called "Remembering, Repeating and Working Through," Freud (1914a, p. 145) said:

> The working through of the resistances may, in practice, turn out to be an arduous task for the subject of the analysis and a trial of patience for the analyst. Nevertheless, it is a part of the work which effects the greatest changes in a patient and which distinguishes analytic treatment from any [other] kind of treatment.

The process of "working through" requires the therapist to expose the patient's resistances to him again and again, and help him see what impulses frighten him and create guilt. The patient's conflict is worked through when he can genuinely accept his wishes and thoughts without punishing himself for them.

Anna Freud in *Ego and Mechanisms of Defense* (1937) pointed out that while resistances constitute obstacles to a successful therapeutic outcome, they provide essential material for constructive work. Her classification of resistances is the familiar list of defense mechanisms: projection, reaction formation, repression, and so on. Anna Freud also emphasized the importance of taking into consideration the impulses, superego mandates, and environmental stimuli that are warded off by resistances.

In 1955 Edward Glover distinguished between "gross" and "unobtrusive" resistances. Gross resistances refer to obvious behavior such as consistent lateness for a therapeutic session, defiant silence, and refusal to comply with the fundamental rule of free association. Unobtrusive resistances refer to behaviors of which the patient is unaware: excessive compliance, forgetting the time or date of an analytic hour, and failure to remember to pay the therapist.

Greenson (1967) classified resistances according to their sources (id, ego, superego); their fixation points (oral, anal, phallic-Oedipal, latent, and adolescent); the types of defense utilized (e.g., repression, isolation); the clinical diagnosis of the patient (e.g., anxiety hysteria, obsessive-compulsive neurosis, character disorders); and finally, whether a resistance is ego-alien or ego-syntonic. An ego-alien resistance is one that appears "foreign, extraneous and strange to the patient's ego' '; e.g., the patient, for no rational reason, fears the therapist's condemnation and therefore finds it very difficult to talk. An ego-syntonic resistance refers to one that is a well-established, habitual pattern but also wards off anxiety; e.g., the patient must compulsively arrive for every appointment a half-hour before the scheduled time, and if he doesn't he will feel stress and a need for punishment.

Fine (1971) has provided a classification which divides resistances into those involving refusal to comply with basic requests and those of a more subtle nature. Examples of the first type are lateness, refusal to talk, or refusal to pay. Examples of "indirect resistances" are overemphasis on the here-and-now, unreasonable demands, somatization, and the negative therapeutic reaction.

Sandler et al. (1973) and Greenson (1967) have taken the position that a classification of the *sources* of resistance is especially pertinent, and have listed the following specific resistances as most common: the threat posed by the therapeutic work of interfering with the patient's habitual modes of adaptation; trans-ference-based resistances; resistances derived from epinosic gain and from secondary gain; those that stem from the superego; resistances resulting from difficulties in the patient's outside rela-tionships because of changes brought about by therapy; resist-ances prompted by the danger of cure and the inevitable loss of the therapist; and finally, resistances created by threats to the patient's self-esteem. These authors also have noted that while resistance was originally seen as related to recollection and free association, it has been extended to include all obstacles to the aims and goals of therapy.

Langs (1976) has pointed out that in any discussion or classification of resistances, one must consider the therapist's contribution to the formation of the patient's resistive behavior. Is the therapist behaving in such a way that the patient wants to come late, refuse to cooperate, or quit the treatment?

All the writers cited in the forgoing discussion agree that resist-ance occurs in all therapy, and that the therapist must understand its source and why it takes the form it does, and must then help the patient resolve it. We shall now consider in more detail and from a psychoanalytic perspective some typical forms of resist-ance in therapeutic work.

LATENESS

As we discussed in Chapter 2, the analytically oriented therapist takes the position that behavior in and of itself does not tell us very much. A resistance like lateness to appointments with the therapist can have different meanings for different patients, as the following two vignettes indicate.

Mr. and Mrs. Underwood, a couple in their mid-thirties, were seen for marital counselling. After four sessions with the therapist, during which they expressed a great deal of scorn for each other, they began to arrive about fifteen to twenty minutes late for appointments. When the therapist confronted the couple with their consistent lateness, at first they denied that it had any significance. However, when the therapist suggested that "something about coming here must bother you and it seems that there's something you would rather avoid discussing," the Underwoods were finally able to examine their persistent lateness and its causes. It turned out that both of them were afraid to discuss their mutual criticisms because "if it continues," said Mr. Underwood, with his wife agreeing, "we'll have to split and I'm not ready for that."

The Underwoods' lateness was an expression of their separation anxiety. They both were becoming frightened of their mutual hatred and were worried that continued expression of it would lead to a breakup of their marriage.

Mr. and Mrs. Thomas, a young couple in their twenties, were also involved in marriage counseling. After about six sessions, which they agreed had been productive and helpful, the couple began to arrive late for appointments. When their lateness was pointed out to them, Mr. Thomas acknowledged that he was feeling uncomfortable about something but was not sure what it was. Mrs. Thomas had similar feelings.

When the therapist pointed out to the Thomases that they had begun coming late after they agreed that they were feeling more warmly toward each other, Mrs. Thomas blurted out, "I know what bothers me. Now we're supposed to have sex more often and I don't want that." Mr. Thomas said that during the past few weeks he had found Mrs. Thomas more attractive to him and had thought several times of making love to her.

The Thomas' lateness was an expression of their resistance to deeper intimacy. As they felt increased warmth toward each other, their sexual desires became more intensified and this frightened both of them. By coming late to interviews, they gave themselves less chance to face their sexual conflicts.

SILENCE

When a patient resists by being silent, it usually means that he is consciously or unconsciously unwilling to communicate a thought, feeling, or memory to the therapist. Frequently the patient is anxious about what the therapist will think of his angry or erotic feelings or deeds. Like the child who fears punishment and hides from his parents, the frightened adult tries to handle his anxiety through silence.

Miss Smith, aged twenty-four, was in treatment with a male therapist. Her presenting problems all revolved around difficulties in her relationships with men. Although Miss Smith was quite articulate in her first several interviews, after she recalled some history that involved sex play with an older brother, she became silent. When the therapist asked "What might be making you run away from me at this time?" she with some difficulty told him that she was afraid he might try to seduce her, as her brother had, so she avoided talking to him.

Miss Smith was stimulated by her talks with the therapist, particularly when she discussed sexual matters. Because her sexual wishes made her uncomfortable, she had to project them onto the therapist and then avoid him through silence. The mechanisms she utilized were those operative in a phobia; i.e., she *repressed* her sexual wishes and *avoided* the therapist.

Silence, like all behavior, can have many meanings and many purposes. For Miss Smith, it was a means of resisting expression of sexual feelings. For Mr. Roberts, as is shown in the following case example, it was a way of preventing expressions of aggression.

Mr. Roberts, aged thirty-two, sought help because he never advanced on his job as a computer operator. Although he was a hard and diligent worker, he was very quiet with peers and authorities and seemed unwilling to assert himself with them. When it became clear that Mr. Roberts was frightened of many aggressive fantasies, the therapist interpreted this to him. Mr. Roberts then spent the next few interviews in silence. After several more interviews and with help from the therapist, he was able to say how frightened he was of "telling you [the therapist] off for making irritating comments!"

RELUCTANCE TO PAY FEES

Since money plays such a significant role in our society, it inevitably is used to express resistances in psychotherapy. Analysts and therapists often feel anxiety about charging reasonable fees and can have even more reluctance to charge for missed appointments.

When the patient is late in paying his fee, he is usually expressing some resentment about the treatment and/or the fee.

Mr. Queen, aged forty, was in treatment with a male therapist. After an initial "honeymoon" during which Mr. Queen extolled the therapist for his sensitivity and understanding, he became quite competitive with him. He told the therapist that he was the brighter, sexier, and more athletic of the two, and that if they ever got into a boxing arena the therapist would be on his back in five minutes.

When the therapist did not counterattack but merely told Mr. Queen that he was engaging him in a battle similar to the ones he had repeatedly had with his father, Mr. Queen said, "I'll get you pissed yet. You like to act unperturbed, but I'll get to you!" Mr. Queen then let several weeks go by without paying his usual monthly fee. When he was confronted with his resistance, Mr. Queen eventually said, "This way I can control you and feel some superiority over you. You can't run the show all the time!"

Mr. Queen used his nonpayment of fees to express contempt toward the therapist. This way he could feel like an adequate competitor and try to make the therapist feel helpless, just as he had felt with his father when he was a boy.

Fees can also be used to express seductive desires and wishes to manipulate.

Mrs. Pearson, aged fifty-three, was a wealthy woman who "bought her friends" by giving them expensive gifts and holding lavish parties. Although charming and loved by most of her family and friends, she sought treatment because of depressed feelings, low self-esteem, and lack of sustained pleasure in her life. In her relationship with the therapist she felt insufficiently appreciated, and wanted more praise, more encouragement, and more advice. The therapist did not gratify Mrs. Pearson's demands, but attempted instead to help her better understand her insatiable wishes to be adored and indulged. After a few meager attempts to cooperate with the therapist, the patient made him an offer. She pointed out that because she had a very high income and did not need all her money, she wanted to pay a higher fee for the therapy. She reasoned that the therapist could use some of the money she did not need.

Rather than accept or reject Mrs. Pearson's offer, the therapist explored with her the meaning of her proposal. At first angry and then more thoughtful in subsequent interviews, Mrs. Pearson realized that offering a higher fee to the therapist was her attempt to buy his love. The offer not only protected her against exploring her feelings of low self-worth but also expressed id resistance—a wish to be loved and cared for all the time and to be treated like what Mrs. Pearson termed "Her Royal Highness."

It is always the therapist's responsibility to help the patient understand what meaning money has for him—particularly when money, with all its attendant affects and defenses, becomes an element in the therapeutic relationship. Mrs. Pearson used money to put herself on a fantasied throne and make others "slaves"—a defense against feelings of poor self-esteem.

If the patient uses money to express his resistances, confrontation of the resistive behavior can help him function better, not only in situations that involve finances but in other interpersonal encounters as well.

Mr. Olsen, a single man of twenty-five and a successful salesman, sought treatment for ulcers and other psychosomatic ailments. He was a very driven and competitive man who always wanted "to make a killing." After about three months of what he termed "good, constructive therapy" with a male analyst, he took off from therapy for a two-week vacation without any notice. When he returned, he insisted that he should not pay for his missed sessions because the therapist "did not offer any service."

When Mr. Olsen's behavior was explored, he pointed out that he resented the analyst's "control" and "lofty position" and implied that he felt very competitive with him. His vacation and refusal to pay the fee were his expressions of competition, contempt, and the desire to destroy the gains he had already achieved in therapy.

As Mr. Olsen discussed his competitive feelings and explored some of the dynamics of his competitive relationships in the past and present, he began to realize "how much pleasure I get out of gypping others." He began to understand how his refusal to pay the therapist was his way of expressing his contempt, and that contempt was his underlying feeling in most interpersonal relationships.

The Patient's Situation as a Resistance

People often seek out a therapist because they have some situational problem, such as a poor marriage, a conflicted parent-child relationship, an unsatisfactory job, or educational difficulty. While a patient's spouse, parent, employer, or teacher may not always be a mature individual responsive to his needs, it is very important to recognize that when the patient continually focuses on the problems that significant others impose on him, this is usually a sign of resistance. Most individuals would rather believe that their unhappy marriages, unsatisfactory jobs, or unstimulating interpersonal relationships are caused by forces outside themselves. Frequently patients hope, and sometimes demand, that the therapist manipulate their environment and change the spouse, boss, or teacher. However, it is of much more help to these individuals to see how in many ways they are determining their own fates.

Mr. and Mrs. North, a couple in their mid-forties, Bob (age twelve), and Sally (age ten) were seen in family therapy because they constantly bickered, found it hard to agree on even trivial issues, and seemed to receive little pleasure from life, either individually or collectively.

In their sessions each of the family members projected blame onto the others. Mrs. North accused Mr. North of being too passive, Mr. North accused Mrs. North of being too bossy, and the children complained that their parents demanded too much of them. Sally and Bob also argued with each other, and each of them felt that the other did to take enough responsibility for family chores.

When the therapist observed that the Norths were using the therapy sessions as wrestling matches with each family member deriding the others, the meaning of this resistance slowly became apparent. Mrs. North had to demean her husband because she had many sexual fears, and by criticizing him she could keep him at a distance. Mr. North harbored a great deal of resentment that frightened him, and by being isolated and passive he could control his aggression. Bob and Sally both wanted their parents' love but felt uncomfortable facing their wishes and masked their anxiety by arguing.

Although the Norths' critical statements about one another had a basis in reality, their functioning could not improve until each member of the family was helped to take some responsibility for the family altercations.

It is often tempting for a therapist to support his patient against a spouse, boss, or teacher, but the patient will not feel better or function more maturely until he faces and resolves his own contributions to his neurotic interactions.

OVEREMPHASIS ON THE PAST

Just as a patient can resist exploring himself by focusing on others, he can avoid coping with the present by overemphasizing the past.

Mr. Martin, forty-one, had many problems: He was unemployed, alcoholic, sexually impotent, depressed, and lethargic. He used his interviews with his therapist to complain about his "miserable childhood," when his parents had "neglected" him, his teachers "abused" him, and his friends "scapegoated" him. He obviously received much gratification from pitying himself, and was making virtually no progress in therapy.

When the therapist confronted Mr. Martin with his resistance and pointed out how he avoided discussing his present circumstances, Mr. Martin became furious. He told the therapist that she was a brutal and unsympathetic person who was oblivious to her patient's suffering. The therapist did not respond to Mr. Martin's hostility, and in subsequent interviews he was eventually able to face the fact that he was still yearning to be a little boy who would be taken care of by an indulgent mother. Talking about the past was his way of keeping himself a child and avoiding adult responsibilities.

If the present is uncomfortable, as it was in the case of Mr. Martin, the patient may overemphasize the past. If fantasies and wishes arouse anxiety, the patient may focus his associations on the superficial events of his daily life. If the past is very traumatic, the patient may stay with the present. When there is an overemphasis on any aspect of the patient's life, the therapist should always wonder about what is being concealed.

THE NEGATIVE THERAPEUTIC REACTION

In *The Ego and Id* (1923), Freud noted that many patients who could achieve insight into their problems and accept the analyst's interpretations did not improve. No matter how much self-understanding they derived their symptoms did not disappear, and in several cases they became exacerbated. Freud reasoned that there must be some inner force that prevented patients from utilizing their insights, and he identified this force as the superego.

Many patients cannot tolerate the idea of feeling better and enjoying a more productive life. Each time they are successful, they feel guilty. In the negative therapeutic reaction, the individual with a punitive superego who is plagued by considerable guilt is also one who has strong hostile wishes. When he succeeds at something he feels that he is destroying someone, and for this feeling—an expression of the underlying hostile wishes—he has to be punished. When such a person enters therapy, does not improve, and points out that he probably won't ever get better, he is unconsciously directing his anger toward the therapist. The negative therapeutic reaction evolves because the patient wants to defeat the therapist and therefore feels guilty.

Miss Landy, thirty, sought treatment because she found herself unable to enjoy anything in her life. She went from job to job, man to man, and apartment to apartment. Each time she was in a new situation, she would find fault with it and leave.

It was inevitable that Miss Landy would be dissatisfied with her therapy. After a few months of treatment, in which she reviewed her strong competition with both men and women, and seemed to find the therapist's clarifications and interpretations quite helpful, she said that she was going to quit. She had tried her best and she was sure that the therapist had tried her best too, but, she concluded, "I am just untreatable." When the therapist asked Miss Landy "How do you think I feel about failing you?" Miss Landy imagined that she was probably feeling dejected, depressed, and hurt. Slowly Miss Landy began to realize that this is what she wanted, and that in many ways she was using her treatment to spite the therapist. At first all she could feel was dejection and futility. But when she got more deeply in touch with her spiteful feelings, her negative therapeutic reaction diminished.

IDEALIZING THE THERAPIST

An expression of resistance that is sometimes overlooked by psychoanalysts and psychotherapists is the patient's tendency to overvalue the help he gets, thus resisting becoming autonomous. Experiencing the therapist as the parent he always wanted, he checks with him every time he has to make a decision. It is extremely important for a therapist to understand that helplessness and passivity are resistances to autonomy and assertiveness, and that it is contraindicated to take over the patient's problems for him. If the patient's dependency is gratified, he does not learn what he is afraid of and will continue to seek symbiotic mergers in his relationships.

Fifteen-year-old Kenneth was referred for therapeutic help because he was doing poorly at school, had few friends, was passive and complaining at home, and was frequently depressed. After seeing a male therapist for three interviews he had a "flight into health"; that is, all his symptoms disappeared. He felt happy, started doing good work at school, and made a few friends. "I have found the father I never had. You listen, are kind, and I feel much stronger with you in my corner!" he gleefully stated.

As work with Kenneth continued, it became clear that he was in love with a fantasy. His improved functioning was tenuous because he was on a psychological "honeymoon" with the therapist, in which he made him into a perfect, omnipotent parent who would take good care of him. When the therapist did not respond to Kenneth's seductive attitude or give in to his demands, it took Kenneth many weeks of anger and depression to see that his idealization of the therapist was an attempt to fight independence, assertiveness, and autonomy and be a little boy instead.

As the foregoing discussion implies, when an individual enters into a relationship with a therapist part of him unconsciously works against progress. Every patient, no matter how much he consciously wants his life to be different and regardless of how much he is suffering, still fears change. Resistances are facts of therapeutic life, and understanding the unconscious reasons for their unique expression is crucial to both patient and therapist.

Transference

Anyone who is engaged in helping others make changes in their lives recognizes that in the face of all logic and reason, the patient or client may often behave in a most obstinate manner. In addition to the fear of change, therapeutic progress is always hindered by the patient's major resistance, transference—the feelings, wishes, fears, and defenses that influence his perceptions of the therapist. Transferential reactions are unconscious attempts by the patient to recapitulate with the therapist types of interpersonal interaction similar to those he experienced with significant persons in the past. Every client or patient experiences the therapist not only in terms of how he objectively is but in terms of how he wishes him to be and fears he might be.

If the therapist does not understand how he is being experienced by his patient, he will not be very helpful. Each patient responds to interpretations, clarifications, or environmental manipulation in terms of his transference to the therapist. If he loves the therapist, he will be inclined to accept therapeutic interventions; if he hates the therapist, even the most neutral question such as "How do you feel?" will be suspect. Finally, if the patient has mixed feelings toward the therapist, he will respond to virtually all interventions with ambivalence.

One of the major tasks of the analyst is to help the patient see how and why he experiences him as he does. Why does the patient act like a compliant child and accept everything the analyst says? Or why does he argue with the therapist every time he says something? Why is the analyst's silence experienced by one patient as rejection and by another as love?

Although transference from a strictly technical point of view is a resistance, in most discussions transference and resistance are separated. Resistances, as we have already noted, are defense mechanisms utilized by the patient in therapy to maintain the status quo. Transference also seeks to maintain the status quo: The patient distorts who the therapist is and attempts to interact with him as if he were a figure from the past. Freud (1914b, p. 153) distinguished resistance and transference:

> It may thus be said that the theory of psychoanalysis is an attempt to account for two striking and unexpected facts of observation which emerge whenever an attempt is made to trace the symptoms of a neurotic back to their sources in his past life: the facts of transference and of resistance. Any line of investigation which recognizes these two facts and takes them as the starting point of its work may call itself psychoanalysis, though it arrives at results other than my own.

Freud (1925) singled out the notion of transference for much discussion. He pointed out that it "is a universal phenomenon of the human mind . . . . and in fact dominates the whole of each person's relations to his human environment." He further averred that transference exists in all relationships: in marriage, in the classroom, in business relations, and in friendships. Because of our unique histories, ego functioning, superego mandates, values, and social circumstances, each of us brings to every new relationship wishes, fears, anxieties, hopes, pressures, defenses, and many other subjective factors that have evolved from previous relationships and that may or may not be appropriate in the new situation. Because these universal phenomena are largely unconscious, we cannot will them away or consciously modify them. They influence our perceptions of the people we meet, and very often the reasons we give for responding to people with love, hatred, or ambivalence are rationalizations, i.e., excuses to justify our reactions.

Because every human being has had emotionally charged experiences—positive, negative, and ambivalent—with parents, siblings, members of the extended family, and others; and because these experiences have left indelible marks on him, his attitudes toward intimate relationships in the present are continually colored by past transactions. We continue to seek in new relationships what was pleasant in the past and to resist what was unpleasant.

The intimate relationship of patient and therapist is one in which the patient *depends* on the therapist. This invariably reactivates feelings and ideas that the patient experienced in respect to others on whom he depended in the past. These feelings and ideas cannot be obliterated, avoided, or neglected. They are normal in any interaction and become intensified in helping situations. If the patient has experienced those who nurtured, advised, and educated him as essentially positive and well-meaning, he will in all likelihood experience the therapist in the same way. However, usually there are residual mixtures of love, hate, and ambivalence toward parents and others in all individuals, and every therapist will be the recipient of all these feelings.

While transference reactions are always traceable to childhood, there is not always a simple one-to-one correspondence between the past and present, although sometimes there is a direct repetition such as when the patient is quite convinced that the analyst is almost identical to his father, mother, or siblings. On other occasions there can be a compensatory fantasy to make up for what was lacking in childhood. In other words, the patient fantasies that the therapist is somebody his mother or father should have been, i.e., an ego ideal.

Miss Johnson, twenty-three, after a few months of treatment told her therapist that he was the most wonderful man alive. He was brilliant, handsome, kind, sensitive, and empathetic. As long as he was in her life, she felt wonderful.

The transference reactions to the therapist had to be viewed as a resistance. To compensate for feelings of low self-esteem, "emptiness," and depression, Miss Johnson fantasied that she was in a perfect symbiosis with the therapist. It was important for him to help her eventually see that her transference reactions protected her from experiencing some of her murderous fantasies about both parents and her tremendous guilt about these fantasies. As Miss Johnson was helped to talk about some of the feelings and fantasies that she had experienced many years ago as a child, she could begin to perceive the therapist a little more realistically.

When the therapist recognizes that transference always exists in all the relationships that patients have with him, he can look at his therapeutic results more objectively. If the patient wants him to be an omnipotent parent to whom he can cling, then he will fight interventions aimed to help him become more autonomous. If the patient wants the therapist to be a sibling rival, then he will use the therapist's interventions to continue his sibling fight. Because the patient views all the therapist's interventions through the lens of his transference, the therapist must explore with the patient not just why he resists change, but more specifically, why he wants to perceive the therapist in a childish way.

Just as a positive transference can defend against negative feelings toward figures of the past (as was true with Miss Johnson), so a negative transference can protect the patient against positive feelings toward significant others of which he is frightened.

Mr. Ingersoll, aged forty-five, sought treatment for many problems. He was experiencing a great deal of job dissatisfaction, marital conflict, sexual impotency, and depression. After a few months of treatment he felt less depressed and his sexual functioning improved. However, his polite and cooperative demeanor with the therapist changed, and he became provocative, sullen, competitive, and contemptuous. When he was confronted with his negative transference reactions, he said, "I don't want to like you!" Positive feelings, patient and therapist eventually learned, scared Mr. Ingersoll. He had strong wishes to be held, cuddled, and hugged by his father, who had died when he was twelve; the negative transference protected him from experiencing his strong yearning for a father figure. As he put it, "I'd rather fight than switch."

A very common use of transference is the patient's projection of unacceptable parts of his psychic structure onto the therapist—id wishes, ego defenses, and superego mandates.

Mrs. Harris, thirty-seven, was seen in treatment for marital difficulties. She was a very constricted woman with a powerful superego. Extremely well organized and disciplined, she could not permit herself very many gratifications. During treatment she transferred many of her unacceptable id wishes to her female therapist. She told the therapist her fantasy that the therapist had "probably had many extramarital affairs," "enjoyed getting beaten up by a man," and "took hot showers with him." The therapist neither accepted nor denied Mrs. Harris' transference projections, but encouraged the patient to fully explore her fantasies. Mrs. Harris was eventually able to identify with the therapist's nondefensive attitude and face some of her own sexual fantasies, which had been very repressed.

More often than not, the patient projects his own superego onto the therapist and expects punishment from him. Such projection is related to the way the superego is formed in a child. The process of socialization is one in which the child gives up various modes of instinctual gratification at the request of significant figures. This process is crystallized in the superego, which induces guilt. Guilt is superego punishment. Because the superego is formed in interaction with significant individuals, it can be changed only by interaction. As the client or patient projects his superego onto the therapist, a consistent comparison of this projection with reality serves to break down the superego in the course of time (Fine, 1971).

Twelve-year-old George came to treatment with a variety of scholastic and interpersonal problems. As soon as he started treatment, he mentioned that he had stopped masturbating. When the therapist wondered why he had done that, he replied that it was a bad habit and that surely the therapist would condemn him for it. When the therapist asked George what was wrong with masturbation, George told of his fantasies about going blind, discoloring his hands, and getting pimples. All of these fantasies were expressions of George's strict and punitive superego. Furthermore, he had to learn that the therapist was quite different from his parents. He did not feel that sex was something bad; it was something to be enjoyed.

Whatever the dynamics of transference are—projection of superego mandates, id wishes, or other unconscious elements—a therapeutic relationship is distinguished from all others not by these dynamics but by their place in the relationship, i.e., the therapist's attitude toward the transference and the use he makes of it. When a person asks for encouragement, advice, or punishment, the analytically oriented therapist—in contrast to a friend or relative—wants to know why these responses are requested. As Charles Brenner (1976, p. 109) has said:

> The addition of a dash of encouragement, or a measure of scolding or admonition, however tactful and well intended, may seem to hasten the [therapeutic] process. It can, at times, produce symptomatic improvement. But it is no substitute for analysis of why the patient wants encouragement, admonition, or any other nonanalytic behavior. . . . In the long run it cannot fail to interfere to a greater or lesser degree with progress and with the achievement of an optimal end result.

In sum, transference exists in all relationships. There is no such thing as a patient or a client who has "no transference" or in whom transference fails to develop. As clinician and patient accept transference as a fact of therapeutic life and constantly study the patient's transference responses, they gain an appreciation of the nature of his conflicts and aspects of his history that are contributing to his dysfunctional behavior (Sandler et al., 1973; Menninger, 1958).

Countertransference

Countertransference is the same dynamic phenomenon as transference, except that it refers to those unconscious wishes and defenses of the therapist that interfere with his objective perception and mature treatment of the patient. Frequently the patient represents for the therapist an object of the past onto whom past feelings and wishes are projected. The term "countertransference" was first used by Freud in his paper "The Future Prospects of Psychoanalysis" (1910, p. 141):

> We have become aware of the "countertransference" which arises in him [the analyst] as a result of the patient's influence on his unconscious feelings, and we are inclined to insist that he shall recognize this countertransference in himself and overcome it.... no psychoanalyst goes further than his own complexes and internal resistances permit.

Freud repeatedly stressed the limitations imposed on analytic work by the practitioner's psychological blind spots. Initially he advocated a continuous self-examination for the analyst (1910), but he soon realized that this is difficult because of the analyst's own resistance to self-understanding. By 1937 he realized that in self-analysis the danger of incompleteness is particularly great; one is too easily satisfied with a partial explanation, "behind which resistance can easily keep back something that may perhaps be more important." He recommended that in lieu of self-analysis, every analyst undergo an analysis by someone else. In 1937 he suggested that analysts be reanalyzed about every five years.

As indicated above, countertransference reactions can arise because of the therapist's inability to deal maturely with aspects of the patient's communications that impinge on problems of his own. For example, if a therapist has unresolved problems connected with his own aggression, he may need to placate or be ingratiating with a patient. Similarly, if a therapist is threatened by his own unconscious homosexual feelings, he may be unable to detect homosexual implications in a patient's material (Sandler et al., 1973) or may perceive them where they do not exist.

A major development in the psychoanalytic writings in countertransference occurred when analysts began to recognize that this phenomenon, like transference, is inevitable, ubiquitous, and frequently desirable and helpful to the therapy. One of the clearest statements in this connection has been made by Sharpe (1947, p. 120): "To say that an analyst will still have complexes, blindspots, and limitations is only to say he remains a human being. When he ceases to be an ordinary human being he ceases to be a good analyst."

Annie Reich (1951) has pointed out that countertransference is a necessary prerequisite of analysis: "If it does not exist the necessary talent and interest is lacking." A similar view has been expressed by Little (1960), who says that "without unconscious countertransference there would be neither empathy nor analysis itself." Money-Kyrle (1956) has referred to empathy as the "normal" countertransference.

Brenner (1976, p. 130) has stated:

> Whatever work one does as an adult, whatever satisfactions one finds in a chosen profession, whatever relationships one establishes with persons one meets with, whether in a professional capacity or in any other, all are significantly motivated or determined by psychic conflicts that originated in connection with childhood instinctual wishes. One cannot, therefore, distinguish sharply between countertransference that deserves to be called normal and that which deserves to be called pathological. Just as in the case of neurotic symptoms, the differences [between the neurotic and normal] are a matter of degree.

In a similar vein Greenson (1967, p. 399) has said:

> It does not do justice to the arduous demands of the analytic profession to hope that the obtaining and delivering of insight

might be free from conflict, guilt, and anxiety. These activities ought to be pleasurable to the analyst. . . . The pleasure in listening, looking, exploring, imagining, and comprehending is not only permissible but necessary for the optimal efficiency of the analyst.

POSITIVE COUNTERTRANSFERENCE

Therapy usually proceeds well when the therapist likes the client or patient. If the therapist does not really care for the person he treats, this will be reflected in his interventions and the patient will sense it. While a positive countertransference is a desirable attitude, like a positive transference it must be studied carefully (Fine, 1971).

A temptation for many therapists is to love the patient too much. When this occurs, the patient is not perceived accurately or treated objectively. In his overidentification, the therapist often supports the patient against his real or fantasied opponents, rather than helping him understand his interpersonal conflicts. Overidentification frequently takes place in working on parent-child and marital conflicts.

Frank, aged eleven, was referred for treatment because of academic difficulties, depression, constant arguments with peers and adults, and insomnia. With the therapist Frank appeared very open; he mentioned that he needed help because "I can't get along with others." He also made many other self-critical remarks, and the therapist gradually grew quite sorry for him because he appeared so depressed and helpless.

What the therapist did not understand was the seductiveness in Frank's behavior. Frank seemed to think that if he could present himself as a depressed, self-critical boy, perhaps the therapist would not see his provocativeness. Frank was successful, and induced the therapist to tell him that he was too hard on himself. He went even further and told Frank that he had a right to be angry at his teacher and his parents. The therapist's interventions, based on his positive countertransference and overidentification, did not help Frank. On the contrary, Frank used the therapist's remarks to fight others and to maintain his regressive behavior.

When the therapist is overidentified with the patient, he begins to overlook the patient's contributions to his own problems. This strengthens the patient's self-pity, and both therapist and patient myopically view the patient as a victim of circumstances.

Mr. Ernst, a thirty-five-year-old married man, was being seen in treatment for sexual difficulties. In his presentations of his marital difficulties Mr. Ernst described his wife as tyrannical and overpowering, while he appeared kind, warm, and conciliatory. The therapist joined Mr. Ernst in his attacks on his wife under the guise of "helping him assert himself better." What was overlooked in the therapy was Mr. Ernst's strong masochism, his own wish for passivity, and his own desire to be dominated.

Only when the therapist realized his countertransference problems could he begin to help Mr. Ernst see how he was both inviting and sustaining a sadomasochistic relationship with his wife.

NEGATIVE COUNTERTRANSFERENCE

A therapist is a human being and is more like his patient than unlike him (Sullivan, 1953). Because the therapist has wishes, defenses and anxieties, it is inevitable that his vulnerabilities will be activated in the therapeutic situation and that he will feel hostility toward some of those whom he wants to help. It is often difficult for therapists to acknowledge their hostility toward their patients because in their profession angry feelings are considered a liability. Frequently hostile feelings in a therapist are denied and repressed, and manifest themselves in disguised and subtle forms. Two of the most common expressions of disguised hostility are the use of the clinical diagnosis as a countertransference expression (Fine, 1971) and alterations of therapeutic plans and techniques.

When patients are distrustful, isolate themselves from relationships, and are frightened of the helping situation and helping person, it is quite understandable that the therapist gets discouraged, questions his or her own skills, and feels quite angry at the patient who does not show any progress.

Mr. Daniels, a twenty-six-year-old army veteran, was hospitalized because of hallucinations, delusions, paranoid reactions, and depression. Every time a social worker, psychologist, or psychiatrist approached him, he withdrew and refused to talk. Feeling very discouraged, the staff diagnosed Mr. Daniels as an "incurable schizophrenic," placed him in the back ward of the hospital, and gave him drugs and electric-shock therapy.

When Mr. Daniels was assigned to a student social worker, it became clear that his diagnosis and therapy had been in many ways the result of negative countertransference. The student, unfamiliar with diagnostic terminology and unready to foist an unfavorable prognosis on Mr. Daniels, greeted him humanely. Rather than withdrawing when he said he did not want help, the student sat through his silences, listened to his complaints, and was not too perturbed by his paranoid accusations and grandiose plans. The patient began, at first with reluctance, to discuss his history with the worker, examined his anxieties and terrors with him, and eventually was able to leave the mental hospital and take a job. With further help in an outpatient mental health facility, Mr. Daniels was able to move toward more intimate interpersonal relationships and derive pleasure from them.*

When the client or patient does not respond to questions, confrontations, environmental manipulation, or interpretations, there is a tendency for the therapist to express hostility not only by using pejorative diagnostic labels but by applying "innovative procedures." These procedures, when examined carefully, often turn out to be sadistic attacks. Drugs, shock therapy, and back-ward isolation are frequently administered when the patient or

---

*In a research project conducted by the writer (Strean, 1976), it was demonstrated that first-year social work students, because of their humane approach and absence of hostility, can be very helpful to patients in mental hospitals who have been clinically diagnosed as schizophrenic.

client rejects the therapist's efforts to talk to him. Sometimes the negative countertransference is expressed through verbal techniques.

Mrs. Case, a forty-year-old mother and a patient at a child-guidance clinic, refused on many occasions to take the therapist's advice. The angry therapist diagnosed Mrs. Case as "severely masochistic" and under the guise of "innovative techniques" became quite cruel to her. Contending that Mrs. Case's assertiveness should be liberated, every time the patient said that she was disgusted with herself the therapist replied, "Yes, you are disgusting." When the patient said that the therapist's techniques were not helpful, she was told that she wasn't a helpful patient.

Protecting herself by using "innovative procedures" she labeled "mirroring" and "joining the resistance," the therapist did everything but face with Mrs. Case her wish to defeat her own therapy. Instead of helping Mrs. Case face her fear of therapy and change, and her competition with the therapist, the therapist tried to cope with her own countertransference reactions (feelings of futility and anger) by attacking her patient with "therapeutic techniques." These attacks only induced a deeper feeling of despair in the patient.

Commenting on negative countertransference in the psychoanalytic situation, Fine has suggested (1971, p. 168):

There are a great many instances where the analyst, because of his unconscious hostility to the patient or because of defiance to his own analyst or to the profession, insists that the patient is untreatable, or untreatable by an analytic means, and resorts to all kinds of measures that immediately make the situation worse. In by far the great majority of cases, analytic help is the kind that is most needed.

The Activities of the Therapist

Until now we have concentrated on concepts that relate to the communications brought by the patient or client and to those factors in patient or therapist that either facilitate or hinder the free flow and understanding of these communications. We now turn to a discussion of some of the contributions of the therapist in psychoanalytically oriented therapy.

As the patient tries to observe the fundamental rule, saying everything that comes to mind, he will develop resistances and transference reactions that evolve from his unique metapsychology. Much of the therapist's efforts are devoted to helping the patient understand his resistances and transference reactions. What specific therapeutic activities will help the patient resolve his conflicts?

One of the primary tasks of the analytically oriented therapist is to *listen*. As the patient produces material, themes emerge and the therapist *asks questions* so that persistent themes receive further elaboration. As certain resistances and other maladaptive behaviors become clear to the therapist, he *confronts* the patient with them; i.e., he draws the patient's attention to a particular phenomenon, such as persistent lateness to appointments, and tries to help him recognize something he has been avoiding that will have to be further understood. Usually confrontation is followed by *clarification,* which involves bringing the psychological phenomena with which the patient has been confronted (and which he is now more willing to consider) into sharp focus. Clarification involves the "digging out" of significant details from the past that contribute to the etiology of the uncovered phenomena (Greenson, 1967; Sandler et al., 1973). *Interpretation* of the psychodynamic meaning of the patient's thoughts, feelings, fantasies, and dreams—especially in terms of their psychogenetic origin—is the hallmark of psychoanalytic therapy. Its goal is *insight,* or self-understanding. *Working through* is the integration of understanding by repeating and deepening insights, and extending the meaning of the patient's resistances and transference. Finally the patient *synthesizes* the insights by working out an adequate way of coping in which anxieties are kept to a minimum and pleasure is derived from living.

Let us look at some of these dimensions of the therapeutic process in more detail.

LISTENING

It usually takes many years of experience for a therapist to firmly believe that when an individual is given an opportunity to express thoughts, feelings, memories, fantasies, and dreams to an attentive listener, tensions are reduced, understanding is achieved, and psychic energy that had been used to repress disturbing affects and ideas becomes available for more productive functioning.

Most individuals who seek psychotherapy do so because there is no one in their immediate environment to hear them out. Most listeners, when hearing someone else describe a conflict, voice indecision, or discuss feelings of helplessness and hopelessness, and feel obligated to appear ''helpful.'' They fail to realize that one of the most effective means of being helpful is to give the interviewee plenty of latitude to voice what is on his mind (Barbara, 1958).

In most societies it is a unique experience to talk with someone who, instead of advising, criticizing, or bringing attention to himself, listens attentively and does not judge. When a patient is given the opportunity of being with someone who does not ask anything for himself but focuses his interest solely on that patient and listens, many things can happen. The patient begins to feel that he is a person of value, and this feeling of self-worth induced by an accepting interviewer often strengthens him to use his coping mechanisms more freely and effectively. He begins to see that his problem with his boss, his marital distress, or his psychosomatic symptom does not mean that the end of his world is in sight.

When the patient feels he is being regarded positively by the interviewer, a feeling that is usually transmitted by nonintrusive listening, he begins to regard *himself* more positively (Rogers,

1951). The interviewee who is full of self-hatred often reacts with suspicion to compliments and other supportive remarks. He may feel he is being patronized and demeaned when the interviewer uses these well-intentioned procedures. However, the patient can begin to learn to value himself much more when the interviewer values what he says by listening to him carefully (Benjamin, 1974). Most interviewees sense when the interviewer is somewhere else, so that silent listening without being attentive to a patient's spoken and unspoken messages rarely achieves very much.

The value of attentive listening may be seen from the following interview between a resident in a home for senior citizens and her social worker.

Mrs. Clark, aged seventy-four, was brought to the social worker's office because, after two days of living in a home for senior citizens, she was refusing to eat, participate in activities, or have anything to do with residents or staff members. She sulked most of the time and appeared very depressed, keeping her head in her hands and her thumb in her mouth.

When the social worker and Mrs. Clark sat down, there was an initial silence. The worker then said, "You seem very unhappy since you have been here. Would you like to talk about it?" Mrs. Clark was at first a little reluctant to talk; then she said that she did not like the food, the people, the room, or the activities at the institution. She felt that being in her own home was much better; at home, where her daughter, son-in-law, and grandchildren resided, she knew everybody and they really cared about her. She could tell her daughter or grandchildren what was going on in her life and they would listen. "Nobody at this place wants to listen to me," Mrs. Clark said tearfully. After another short silence she said, "You see, my social worker thought I would like this place because I could be with lots of people and do things; and because she always listened to me I thought I'd do her a favor and come here. But I hate being alone!" Mrs. Clark then looked at her interviewer and asked, "Will you be at the buffet tonight?" When the social worker said "Would you like me to be there?" Mrs. Clark replied, "Maybe you'll sit next to me and we can talk some more. I think I'll go to the bingo game now."

Like so many patients and clients, Mrs. Clark needed some-body to listen to her. When she was given the opportunity to ventilate anger, criticize the institution, and voice her longing for what was comfortable, she felt accepted and valued. Feeling accepted and valued, she became less depressed for a while and could begin to enjoy the here-and-now of the institution. It will be noted that the interviewer in the above vignette, after her opening remark, did not say a single word but instead listened attentively. As a result, Mrs. Clark endowed the interviewer with the positive characteristics that she was searching for in another person and then could use her effectively as a means of making the break from home and using the institution to her advantage.

Whether the problem of the patient is homesickness, job dis-satisfaction, marital conflict, or any other form of distress, effec-tive listening by the interviewer inevitably reduces anxiety and unleashes energy for more constructive problem solving.

ASKING QUESTIONS

An attentive listener must demonstrate that he has grasped the essential points of his patient's story. The patient usually feels that he is being heard if the interviewer, through questions and comments, illuminates and clarifies significant features of the interviewee's own account. If the interviewer demonstrates that he is attending to the major details of the interviewee's story, it gives the latter the stimulating feeling that the listener not only wants to but does understand what he is trying to say.

One of the central procedures in good interviewing is posing good questions. Questions are asked to get pertinent data so that the therapist can arrive at an assessment of the patient; they are also asked to help the patient explore and reflect upon his role and the role of others in his interactions, and to direct the patient's conversation to fruitful channels. A question that truly engages the patient is one that clarifies ambiguities, completes a picture of the situation he is describing, obtains more detail about his thinking, and elicits emotional responses (Kadushin, 1972).

In order for a question to be considered helpful by the interviewee, he has to experience it as one that, if answered in full, will enhance him in some way. Questions that can be answered with "no" or "yes" or "I don't know" do not really aid the person to discharge distress, explore his distress more fully, or increase his self-understanding. For example, if a patient is asked "Do you love your husband?" she is given little opportunity, because of the way the question is phrased, to really reflect on her marriage, examine her role in it, or discharge her complaints. However, if she is asked "Can you tell me about your marriage?" or "How do you and your husband get along?" more data will be elicited.

Questions have to be phrased so that they can be understood. They should be unambiguous, and simple enough for the patient to remember what is being asked. When the therapist asks a question, he should have a clear purpose in doing so.

Perhaps more important than the exact formulation of a question is that attitude with which it is conveyed. The patient must feel that the question evolves from the interviewer's empathy and identification with him. This helps the patient to talk freely, communicate in greater depth with the interviewer and himself, and really tell his story.

CONFRONTATION

In order to help the patient discover the unconscious forces that are contributing to his problems, the therapist has to confront him with certain behavior of which he is unaware. It is extremely important when confronting a patient to have enough evidence available to support the confrontation and some assurance that the confrontation will be meaningful to the patient. Premature demonstration of resistive or transferential behavior not only is a waste of time but often compounds anxiety, intensifies resistance, and dissipates material that might be effective at a later point (Greenson, 1967).

After four months of treatment with Mr. Bernstein, aged forty-one, it became clear to the therapist that he would inevitably arrive late for any session immediately following one in which he had expressed positive feelings toward the therapist. After this had occurred several times and after Mr. Bernstein had talked about how he would rather "fight and feel strong" than love, the therapist confronted him with his pattern of lateness. At first Mr. Bernstein seemed dubious, but later on he said, "It has happened a lot, so I better look at it." Mr. Bernstein could acknowledge that "he felt uncomfortable when I like you." Exploration revealed that Mr. Bernstein was afraid of closeness and love because "I might get trapped into a homosexual affair with you."

Confronting Mr. Bernstein with his lateness to appointments after he expressed positive and warm feelings toward the therapist enabled him to get in touch with his unconscious homosexual wishes and fears. As Mr. Bernstein became willing to consider the dimensions of his homosexual transference, the therapist could then begin to help him clarify the meaning of his homosexual wishes.

CLARIFICATION

It is not enough for the patient to become aware of an impulse, wish, or idea that has been unconscious; equally important, he should understand why he is seeking the gratification of the impulse or wish, and what impact it has on his life.

Mr. Bernstein, in the above example, needed help in *clarifying* why he was frequently hostile and/or avoided people. By studying his transference behavior with the therapist, he slowly realized that he was afraid of "falling in love with older men." The therapist, after Mr. Bernstein revealed several memories of his father and his yearning for him as a boy, could clarify for Mr. Bernstein that he was avoiding looking at how much he missed a father, and how much he secretly craved to hug, kiss, and fondle his father.

INTERPRETATION

Freud's first references to interpretation were in *The Interpretation of Dreams* (1900), in which he discussed the analyst's understanding and reconstruction of the hidden sources and meaning of the dream ("latent content"). This was arrived at by an examination of the free associations of the patient to the conscious memory of the dream ("manifest content").

In the early years of psychoanalysis, the analyst conveyed and explained this interpretation to the patient, but this was a relatively didactic communication (Sandler et al., 1973). By the time Freud came to write his papers on technique, he began to distinguish between the interpretation and its communication to the patient. In 1926 (p. 160) he wrote:

> When you have found the right interpretation another task lies ahead. You must wait for the right moment at which you can communicate your interpretation to the patient with some prospect of success ... you will be making a bad mistake if ... you throw your interpretations at the patient's head as soon as you have found them.

As understanding of resistances in treatment has advanced, Freudian therapists have increasingly realized that resistances must be interpreted to the patient before id material can be exposed. In other words, first the patient needs help in realizing that he is avoiding the therapist and wanting to defeat him (as was true in the case of Mr. Bernstein). Later, the id wishes (in Mr. Bernstein's case, desires for closeness and sexuality) can be examined.

Currently, the term "interpretation" is being used in the psychoanalytic literature to mean a variety of activities (Sandler et al., 1973):

1. The analyst's inferences and conclusions regarding the uncon-

scious meaning and significance of the patient's communications and behavior.
2. The communication by the analyst to the patient of these inferences and conclusions.
3. All comments made by the analyst—confrontations, clarifications, questions, and so on.
4. Verbal interventions specifically aimed at bringing about "dynamic change" through the medium of insight.

In order to differentiate interpretation from other therapeutic activities such as questioning and confrontation, we shall consider interpretation as that activity which makes the patient aware of the unconscious meaning, source, history, mode, or cause of a given psychic event (Greenson, 1967). Interpretations are of three types: uncovering, connective, and integrative (Fine, 1971).

THE UNCOVERING INTERPRETATION

The uncovering interpretation is one through which some concealed wish is brought to consciousness. Sometimes the wish is explicitly expressed in the patient's associations and sometimes it is inferred by the therapist from the material. As a rule, an inference presented to the patient cannot be too far removed from his associations; otherwise it will leave him far behind the therapist and an unfruitful dialogue will ensue.

Once a trusting relationship has been established between patient and therapist, the uncovering interpretation is the one that is used most frequently. The therapist is almost always attempting to help the patient reduce his anxiety, self-hate, and maladaptive defensiveness, and he does this by trying to uncover id matieral so that the patient can develop more awareness and more acceptance of his libidinal wishes.

Miss Arlington, a twenty-three-year-old unmarried woman, sought help because she had poor interpersonal relationships, particularly with men. She alternated between socially isolating herself and getting involved in vengeful disputes. After about nine months of treatment, when her relationship to her male therapist was quite well established and considerable evidence had been amassed, the therapist was able to make an interpretation of her withdrawal and belligerence.

After several confrontations and clarifications, during which Miss Arlington was quite combative with the therapist, she dreamed that she was opening and closing a pantry that was on the therapist's chest. He interpreted this as meaning she would rather maintain a distance and fight with him than "eat him up."

Because the interpretation was well timed, Miss Arlington was able to use it to her advantage. She talked of her insatiable desires and said, "If someone isn't around for me I go nuts!" She was able to see that she used her relationship with her therapist to protect herself from recognizing her wish to "devour" him.

By using one of Miss Arlington's dreams the therapist was able to interpret her wish to "devour people emotionally" (and to eventually help her see what this wish was all about). It should be remembered that a dream is just another form of communication, and that the best way to uncover its meaning is to help the patient associate to it. In addition, the meaning can become clearer when therapist and patient bear in mind what was transpiring in the therapy and the patient's daily life before the dream was presented.

THE CONNECTIVE INTERPRETATION

On of the major findings of psychoanalysis is that the individual is constantly experiencing the present as if it were the past. He frequently makes relatives, friends, and colleagues into significant figures of his childhood. This resistance to perceiving people as they really are contributes to many of his difficulties— e.g., he wants his wife to be his mother, his boss to be his father, and his children to be his siblings.

Through the connective interpretation, the present is related to the past so that the patient can see how he is distorting the present by waging old battles and seeking childish gratifications.

Mrs. Crane, aged thirty-five, was a patient at a child-guidance clinic because her daughter Faye, aged ten, had a severe school phobia. In discussing her inability to release Faye and let her go to school, Mrs. Crane recalled several incidents from her own childhood, when she had been Faye's age. One of her memories involved a teacher who was very sadistic toward the children. Mrs. Crane, as a girl, had wanted to "tell her off and quit school." The therapist was able, with this information, to make a connective interpretation. She showed Mrs. Crane how she was experiencing Faye as if Faye were the same ten-year-old that she had been twenty-five years previously. The therapist also helped Mrs. Crane see that she was misperceiving Faye's teacher by making her into the sadistic teacher of her own past.

The Integrative Interpretation

The integrative interpretation involves pulling together material from a variety of sources. It is offered to help the patient see his problems and life situation in a more adequate perspective. Like all interpretations, integrative interpretations have to be repeated a number of times until the patient is able to formulate a perspective in his own terms.

Mr. Darwin, aged thirty-seven, sought treatment for sexual impotence, "homosexual panics" (fear that he would seduce men or boys), depression, and poor work habits. After a few months of therapy, during which he was quite euphoric, Mr. Darwin became even more depressed than he had been when he initially sought treatment. His impotence returned, and he found going to work almost impossible.

One of the important etiological factors in Mr. Darwin's life was that his father, whom he had "loved with a passion," had died suddenly when he was ten. Mr. Darwin "never forgave" his father "for not being constantly available to me."

Integrative interpretations helped Mr. Darwin see that he was engaged in a futile battle with his father for not being with him all the time, and that this same fight was being recapitulated in his relationship with the therapist. As he became more aware of the reasons for his wish to fight, he felt less depressed and more loving. Later he learned that he was using his aggressiveness to ward off loving feelings, which frightened him.

Insight, Working Through, and Synthesis

As the patient associates to his past and present—examining fantasies, dreams, defenses, and interpersonal relationships—it is the goal of analysis that with the therapist's help (confrontations, clarifications, interpretations) he will achieve *insight*.

Insight is a dimension of psychotherapy that has been very much misunderstood. The popular literature seems to imply that one insight will heal a neurosis. This *never* takes place; an insight has to be "worked through"—i.e., elaborated, reviewed, and reconsidered—before it can have a real effect on the patient's functioning. Furthermore, it is important to differentiate between emotional and intellectual insight. A time-worn joke has a student of psychoanalysis ask, "If Van Gogh had been psychoanalyzed, would he have cut off his ear?" The teacher answers, "Yes, but he would have known why."

Insight, to be effective in altering functioning, involves the lifting of repressions, the recovery of lost memories, the feeling of affects that were suppressed, and a new grasp of the significance and interrelations of events (Schafer, 1977). Recollections take on a new meaning. The patient may say, as Freud (1914b) pointed out, "As a matter of fact I've always known it; only I never thought of it."

Intellectual knowledge of dynamic defenses and other sources of disturbance is manifestly ineffective in altering pathology; otherwise, giving a patient or client a book to read would help him. Insight, to be effective, *always* must be accompanied by genuine affect and a real awareness in the patient of how he has distorted his perceptions. Usually, when a patient verbalizes insights without functioning differently in any way he is defending against the recall of a memory, is repressing a fantasy or an idea, or is refusing to experience certain feelings.

After the patient comes to an insight—e.g., understands that his job failure is part of his battle with Father—the same interpretation usually has to be reviewed several times by patient and therapist before the conflict ceases to be a problem. This is what is meant by "working through." Greenson (1967, p. 42) has described working through as "the repetitive, progressive, and elaborate explorations of the resistances which prevent an insight from leading to change. . . . A variety of circular processes are set in motion by working through in which insight, memory, and behavior change influence each other."

If insights are worked through, there will be sustained change. Symptoms and maladaptive defenses will be given up. However, working through is like any learning process. Hobbs (1968, p. 19) has spoken of the therapeutic experience as one of "specific and concrete opportunities for learning new ways of responding, new ways of relating to other people, and new ways of perceiving oneself." It takes time to integrate new ways of looking at attitudes, thoughts, and interpersonal behavior. The patient characteristically moves two steps forward and one step back. The same issues, fears, and decisions must often be worked through over and over before the patient can assimilate them and make them his own (Wood, 1971).

Writers in the field maintain that although working through is an essential part of the psychoanalytic process, interpretation of unconscious mental content and of transference repetitions, together with the gaining of insight, are equally vital. The fact is that any technique that does not make use of all these elements cannot be regarded as psychoanalytic.

When neurotic problems have subsided and insights are worked through, the individual is ready to pursue love and work with enjoyment. *Synthesis* means that the patient has worked out an adequate way of living in which anxieties can be kept to the minimum and pleasure from realistic ventures is at the maximum.

The Patient's Responses to the Therapist's Interventions

As has been suggested already, when a therapist questions, confronts, clarifies, or interprets, the patient will respond to the intervention in his own idiosyncratic manner. The patient's unique transference to the therapist and his unique resistances are always going to influence how he will respond. It is a commonplace observation that the most carefully worded statement is not received by a patient the way it was intended. A statement of support may be experienced as criticism, and a statement designed to challenge may be experienced as supportive and laudatory. Even a simple question such as "Why not?" may be perceived as a command as illustrated in the following example (Herma, 1968).

Mrs. Enter, aged thirty-one, in her first interview with her therapist, asked the therapist if she thought that she could take a job as a teacher's aide. The therapist—interested in exploring Mrs. Enter's feelings, thoughts, and doubts about the matter—asked "Why not?" The patient presented several reasons why she could not take the job: the hours, the job's demands, family responsibilities, and so on. In the next interview she informed the therapist that she had taken the job "because you told me to." When the therapist looked puzzled, Mrs. Enter said, "Don't you remember? I said 'Should I take the job?' and you said 'Why not?' To me that meant I should take it!"

The patient frequently contributes a meaning to the therapist's questions, interpretations, or silences beyond the one intended. Silence may be experienced as anything from reassurance to rejection. The patient always experiences the therapist's activity or inactivity through the lens of his transference and resistances, and hence there is always some subjective, nonrational distortion.

In order to promote a progressive and productive helping relationship, the therapist must observe, understand, and relate to the patient's responses to his interventive acts. The decisive question with regard to the therapist's remarks (clarifications, confrontations, questions, or interpretations) is not whether a statement is correct but how the patient reacts to it, and what the therapist does with the patient's reactions (Fine, 1968). On most occasions the therapist presents the "correct" interpretation or performs the "correct" activity; yet his intervention may not bring about the results he strives for if he has not paid sufficient attention to how his words and actions are received and elaborated on by the patient. Is the patient listening to the therapist? Fully or partially? Is he accepting the therapist's statement or rejecting it? Is he ambivalent about it?

Just as the patient's verbal acceptance of the therapist's intervention is no proof that it will be used constructively, his rejection of it is no proof that it will not. Patients may accept an interpretation out of a wish for love and reject one out of a need to compete with the therapist. What is of crucial importance is how the therapist responds to the patient's rejection or acceptance of his intervention. The patient may need help to see why he is compliant, or he may need to understand more about his negative and competitive transferences (Fine, 1968).

Frieda, aged seventeen, balked at every one of her therapist's statements. On hearing an interpretation she would call him "a bald old jerk," "stupid," and "uptight." After blasting the therapist for one or two sessions, she would then come in and report, "I've got an insight!" The insight usually consisted of one of the therapist's interpretations, which she had to repudiate consciously but could unconsciously use to help herself. As long as she could feel it was her own interpretation and not the therapist's, it was valid.

The therapeutic situation is a dynamic dialogue. In this dialogue the patient's responses to interventions must always be subjected to careful study. The primary emphasis in psychoanalytic therpay is placed on the ways in which the patient responds to interventions, rather than on whether the interventions are correct or incorrect.

Limitations of Psychoanalysis

Psychoanalysis has several limitations as a science. First, the theory has shortcomings in its empirical procedures in that Freud made his observations under uncontrolled conditions; i.e., he never used "experimental" and "control" groups in his research. These same uncontrolled conditions tend to be the rule in most psychoanalytic research today.

Critics of Freud's methods have objected to his accepting at face value what a patient said without attempting to corroborate it by some form of external evidence. This also tends to be the practice of most psychoanalytic clinicians today. However, those analytically oriented therapists who have moved into family therapy have been able to observe different perceptions of the same phenomenon by a patient and members of his family (Wood, 1970).

What we find in Freud's writings is the end result of his thinking without the original data upon which it was based. Even in Freud's case histories (e.g., Little Hans, Wolf Man) we do not have the benefit of Freud's hypothesis testing, proof and disproof of notions, quantification of empirical data, and all the other processes that take place in good scientific thinking.

Freud's theories are primarily based on his interviews with psychoanalytic patients of middle and upper-middle socioeconomic classes. For social workers and other professionals who are very much interested in the person-situation constellation, Freudian theory offers limited understanding of the impact and salience of the client's social-cultural milieu, and virtually no understanding of how to intervene in it. Freud's therapeutic procedures such as as free association, dream analysis, interpretation, and analysis of the transference are essentially designed for the more articulate, introspective individual who has many ego resources.

As a psychotherapy, Freudian psychoanalysis also has some limitations. It was designed exclusively for one-to-one treatment and as the unit of diagnosis and treatment enlarges to a dyad, a family, a group, or even a community, notions like transference and resistance have to be increasingly supplemented with concepts from the social sciences. Psychoanalytic psychotherapy, as mentioned above, is a talking and introspective type of therapy. Consequently, the classical psychoanalytic treatment model that we have discussed in this chapter can be of only limited help to clients and patients who have verbal and cognitive deficits.

Despite the limitations of Freudian theory, it is a patient, meticulous, and complex view of man that can be of enormous help to those who wish to understand people in depth and help them resolve psychological conflict.

ner; parents may *repress* unacceptable wishes and feelings that become activated in the parent-child relationship; and group members, through *reaction formation,* may condemn their colleagues without noting how they are protecting themselves. If applicants' *defenses* are understood but not attacked they may find it easier to become clients (A. Freud, 1937; Strean, 1978), because their sense of vulnerability is being protected rather than prematurely exposed.

As was true of Mr. Addison, many individuals who seek out social agencies cope with their anxiety by making requests and demands of the worker rather than facing their distress. Frequently these requests appear outlandish, but they must be respected and evaluated objectively.

Miss Beck, aged twenty-four, sought out a social worker because she "wanted a man." She was quite convinced at her initial consultation that if she presented what she required from a husband, the social worker would find one for her. Although Miss Beck appeared very demanding, the worker neither gratified her requests nor told her that they were preposterous; instead he explored them with her.

During the course of several interviews, as the applicant discussed with the worker her fantasied lover—"a man who is tall, handsome, rich, warm, brilliant, loving, attentive, and a good dancer"—she slowly became more realistic. During the fourth interview she said to the social worker, "Do you think I'm asking for too much?" Recognizing that her fantasies protected her from facing certain realities, the worker respected Miss Beck's defenses and queried, "What makes you ask this question?" Not feeling attacked, Miss Beck went on to describe how she was frightened to converse with a man, was usually silent on dates, dreaded sexual intimacy, and kept hoping that her dates would take full control of the situation and "anticipate my needs."

Miss Beck and the worker could eventually agree that what seemed necessary was an exploration of her weak self-image, sexual guilt, discomfort in intimate relations, and anger at her inability to find an omnipotent parent.

Whether the applicant's request seems reasonable and understandable or unreasonable and far-fetched, it needs to be explored so that its unconscious meaning can evolve for both worker and client. When a couple makes an adoption application and their infertility is explored, it may turn out that they are capable of having their own child (Renne, 1977; Bernard, 1953). Similarly, parents who want to institutionalize their child may learn during exploratory interviews with the social worker that they are troubled by their aggressive fantasies toward the child; they may later decide to examine their aggressive wishes in treatment and try to live with the child while doing so (Sobel, 1953). A married couple may decide after reflecting on their relationship under the guidance of a social worker that it is better to divorce than "learn to communicate better."

Regardless of the social worker's unit of attention and field of practice, it is always necessary to understand the unconscious meaning of a client's request and the unconscious contribution he is making to his problem. As was suggested earlier in this chapter, when the worker does not accept the applicant's statements literally but recognizes that they evolve partially from id wishes, superego mandates, defense patterns, and unique personal history, he can frequently help the applicant become a client.

It should be borne in mind that many individuals who are referred to social agencies do not wish to be there in the first place. Nevertheless, it is important to understand what is operating unconsciously when a client wishes to reject the social worker's help.

Mr. and Mrs. Cameron, a couple in their mid-thirties, were referred to a child-guidance clinic by school officials because their ten-year-old son, Joshua, had many scholastic and interpersonal problems. During their first interview both parents expressed indignation at being referred for help. Said Mr. Cameron with his wife nodding in agreement, "We work hard so that he'll have everything and we know he's a good kid. That lousy guidance counselor doesn't know what he's talking about. Josh doesn't need help and neither do we!"

When the worker encouraged Mr. and Mrs. Cameron to voice their anger and assured them that neither they nor Josh would be required to come to the clinic, they began to look at their relationship with their son a little less defensively. Both of the Camerons acknowledged that they were somewhat indulgent at times and on other occasions were too punitive. The more the social worker emerged as a noncritical, nonpunitive, and nonjudgmental figure, the more the Camerons could explore their relationship with Josh.

Just as it is essential for the worker to listen empathetically to clients' irrational requests and subjective analyses of their problems, it is equally important to grant them the privilege of *not* participating in a helping process. In most situations, when resistances are respected and anger accepted, the reluctant applicant does become a participating client.

Psychoanalysis and the Diagnostic Assessment

Having clarified the applicant's initial problem and helped him move toward participating in a helping process as a client, the worker must then formulate a diagnostic assessment. The process of assessment is an attempt to ascertain what is troubling the client and what seems to be contributing to his problems. Obviously such professional judgments should be supported by evidence and reason and should be checked and rechecked. The diagnostic assessment takes into consideration the client's current behavior in and out of the social work interviews, his personality, his situation, and his modes of relating to the social worker. The social worker does not rush to any conclusion but makes sure that the diagnostic assessment meets logical and professional criteria for validity and reliability, i.e., that it derives from facts that are clearly apparent and can be seen by any other professional observer (Siporin, 1975; Hollis, 1964).

As we shall see, diagnostic processes differ depending on the unit of attention; however, there are several dimensions of any diagnostic assessment that are essential to the process regardless of the size of the client system.

Dimensions of a Diagnostic Assessment

The Role of the Environment

Social work theory contends that the diagnostic assessment is always "psychosocial" because people and their situations are always in dynamic interaction and both contribute to adaptation and maladaptation. Consequently, in order to understand what is troubling a client and contributing to his or her problems, the social worker begins by scanning the whole "field"—all the known variables in the client's person-situation gestalt (Hollis, 1972).

In assessing the client's situation, ego psychologists have referred to the "average expectable environment," the environment that provides "normally healthy . . . experiences" (Hartmann, 1958). According to this standard, an income below the poverty line would constitute an external pressure, as would inadequate housing, a poor school, lack of employment opportunity, or inadequate medical care.

The Personality

Just as the social worker scans the field of the client's milieu and notes the contribution of each of the client's subsystems (family, school, neighborhood, and so on), so he scans the various systems of the client's metapsychology.

The worker will want to assess how the client is functioning dynamically—i.e., how are drives expressed? Are they being used in the service of mature love and work or are they being used to discharge childish impulses? To what extent is the client trying to gratify childish narcissism and infantile dependence? Is the client relatively consistent in expressing feelings and impulses or is there an unusual amount of ambivalence? Are there unresolved angers toward parents and siblings? Is the client able to love and sustain an intimate sexual relationship with someone of the opposite sex or is he/she attracted to members of his/her own sex? In handling aggression, is the client able to stand up for his/her rights without being cruel? Is aggression turned inward? Does the client need immediate discharge and gratification of tensions and impulses or is there sufficient ego control to handle impulses constructively? Is the client Perlman's "diminished man" (Perlman, 1970), so bureaucratized by our culture as to have lost touch with instinctual roots?

In reviewing the client's history (the *genetic approach*), the worker will want to assess how much the client is recapitulating the past in the present. Is he/she attempting to make a spouse, employer, or colleague a parental figure? Or still seeking gratifications that were more appropriate in childhood (i.e., engaging in a strong quest for oral gratification; yearning to express anal sadism or phallic narcissism)? Where is the client fixated? Or has some external stimulus that caused anxiety triggered a regression?

In focusing on the contribution of the client's life story to current functioning, the worker should consider not only the history of the client's adverse experiences and their meaning to him, but also, as Perlman has advised,

> "the history of his successful or unsuccessful adaptation to them—his "solution" of his difficulties... by retreat, by entrenchment, by blind fighting, or by compromise, detour, and constructive substitutions—this history of his development as a problem-encountering, problem-solving human being may provide... an understanding of what the client suffers from and what the extent of his coping ability is likely to be. (Perlman, 1957, p. 176)

As social workers have assessed the broad patterning of their clients' past experiences, successes and failures, interactions with significant others, and areas of fixation and regression, many of them have found Erikson's formulations (1950) helpful. Erikson accepted Freud's theory of genetic stages of instinctual development but generalized beyond it, placing development within its social and cultural matrix and emphasizing the tasks of ego mastery presented by each stage of maturation. As the worker evaluates the client's psychosocial functioning, he can ask: "Is this client trusting? Has he sufficient autonomy or is he full of self-doubt? How much initiative can he take without feeling guilty? Can he act and feel industrious without too many feelings of inferiority? How stable is his sense of identity? Is he capable of intimacy? If he is a senior citizen is he able to love others and devote himself to absorbing interests, or is he stagnating? How much despair does the client feel?

An important feature of the client's metapsychology is the *structural* dimension. In making a diagnosis the worker will want to assess the client's *ego* functioning. How realistically does he perceive relationships, himself, and life events? Is he able to test perceptions and plans for action against reality before coming to conclusions about them? How sound is his judgment? What are his major identifications? How rigid or flexible are his defenses? What is the nature of the anxiety that he defends against? What about relationships with others? Is he capable of genuine empathy?

The quality of the client's *superego* functioning also has to be evaluated. Is he capable of guilt? Is the guilt excessive or insufficient? Which aggressive and sexual impulses cause anxiety, and which induce guilt?

Because the *unconscious* is part of every client's functioning, it is important for the worker to understand what unconscious wishes are propelling the client's sexual problems, parent-child conflicts, and other difficulties. As we discussed earlier in this chapter, the client's presenting problems are not only a result of external pressures but usually provide a certain amount of unconscious gratification; in many ways the client has unconsciously created them. Consequently, the client's *topography* should always be assessed so that the worker can ferret out what the unconscious gratification is.

Assessment of the *economic* weightings and equilibria involved in the client's functioning helps to answer such practical questions as: What is the equilibrium in this marriage or in this family—i.e., which forces are helping achieve complementarity and which forces are inducing role strain? How does the problem of a child support the defenses of other family members? Does a particular welfare mother, burdened and harassed by a destructive reality situation, have a sufficient quantity of inner resources to "make it" if the worker provides a certain amount of relief from some external pressures? (Wood, 1970)

SYMPTOMATOLOGY

In any diagnostic assessment the social worker should determine wht neurotic or psychotic symptomatology and/or pathological character traits are present—obsessions, compulsions, hallucinations, depression, or psychosomatic symptoms. As the worker evaluates these signs of distress, he integrates this understanding with his knowledge of ego psychology and system theory. It is one thing for a child to be afraid of attending school when the environment is benign and quite another when he has to attend overcrowded classes and deal with punitive teachers and peers. It is one thing for a man to accuse his wife of belittling him when she does devalue him and quite another for him to distort her remarks and project his negative self-image onto her in a paranoid manner. In most cases, both person and situation are providing the fuel that sustains the client's distress. As Hollis (1972, p. 269) has pointed out:

> A problem does not lie simply in a given weakness in the personality or a specific lack or condition in the milieu but rather in the way in which various weaknesses or idiosyncrasies in the total system interplay and affect each other. . . . Every factor in a system affects every other factor in that system.

CLASSIFICATION

As was suggested in Chapter 2, there are many dangers in classifying a client as "neurotic," "psychotic," and so on. One danger is that of stereotyping, i.e., assuming that all individuals in the same category are exactly alike. Another danger is that of careless labeling, i.e., assuming a person belongs in a given group on the basis of a few superficial qualities. Erikson (1968) has suggested that high on the list of therapeutic mistakes is "diagnostic name calling" and that a person's potentialities for uniqueness "can be burdened by a diagnostic curse." He has also pointed out the realistic danger that clients or patients, by assuming roles that have been diagnostically suggested, may find their identities in neuroses or psychoses.

Because of these hazards some social work writers (e.g., Perlman, 1957) have questioned whether a clinical diagnosis has any value at all. As was noted in Chapter 3, a clinical diagnosis can be utilized in the service of countertransference problems (Fine, 1971) and for other destructive purposes. However, when the social worker attempts to determine if a client is neurotic or psychotic or has a character disorder, he may be able to relate his observations to the cluster of factors characteristically found together in a given clinical diagnosis. Also, in marshaling facts to make a classification the worker may be able to rectify an incompleteness in the rest of the diagnostic assessment.

Diagnostic assessment involves a many-faceted but orderly understanding of the client-situation constellation. In planning treatment, everything that is known—strengths and weaknesses—is reviewed and assessed for the purpose of learning how best to help the client-system (Hamilton, 1951; Hollis, 1972).

Assessing Different Units of Attention

As was mentioned earlier in this chapter, different units of attention require different diagnostic considerations. We will attempt in the remainder of the chapter to elucidate some of the differences in diagnosing an individual, a dyad, a family, a small group, or an organization.

ASSESSING INDIVIDUALS

One of the frequent oversights in social work assessment is a failure to individualize the client's person-situation constellation. Although two individuals may be part of the same "descriptive problem classification"—e.g., alcoholism, unemployment, old age—the individual's unique metapsychology and unique environment must be understood. (This also applies to other client systems, as in marital, parent-child, and family conflicts. Here, too, the social worker must always try to avoid stereotyping.)

All too frequently, those who work with individuals in financial straits lump them into one diagnostic group, referring to "the poor client," "the charity case," "the blue-collar worker," and so on. In contrast, we rarely hear of diagnostic labels like "the middle class client" or "the white-collar client." The following two case vignettes are presented to illuminate the particular importance of differential diagnosis (and differential treatment) in work with "poor" individuals.

Mrs. Dodd, aged thirty-two, was referred to a family agency by the worker she was seeing at the County Welfare Office. The client was very suspicious of her welfare worker's motives, resented reviewing her budget with her, and according to the welfare worker, "refused to see the reality of anything." She constantly berated her children, disliked her neighbors, and stayed away from most interpersonal situations.

Although Mrs. Dodd was reluctant to accept the referral to the family agency, she did keep her appointment for an intake session. In her first interview she castigated all social workers and the welfare system, demeaned her own worker's "stinginess," and told the social worker at the family agency that her work with her would probably be a failure too.

The family social worker noted the client's enormous distrust, which bordered on paranoid thinking, and observed that her powerful rage interfered with the smooth operation of her ego functions: Her judgment was poor, her reality testing was weak, and in her interpersonal relationships she exhibited much narcissism and wishes to be omnipotent. As the worker considered Mrs. Dodd's impoverished reality and came to understand her metapsychology, she could devise an individualized treatment plan. Recognizing that Mrs. Dodd was probably a "borderline personality," who would be distrustful of therapy, the family social worker concluded that only by helping her verbalize her resentment and distrust could treatment take place.

The therapist invited Mrs. Dodd to prescribe how treatment should be conducted so that she would not fail her by making numerous mistakes. Mrs. Dodd, pleased to be placed in the role of consultant, advised the worker "to listen to my anger and don't correct me!" The worker complied.

Because the social worker was able to recognize that Mrs. Dodd was fixated at a trust-mistrust level of psychosocial development, she was able to respect her paranoid mechanisms and help her ventilate her rage. Knowing that Mrs. Dodd would not be very cooperative in treatment because she experienced the worker as an aribtrary and powerful authority who would render her powerless, the worker abdicated her own role of authority and utilized Mrs. Dodd as a consultant. The worker reasoned that only after Mrs. Dodd experienced herself as a knowledgeable authority would there be a rise in her self-esteem. Perhaps she would then be able to examine some of her strong but unacceptable dependency wishes.

Mr. Erlich, a depressed man of thirty-four, came to a social agency "for a job." When his job preferences were explored, his grandiose power wishes emerged. "I'd like an administrative and executive position so that I can order people around!" he bellowed.

As Mr. Erlich's wishes to order people around were further investigated, it became clear that he had been indulged most of his life by parents and others. The worker's assessment concluded that he had never been weaned from his narcissistic attitude; like an "oral" baby, he felt that the whole world should cater to him. Apparently Mr. Erlich had never been helped to establish the limits he needed in order to have some tolerance for frustration.

The cases of Mrs. Dodd and Mr. Erlich demonstrate that all individuals have unique psychosocial and maturational needs, fixation points, and ego functions, and form a transference relationship to the social worker based on their life histories. When the diagnostic assessment is individualized, the worker can formulate an individualized treatment plan. Although both Mrs. Dodd and Mr. Erlich were unemployed and received income maintenance from a county welfare department, their diagnoses and treatment plans were very different. Mrs. Dodd initially needed to feel power in the treatment relationship. For Mr. Erlich, this was contraindicated; his therapeutic need was to have some of his omnipotent fantasies punctured. Mrs. Dodd needed the worker to gratify some of her dependency needs and be her advocate and social broker. Mr. Erlich needed to have his dependency wishes frustrated; i.e., he needed weaning and had to be helped to be his own advocate in a socially acceptable manner.

Assessing Marital Interaction

No marriage can be assessed without giving some consideration to cultural factors: the couple's ethnic backgrounds, levels of education, neighborhood, economic status, and other variables. However, the major contribution that psychoanalysis can make to the understanding of marital interaction and conflict is to expose the impact on the marriage of the spouses' fantasies, defenses, superego mandates, ego functioning, and past histories. In contrast to the learning theorist, communications analyst, or systems specialist, who focus on decision making, communication pattersn, and conscious role expectations (Thomas, 1977), the psychoanalytically oriented social worker is interested in learning how certain unconscious wishes and defenses bring and keep a couple together.

Because the psychoanalytically oriented practitioner regards disturbances in marital interaction (whether they be sexual conflicts, communication difficulties, or role incongruence) as frequently the end product of lifelong personality distortions (Marcus and Francis, 1975), his orientation moves him to the assessment and treatment of the spouses' complementary and discomplementary metapsychological systems.

MATE SELECTION

The factors involved in the psychological dimension of choosing a mate are more difficult to describe than the social variables like race, social class, education, religion, and propinquity, because they are subtle and unconscious. Although most individuals like to conceive of marriage choice as a free, conscious mental process, reports from writers who have investigated the phenomenon consistently allude to the strong unconscious determinants in the decision (Blanck and Blanck, 1968; Eisenstein, 1956; Bolton, 1961).

It should be mentioned first that the mental health and maturity of individuals are not exclusive factors in determining successful mate selection (Eidelberg, 1956). Rather, it is the complementarity or "fit" of the two individuals that is of enormous importance (Lutz, 1964). The complementarity of the sadist and masochist, the dependent alcoholic man and his nurturing wife, the deceiver married to the naive individual who unconsciously enjoys being deceived, have been recognized for some time (Waelder, 1941). Emotional pathology in a marital pair may sometimes be a binding factor if it provides for a complementarity in the marital interaction.

Bill, aged thirty-eight, and Hilda Fitzgerald, aged thirty-two, sought marital counseling for many reasons. When Hilda desired sexual relations Bill was usually impotent, and when Bill was potent and took some sexual initiative Hilda resented his "ineptness," which made her "sick to my stomach." Bill's "arrogance" antagonized Hilda, making her feel very "demeaned," and Bill complained about Hilda's wish to "constantly castrate me."

As a child Bill had been very attached to his mother and very competitive with his father, often wishing that his father would die. When Bill was thirteen his father did die, and Bill blamed himself for this event. He became very depressed and withdrew from most people, including his mother.

Hilda, as a child, had been called her father's "sunny girl"; she had had a strong erotic attachment to her father and a very ambivalent relationship with her mother. When Hilda was twelve, *her* father died.

She felt that her sexual feelings toward her father upset him, and that was why she unconsciously experienced his death as punishment for these feelings.

Because both the Fitzgeralds had strong incestuous wishes that induced guilt in both of them, they both had to defend themselves against enjoying themselves sexually. Recognizing their individual anxiety and guilt was too difficult for them, they unconsciously chose each other so that they could avoid sex; however, consciously they blamed each other for their sexual incompatibility.

Needs that are obscure to the husband or wife often take forms that are transparent to everyone else. However, when well-intentioned friends or relatives point out neurotic patterns to the couple, they frequently resist facing the emotional truth.

Jane, aged twenty-eight, was an intelligent and highly educated woman. Despite her many accomplishments she had low self-esteem and a poor self-image. Whatever she achieved she repudiated; she felt that if she were a man she would be "somebody." To compensate for feelings of low self-worth she married a famous athlete who was intellectually limited. Bob, aged twenty-six, her husband, despite his athletic successes felt very fragile and often referred to himself as "a patsy." He thought Jane's brilliance would "present a good front to the world." Although Jane and Bob were told by friends and relatives that they had little in common with each other, they ignored their warnings and married. It did not take Jane and Bob long to discover that a marriage never cures a neurosis. The reassurance that each of them needed was much too strong to be adequately supplied by the other, and each became depressed, irritable, and hostile toward the other. Eventually, they sought marital counseling.

As we have suggested, many men and women marry with the unconscious purpose of finding a parent. Unconsciously, the women may seek an older man or the man may seek an older woman. Sometimes the individual may marry because he or she is unconsciously attracted to the future spouse's mother or father. During the courtship, while the marriage is still in the offing, any vague feelings of resentment or discontent will be balanced by the reassuring hope that fulfillment merely awaits the consummation of the marraige (Kubie, 1956).

When marriages founder it is usually not because the couple has incompatible interests and habits but because each of the pair is ignorant of the unconscious purposes that determined their respective choice.

To most psychoanalytically oriented therapists the concept "neurotic choice of mate" (Eidelberg, 1956) connotes a marital selection which interferes with enjoyable interaction and in which the displeasure exceeds the pleasure derived from the marriage. When such an error in judgment occurs, it can be conjectured that it was caused by the client's neurosis. It is then necessary for therapist and client to amass the evidence that will establish with relative certainty how the unconscious is interfering with the client's adaptation.

When clients seek help for marital conflict, they usually see the conflict as a result of the other partner's problem. Much like clients who suffer from a phobia, compulsion, or psychosomatic problem and do not realize how they are unconsciously arranging for a good part of their troubles, unhappy spouses rarely know what their contributions to their marital woes really are.

Mr. Routh, aged forty-two, came for treatment after his fourth divorce. He had many rationalizations to account for his failure, but it was only through an investigation of his fantasies and history that he was able to ascertain the cause of his troubles. Mr. Routh had a strong unconscious wish to be close to a mother figure, and he transformed all his wives into incestuous objects. After a jubilant love affair and exciting honeymoon he would become sexually impotent and guilty, and would seek out other women. His extramarital choices were experienced as nonincestuous objects, so he could be relatively comfortable with them. But whenever a woman showed enough interest in him to make her a realistic possibility as a wife, his initial excitement turned to anxiety and his impotence eventually returned.

Although Mr. Routh blamed the institution of marriage for his woes and was very contemptuous of his wives, he was not able to tolerate a wife until he could understand his strong sexual yearnings for a mother figure.

NEUROTIC MARITAL INTERACTION

Successful marital interaction is difficult to achieve. To live with another human being on an intimate basis requires a great deal of maturity. The individual must be able to curb his narcissism and empathize with his partner. Ego functions such as frustration tolerance, judgment, and reality testing must be reasonably well developed. The individual should have overcome infantile wishes such as the impulse for oral merger, incestuous desires, and Oedipal competition. Few people in our society have attained this level of maturity; consequently, one out of two marriages ends in divorce (Ekstein, 1977), and thousands of individuals seek help to cope with their neurotic marital interaction (Eisenstein, 1956).

Some of the vignettes that we have examined in this chapter have demonstrated that when an individual has unresolved conflicts—such as incestuous wishes, excessive dependency, and sexual anxiety—he or she will not be able to enjoy marriage and will usually provoke a spouse in a manner that will diminish the partner's enjoyment of the marriage as well.

It is important to reiterate that individuals usually find marital partners whose dynamics parallel and complement their own. The narcissistic personality usually finds someone to cater to him, the dependent client finds someone to minister to him, and the domineering person finds someone to abuse. Despite the suffering inherent in these relationships, the emotional patterns of the mates complement each other in such a way as to keep them involved with each other; their pathological reactions are perpetuated through an intrapsychic vicious circle of neurotic interactions (Mittlemann, 1956). Let us briefly review some examples of marital dyads that the social worker frequently meets in practice.

THE SADOMASOCHISTIC RELATIONSHIP

This type of marital pattern is characterized by one spouse's aggressive and sadistic attempts to humiliate and hurt the other, thus relieving personal anxiety and self-doubt. The mate often responds initially by becoming very dependent, submissive, and conciliatory. However, the masochistic partner eventually feels resentment toward the spouse for the humiliation that is experienced, and in revenge becomes quite sadistic. The partner who initially behaved in a sadistic fashion finds the rage from the spouse threatening, and retreats to a masochistic position. The partners endlessly reverse roles, often bickering and reconciling several times a day. They forgive each other because unconsciously they are psychologically needy children who cannot enjoy too much autonomy.

Murray and Lillian Green, a couple in their late thirties, sought marital counseling because they were perpetually arguing, threatening each other with divorce almost daily, and "making each other miserable." When Murray told Lillian what he wanted done, she would initially comply and "walk the dog," "clean the pipes," or "buy the newspaper." After a few days of what she referred to as "being a dutiful wife," Lillian would resent Murray and deride him for being so dependent. At first Murray would be contrite and conciliatory and try to curb his demands. However, within a few days he would be angry at Lillian for "putting me down" and would then reissue commands and reestablish the power struggle.

Both Murray and Lillian were very dependent individuals who clung to each other desperately. That is why both were inclined to be very submissive and easily intimidated. However, neither of them could tolerate the feeling of vulnerability when they were very acquiescent, and they defended against this feeling by becoming sadistic and contemptuous.

IDENTITY CONFLICTS

Many men and women are not secure in their knowledge about the appropriate rights, privileges, and immunities that are compatible with their sexual roles. Clients frequently express these doubts by challenging a spouse's attitudes toward domestic responsibilities, workloads in and out of the home, sexual initiative, and so on.

Jerry and Linda Harris, a couple in their late twenties, were arguing in the waiting room when the social worker greeted them. Jerry felt that he should present his side first "because I am the man." Linda felt that this prerogative was not a uniquely masculine one and that she had her rights too.

The argument continued in the consultation room, and many aspects of the Harris' marital interaction were debated. Linda resented Jerry's introducing her as "my wife" because "I am a person," and Jerry felt that this sort of thing "builds my ego, so why should you object? I am pleased to show you off because you are attractive!" Linda felt that she was "being used," and later, when Linda asked Jerry why he couldn't help her with certain domestic chores, he pointed out that *he* was "being used."

Jerry and Linda both had doubts about their self-images, and both wondered unconsciously how much of "a man" or "a woman" they were. Rather than face their anxieties and questions about their respective shaky sexual identities, in a mutually sadistic manner they tried to demean each other in order to bolster themselves.

THE DETACHED-DEPENDENT DYAD

A very common dynamic in marriages is that individuals seek characteristics in a partner which they lack but would like to have. The detached person often admires the dependent person, and vice versa. Freud (1914a) referred to this phenomenon in his paper on narcissism, in which he described how individuals strengthen their self-image by attaching themselves to spouses who appear to own what they lack but would like to have.

Often a detached person's behavior appears to his or her spouse as strength, and the vivacity of the dependent spouse can be experienced by the partner as autonomy. Because each partner is unaware of the defensive function of the other's overt behavior, they both become disillusioned rather quickly. When the dependent spouse demands love this provokes the detached partner's fears, and that partner becomes more detached. The deprived spouse feels humiliated and rejected, and the battle continues unabated.

Sally, aged thirty-two, and Dick Ingersol, aged forty, admired each other a great deal during their courtship. Sally thought that Dick's detachment was a sign of "strength and autonomy," and felt that if she married him he would "protect me and show me how to get along in this world." Dick, on the other hand, was really a depressed man who thought that Sally "would bring some color into my life."

After the Ingersols were married, life became miserable for both of them. Dick became very frightened of emotional involvement and withdrew every time Sally sought him out. This in turn made her feel very rejected, and to cope with her anxiety she sought reassurance by asking Dick over and over again if he loved her. Dick was very frightened of being "swallowed up" by Sally and withdrew. The more he withdrew, the more demanding Sally became, and vice versa.

The Helpless-Considerate Dyad

A marital dyad that is well known to social workers consists of the helpless alcoholic and the seemingly considerate, nurturing spouse. This helpless-considerate dyad appears not only in situations that involve alcoholism but in other marriages as well. The suffering, helpless partner expects his or her spouse to be omnipotent, while the devoted and nurturing mate derives some reassurance and strength from taking care of this person. Because the considerate mate is never considerate or omnipotent enough, and the helpless mate never grateful enough, both parties begin to resent each other.

As with most marriages, the spouses in this dyad receive a great deal of unconscious gratification from their neurotic interaction. The considerate spouse often enjoys the partner's weakness, and the helpless partner usually gets gratification from feeling deprived and complaining about it.

When Larry Joseph, aged thirty, sought treatment for his heroin addiction, his wife, Sandra, also aged thirty, fought the idea. She told Larry that she could help him more than any social worker could. Interestingly, her resentment did not become apparent until Larry mentioned to her that the social worker was helping him and that he was about to "kick the habit." When Larry saw how furious Sandra became, he eventually quit treatment.

THE SYMBIOTIC DYAD

Another dyad well known to social workers is the symbiotic marriage, in which each partner must examine every movement of the other; neither of these individuals can grant much autonomy or independence to themselves or to the other. Like two dependent children who feel worthless, abandoned, and isolated when not in the presence of a parent, the partners unconsciously conceive of themselves as joined together anatomically.

Although there are probably residues in every adult of symbiotic wishes and resistance to individuation (Ekstein, 1977), symbiotic partners are convinced that they cannot function in the world unless they are supported and protected by each other. Since the quest for an omnipotent parent can never be fully gratified, the symbiotic partners are constantly frustrated by each other. Each is not only resentful that the other does not take over with the love, honor, and obedience he is supposed to give, but both partners resent the demands that are placed on them. In addition, a symbiotic relationship usually makes the individuals feel weak, and husband and wife often attack each other for just this reason.

Jack and Irene King, a couple in their early twenties, were artists who shared the same studio, had the same clients, painted together, ate three meals a day with each other, and always showered together. Although they could feel blissful and excited at times, each of them would periodically accuse the other of making too many demands, "never letting me alone," and "wanting too much from me." Even the words they used to formulate their complaints were similar.

When the social worker suggested that each of them have individual therapy so that they could both learn to give and get some privacy and autonomy, both of them were extremely resentful and felt that it would be intolerable to "go it alone." It took six months of joint counseling before the Kings would even consider therapy on an individual basis.

Implied in all the neurotic interaction in marriage that we have discussed in this section is some form of maturational incompleteness. The individuals involved are utilizing their partners to gratify childish fantasies, and as a result are being continually frustrated because what they desire is unreal. In order to assist a couple who are experiencing marital distress, both individuals have to be helped to distinguish between their conscious and attainable goals and needs, on the one hand, and their unconscious and unattainable goals and needs, on the other. Until this is done, marital conflicts will remain unsolved (Kubie, 1956), because a mature and happy marriage requires two mature and happy individuals.

ASSESSING CHILD-THERAPY PROBLEMS

THE CHILD-GUIDANCE MOVEMENT: A BRIEF HISTORY

The child-guidance movement has witnessed many modifications in its therapeutic modalities and in the theoretical perspectives that guide its practice. Originally the movement was conceptualized as one in which the child was the complete focus of diagnostic and treatment attention; the therapist devoted virtually all of his or her efforts to understanding and alleviating the child's intrapsychic conflicts. Until the late 1930s the parents' contribution to the child's therapy was to present the child's problems and history to the therapist as they saw them and then be relegated to the waiting room for the duration of the child's treatment.

With the aid of psychoanalytic theory, child-guidance workers by the 1940s began to realize that a child had unconscious meaning to parents and that their own anxieties and fantasies influenced the growth and development of the child. Professionals learned that a childhood behavior disorder or neurosis was often, if not always, unconsciously induced and sustained by the parents and that therapeutic modifications in the child's behavior, no matter how positive, adversely affected the parents' equilibrium (Colm, 1970).

First mothers were made clients and their participation in the treatment process helped the child's therapy. When the mother's wishes, fears, and neurotic conflicts were addressed, the child's therapeutic gains did not threaten her so much. However, as mother and child improved in their internal functioning and modified their transactions with each other, the father often felt excluded and became threatened by their changes (Burgum, 1942; Beron, 1944). Although it took much longer for child-guidance personnel to help fathers become clients of child-guidance clinics, family agencies, and other social agencies, by the mid-1960s many fathers were actively participating in their children's treatment (Grunebaum, 1962; Strean, 1970; Grunebaum and Strean, 1970).

A natural step in the evolution of the child-guidance movement was the realization that the family could be viewed as a social system with interdependent parts; a change in one part of the system could alter the entire system. Hence family therapy came into vogue, and the disturbed child began to be considered as a symptom of dysfunction in the family system.

Lately the child-guidance movement has moved into larger orbits: the extended family, the neighborhood, and the community. Community mental health units are frequently manned by child-guidance workers, and the problems that they confront are frequently assessed within the framework of a psychoanalytic perspective.

In this section, we shall discuss how a psychoanalytic orientation can help in the assessment of children's psychopathology. Throughout our discussion we shall note the influence of parents' unconscious wishes and defenses—as well as the impact of significant others—on the formation of childhood neuroses and other disorders. In conclusion, we shall turn to "the family" as a unit of diagnosis.

WHY DO PEOPLE HAVE CHILDREN?

Just as it is important in dealng with marital conflict to ask what unconscious factors motivate individuals to marry, so in diagnosing conflicted parent-child interaction and childhood pathology it is equally crucial to understand why the child was wanted in the first place. Despite the fact that clients of social workers and other professionals for some time have included people who are parents, there is a limited amount of research available to document scientifically what factors induce individuals to have children.

Most psychoanalysts agree that the wish to have a child is an expression of narcissism. For most individuals, a child represents the parents reproduced, and it is frequently observed that parents endow their infant with traits that they pride or wish for in themselves. Those parts of themselves that they love or wish to possess are frequently "perceived" in the child, and that is why the child is often experienced as "His Majesty the Prince" (Freud, 1914a).

The dynamic of narcissism is observed in the proud and oft-repeated statement of parents and grandparents that the child "looks like me." When negative attributes are perceived by parents, it is not uncommon for one parent to blame the other for causing them or to claim that the locus of the difficulties is in the genetic history of the other parent. The narcissistic element in parenthood also becomes quite clear when one views parental reactions to Little League baseball games, children's report cards, or their artistic or other accomplishments. "That's my son!" or "That's my daughter!" are only thinly veiled exclamations that really imply "Look how great *I* am!" Similarly, it is difficult for many parents to acknowledge psychological difficulties in their children because unconsciously this means acknowledging difficulties, limitations, and vulnerabilities in themselves.

WHEN PARENTS SEEK HELP

Because one's child is so frequently experienced as a part of oneself, it is frequently difficult for a parent to ask a therapist for help with or for the child. Just as we noted earlier in this chapter that many applicants to social agencies prefer to ascribe the source of their difficulties to forces outside themselves, the parents who consult a social worker are usually quite defensive about facing the psychological truth of their children's limitations.

The psychoanalytically oriented therapist recognizes that as a parent describes a child, the parent's unconscious wishes, anxieties, and defenses frequently distort the presentation of the child's problems. Earlier in this chapter we saw in the case illustration of Mr. and Mrs. Cameron how both parents experienced the recommendation that they receive help for their child as an attack. In response they had to attack both the school their son was attending and the guidance counselor who referred them to the social worker.

A psychoanalytic perspective on child pathology alleges that if a child is emotionally disturbed, one and probably both of the parents have unresolved maturational conflicts of their own, which the child reactivates (A. Freud, 1951; Despert, 1965; Feldman, 1958). For example, the social worker can recognize that the statement "My child doesn't respond to limits" reflects anxiety in the parent that interferes with his or her limiting the child. As the worker interviews this parent, he will look for clues that pinpoint why the parent unconsciously does *not* want the child to respond to limits. Similarly, when a parent says "My child needs sexual information," it can be inferred that it is the parent who is probably in need of such information (Strean, 1970).

If the social worker realizes that a parent, in discussing features of a child's life, is also unconsciously referring to the child within himself, the worker will then relate to the parent's anxieties and defenses. This approach frequently helps a parent to become a client in his or her own right.

During his second interview at a child-guidance clinic Mr. Lazurus, aged thirty-six, reported that his son Peter didn't want to come for therapy. When the social worker asked what Mr. Lazurus thought bothered Peter about coming to the clinic, he replied that Peter *"doesn't like to talk about himself.* He has some hesitancy about revealing himself to a stranger!'' Asked what he thought Peter's hesitancy was about, Mr. Lazurus said that any relationship was threatening to Peter because he *"wants to preserve his privacy.''* When the social worker asked Mr. Lazurus which parts of Peter's life he thought Peter would not want to reveal, Mr. Lazurus said that he was too embarrassed to talk about it. After a long silence he said, ''I'm not sure what embarrasses me and what embarrasses Peter. I guess in many ways we are one and the same.''

When the social worker recognizes that a child's problem in ego functioning and his symptomatology are frequently mirror images of his parents' unconscious ego, he realizes that advice to the parents will not usually be effective unless their unconscious contribution to the child's pathology and their need to sustain it are respected and addressed.

DIAGNOSING THE CHILD'S PATHOLOGY

In diagnosing a child, all the generic principles alluded to earlier in this chapter are pertinent: ego functioning, superego mandates, history, and so on. Of greatest import, however, is how the child's maturational problems are activating conflicts in the parents, and how the parents are inevitably reinforcing and sustaining the child's conflicts. Whatever a parent's reason for coming for help for his difficulties, ''sooner or later we become aware that a parent, too, is emotionally disturbed now or was emotionally disturbed as a child, and that his or her difficulties are very similar to the child's. The more we study the parent, the more we see the similarity of the disturbance'' (Feldman, 1958, p. 23).

Clinicians have noted that parents of acting-out children usually offer them subtle rewards for their behavior and help the child behave as they behaved or would have liked to behave (Love and Mayer, 1970). They have also observed that parents of neurotically inhibited children characteristically prevent assertive behavior in their children because such behavior induces anxiety in them. They withdraw friendliness and other forms of positive recognition except on those occasions when the child inhibits himself or submits to parental dictates (Sternbach, 1947). The child becomes unwilling to relinquish neurotic or acting-out pleasures because he is so frequently the recipient of love premiums when he demonstrates his sensitivity and acquiescence to parental desires.

Ronald Metcalf, aged eleven, was referred to a child-guidance clinic because his reading level was very much below his capacity. Despite his poor reading performance, most of his ego functions such as judgment, reality testing, and relations with people were quite mature. Furthermore, his history showed nothing that appeared eventful or traumatic.

As reports from Mrs. Metcalf were carefully reviewed and as her interaction with Ronald was observed, it became quite clear that almost every time Ronald asserted himself, Mrs. Metcalf would squelch his spontaneity and finish his sentences. Ronald, in effect, was obeying an unconscious mandate from Mother: "Don't assert yourself! Don't be too individuated! I am your mouthpiece and in many ways your eyes and ears, too!"

When Ronald started treatment, Mrs. Metcalf made strenuous efforts to sabotage it. She spoke negatively to everyone of the boy's therapist and told Ronald that he was not being helped. When the boy actually did improve his reading, Mrs. Metcalf made her most determined effort to stop the treatment.

As work with Ronald and his parents continued, the social worker was able to conclude that Ronald was extremely frightened of his aggression and independence. To assert himself was—in his mind—to destroy his parents, and this thought overwhelmed him. It was much easier for him to be passive and ineffectual; this made him nonthreatening to adults and in this way he could maintain their love. In many ways he was "better off" *not* being a good reader.

Mrs. Metcalf was extremely frightened of having an assertive, independent son and had to castrate him psychologically. When Ronald appeared potent, as he did when he started to read at a higher level, this activated enormous terror in his mother and she tried to undo his progress. It turned out that Mr. Metcalf was an extremely poor reader himself, thus confirming the worker's notion that Mrs. Metcalf wanted the males in her life to be weak. Ronald unconsciously realized this, and in many ways identified with his weak father.

As a child progresses in his maturation, he has tasks to resolve—to trust, become autonomous, take initiative, and so on (Erikson, 1950). If the "radius of social relationships" is a supportive one, he has a good chance to accomplish the tasks. However, if parents are disturbed, ill, or absent, if schools are not attuned to the child's needs, if neighborhoods are unsafe, then the child will suffer. It is the social worker's diagnostic task to pinpoint not only what significant others are contributing to the child's life but how the child is experiencing them.

Mary North, aged twelve, lived alone with her mother because her father had died when she was nine. Mary had been very attached to her father, but Mrs. North mentioned that she had detected very few signs of grief in the child when her father died. She continued to do well in school, was cooperative with her mother at home, and seemed to be well liked by her peers.

In contrast to her academic performance and seemingly good adjustment for many years, Mary's schoolwork deteriorated when she was twelve. She became very withdrawn and depressed, and spent most of her time alone, in fantasy.

Through several interviews with Mary and Mrs. North, as well as through a school visit, the social worker was able to make the following assessment: In contrast to her latency years, when Mary's sexual impulses were quiescent, preadolescence activated them. Mary's strong yearning for a father reasserted itself, as did her competition with her mother. In addition, for the first time Mary had a male teacher, and his presence in her life intensified her Oedipal longings. Both Mrs. North and the teacher were unaware of Mary's sexual fantasies and consequently could not help her very much. Also, Mary's burgeoning sexuality activated longings in Mrs. North; she realized that she, too, was thinking of her husband more often now.

Mary's deteriorating schoolwork and declining adaptation could be attributed to her stage of development, her unresolved attachment to her father, her competition with her mother, the presence of an Oedipal figure in her life (the teacher), and an environment that was not responsive to her needs and conflicts.

One of the best ways to pinpoint a child's conflict is to reflect on his level of maturational development. When the child's maturational tasks are confronted, the next question is to determine how people in his social environment are responding to him. Inevitably, the social worker will find that the emotionally disturbed child's significant others are unaware of his needs and/or their own conflicts are interfering with the child's resolution of maturational tasks. The following two vignettes illustrate this phenomenon quite poignantly.

Sally Offer, aged two, was unable to be weaned from the breast. Although Mrs. Offer, aged thirty, made many efforts to do so, Sally cried unconsolably, had temper tantrums, and was totally uncooperative each time her mother attempted to wean her. Advice from physicians did not seem to be effective when Mrs. Offer tried to put their suggestions into practice.

Although Mrs. Offer was critical of the physician who referred her to the mental health clinic, support and empathy from the clinic's social worker enable her to start talking about herself and the story of her own life. It turned out that her own mother had been hospitalized with depression when she was less than one year old. Mrs. Offer also mentioned that she herself had been weaned abruptly. When the worker asked her how she thought she experienced her own weaning and separation from her mother, she began to weep, voiced strong rage, and said that she didn't "see the purpose of this interview."

It became clear to the social worker that just as Sally cried, became angry, and refused to cooperate when she was being weaned, Mrs. Offer reacted to a question about her own separation from her mother with crying, anger, and stubbornness. Mrs. Offer had enormous resistance to weaning Sally because she herself wanted to be breast-fed. In her fourth interview with the social worker, Mrs. Offer stated with conviction, "There is nothing more beautiful than nursing, and I will not let you or anybody else break us up."

Mr. Pendington, aged twenty-eight, consulted his plant physician about his three-year-old son, Michael. Michael was constantly constipated, and was untrained for bowel and urine control. Mr. Pendington insisted on examining Michael's feces almost daily and discussed bowel training with anybody who would listen to him. When the intake worker at the child-guidance clinic to which he was referred asked Mr. Pendington why Michael's defecating was of so much concern to him, he responded, "It gives me a feeling of . . . importance. . . . I dread the day when I'll have to discuss sex, girls, and all that stuff with him. I want to keep him young, I guess!"

It is clear from these two illustrations that parents who have conflicted relationships with their children unconsciously reward them for maintaining a regressed position which they, the parents, enjoy vicariously. A parent may unconsciously prohibit a child's further psychosocial growth, not out of malice, but because such growth would activate the adult's unbearable anxiety. Unprepared for emotionally healthy living because he himself was improperly nurtured, the parent maintains a relationship with his child that is dynamically similar to the one he experienced in his own childhood.

THE FAMILY AS A UNIT OF ASSESSMENT

Although the diagnosis and treatment of the family as a unit have only recently come of age in social work practice, working with the family is not a new development if one views social work from a historical perspective. It was the founder of social casework, Mary Richmond, who said that in planning treatment there is need to consider "the family group . . . which includes all who share a common table" (Richmond, 1917). She also declared that "the family life has a history of its own" and indicated that it must be understood in terms of the family members "interactions, values, activities, external circumstances and the nature of the two homes from which the parents came to make a third one." Richmond cautioned that "the caseworker who ignores these aspects . . . will never win lasting results in social casework."

It should also be recalled that until the late 1940s the journal, *Social Casework*, was called *The Family*, again indicating that this unit was the diagnostic and treatment concern of the social worker for many years.

That caseworkers and most social workers have always felt that the well-being of family members is pertinent in their work is certainly true; that occasional diagnostic formulations and treatment of more than one family member at a time have occurred since social work's inception is also true. However, it has only been in the past decade and a half that social workers have acquired a vocabulary, a conceptual framework, and treatment procedures to diagnose and treat the family as a distinct entity.

Perhaps one of the more important reasons why social work for many decades did not pursue its interest in "the family" was because of its allegiance to and identification with the treatment model of psychoanalysis. Although Freud wrote quite early in his career (1909) that "above all, our interests will be directed towards the family circumstances of our patients," and although in that same year, in the case of Little Hans, he used the actions and statements of both parents to understand the boy's phobic illness, Freud and most of his adherents until the 1950s were essentially concerned with the diagnosis and treatment of the individual. In the writings of many psychoanalysts one can detect a certain antipathy toward the family. Freud himself spoke with particular vehemence about members of a patient's family who, frequently for neurotic reasons of their own, actively interfered with the therapeutic effort. He compared this problem to family members looking over the surgeon's shoulder in the operating room.

A number of factors coalesced so that by the late 1950s and early 1960s the family as a unit of diagnosis and treatment became very popular in social agencies. The knowledge explosion of the 1960s brought concepts from system theory, role theory, and communication theory to social workers' attention; these concepts emphasized that the family is a system with a communication network, and that to help an individual modify attitudes and behavior an understanding of his familial context is crucial (Stamm, 1972). In addition, therapists in and out of social work began to recognize that if one member of a family received psychotherapy, resulting modifications in his behavior required a new family homeostasis (Heiman, 1956; Neubauer, 1953; Rosen, 1956). As was pointed out earlier in our review of the child-guidance movement, it eventually became apparent to workers that the child could not be assessed or treated in isolation, but that the parents had to become part of the treatment plan.

Insights from ego psychology also contributed a great deal toward bringing the family to social workers' attention. Ego psychology—with its emphasis on adaptation (Hartmann, 1958), mutuality, and interpersonal relations (Erikson, 1950)—helped social workers recognize the importance of such phenomena as the complementarity of neuroses, unconscious communication, double-bind messages, and role expectations (Ackerman, 1958).

By the early 1960s, social workers were reevaluating the dynamics and treatment of the school phobic, the unmarried mother, and one-parent families (Strean, 1970). Traditionally most social workers had viewed school phobia exclusively as an expression of the child's anxiety in separating from Mother. They now began to recognize that not only was the child fearful of separation (because the mother might die) but the mother was equally frightened of releasing him, and in most cases the father's attitude and behavior were aiding and abetting the problem.

By the end of the 1960s many social workers, regardless of their field of practice or theoretical view of the human being, were able to recognize the importance of the client's familial context in making an assessment. Not only were the contributions of parents and in-laws pertinent; assessment was to include all those "who live under the same roof with the paterfamilias; those who form the fireside. Even the maid or the animal pets are psychologically important" (Heiman, 1956, p. 234).

THE UNIQUE CONTRIBUTION OF PSYCHOANALYSIS TO FAMILY ASSESSMENT

Family treatment is practiced by clinicians with varying orientations—systems theorists, communication experts, Gestalt therapists, and so on. It is now an eclectic field; contributions from a variety of perspectives form the role armamentarium of the family therapist. What contributions to family assessment has psychoanalysis made?

The notion of "family homeostasis" (Jackson, 1957), or "family balance," provides a framework for the study of those unconscious forces that help to keep the family in equilibrium and those "inputs" that disturb the equilibrium. For example, a couple may be able to interact harmoniously until the birth of a child. In helping the couple reach a new homeostatic balance that includes their child, the family therapist will study not only how each of the marital partners emotionally experiences the baby; in addition, he will want to evaluate how the couple now experience each other as parents and how the advent of the baby influences their perception of each other as sexual partners (Zilbach, 1968).

Perhaps one of the most useful contributions of psychoanalysis to family diagnosis is the concept of the unconscious. Communication and interaction have to be evaluated in terms of the family members' unconscious wishes, fantasies, and defenses. For example, the operation of the unconscious in communication between family members may be observed in a "double-bind" message (Bateson et al., 1956), in which the speaker says one thing and means another.

In the Rider family everyone was overtly polite to each other. Mother, aged forty, father, aged forty-two, and son Jack, aged eleven, frequently complimented each other, often smiling and appearing physically affectionate. However, whenever they were with members of their extended family or with friends, they would try to provoke a discussion in which the others would participate with them in family feuding. Jack often complained about his parents at his grandparents' home, and Mr. and Mrs. Rider criticized each other and Jack at the homes of family and friends.

In the Rider family there was a great deal of unresolved hostility, which was repressed and unconscious in their own home. Each member was so frightened of his or her hostile impulses that the hostility could be expressed only when it was supported by outsiders. It was the task of the family therapist to help the Riders confront not only the anger that each harbored toward the other, but, of equal importance, why they feared expressing it in their own home.

As we discussed in the section on marital interaction, each spouse's perception of the other can be distorted because of unrealistic wishes and fears originating from their relationships with their own parents. Transference always exists in a marital relationship, and likewise, parents can experience a child as sister, brother, mother, or father. The transferential factor is particularly important in family assessment in a foster-home placement, because the foster child "brings his natural parents with him" (Kaplan, 1953).

Tom Stone, aged eleven, was placed in a home where the foster parents, the Bakers, were very warm, tender, and considerate; they tried their best to help him feel comfortable and loved. It came as a shock to both of them when Tom would demean them, curse them, and tell them how horrible they were and how much he wanted to leave their home.

It was not until the social worker helped the Bakers realize that Tom was displacing much of the hatred he felt toward his natural parents onto them that they could relate with him comfortably. Actually Tom felt safer in his foster home, and therefore could express his defiance more openly.

Because all members of a family are unconsciously engaged

with each other, when one or more members seek out a social agency this event has meaning for everybody and they are all unconsciously participating in it. For example, when Mrs. Taylor applies to an agency so that Bill can attend its summer camp, her request must be evaluated not only in terms of the meaning of a vacation to the child, but also with a view toward understanding how the request is experienced by the whole family. What does the request mean to the mother? Does she want to get rid of Bill to give herself a rest? If so, what does this mean to Bill? Do Bill's brothers and sisters feel that he will have an advantage by being at camp? Or do they feel that they will have an advantage? Does Mr. Taylor agree that Bill should go to camp? Neubauer has stated:

> A step forward of one family member may disturb several of the others and could, therefore, create additional disturbances. . . . In making recommendations, the agency that is family-oriented must be aware of the effect of any treatment (has) on the total family. It might at times exclude a procedure which may be helpful to one member of the family, if it would be inadvisable for the family as a whole. (1953, p. 115)

Another contribution that psychoanalysis can make to a family diagnosis is its understanding of defenses. As the social worker observes repetitive behavior that is dysfunctional for the family, such as constant bickering or hostile withdrawal, he can use his understanding of defenses to help the family try to resolve the dysfunctional behavior.

Mrs. Unger, aged thirty-three, a woman with strong symbiotic wishes and omnipotent fantasies, was married to a man who admired her for her assertiveness and aggressiveness. Mr. Unger, aged forty, very rarely questioned his wife's dominating or demeaning treatment of him. When Gerald, the Ungers' son, became six years old and began to assert himself a little, Mrs. Unger became even more critical of her husband. As the social worker studied the family interaction, she began to realize that Mrs. Unger's increased contempt for Mr. Unger was a displacement of her anger toward Gerald. Gerald was now behaving in a less passive manner, and this induced enormous anxiety in Mrs. Unger that she could not face directly.

Very often certain id impulses that are forbidden to all the family members but that each member would like to gratify—e.g., exhibitionistic or sadistic wishes—are projected onto one family member and he is unconsciously encouraged to act out the impulse. As the family members observe their son, daughter, brother, or sister stealing or acting sexually promiscuous, they receive vicarious gratification from the behavior. However, the family members usually condemn this acting out, and to appease their own superego mandates consciously disown it (Szurek and Berlin, 1973).

Willie Thomas, aged fifteen, was the son of a minister. Mr. and Mrs. Thomas were extremely upset to learn that Willie stole, smoked pot, and had group sex several times a week. When the family therapist interviewed the Thomases, it became quite clear how the parents and Willie's sister unconsciously enjoyed Willie's behavior. Although they were all committed to the idea of being "a minister's family and standing for the good things in life like 'abstinence' and 'self-control,'" when the Thomases discussed Willie's activities they became animated. They laughed and smiled and their faces flushed as they reviewed Willie's escapades in detail, thus betraying their unconscious approval.

When the social worker maintains a family focus during diagnosis and recognizes how the conflicts and presenting problems of one family member invariably involve the other members' participation, the treatment plan will be more comprehensive and will meet the client where he or she is emotionally. Treatment of the school-phobic youngster will take into consideration not only the child's separation anxiety but the parents' separation problems. Similarly, treatment of the unmarried mother, the dependent alcoholic, and the antisocial teen-ager will be enhanced when familial interactions are assessed. Contemporary psychoanalytic thinking avers that familial interactions always are etiological in the maladaptation of every client.

APPLYING PSYCHOANALYSIS TO THE ASSESSMENT OF
SMALL-GROUP PHENOMENA

Although most people regard psychoanalysis as a theory that is concerned exclusively with the individual, it has never ignored the individual's interpersonal relationships. As early as 1922 Freud stated:

> In the individual's mental life someone else is invariable involved, as a model, as an object, as a helper, as an opponent, and so from the very first Individual Psychology is at the same time Social Psychology as well—in this extended but entirely justifiable sense of the words. (pp. 1–2)

In the same work from which this statement came, *Group Psychology and the Analysis of the Ego,* Freud addressed a number of group phenomena. He pointed out that the relationships of an individual "to his parents and to his brothers and sisters, to the object of his love and to his physician—in fact all the relations which have hitherto been the chief subject of psychoanalytic research" recapitulate themselves in the individual's group behavior. Freud noted that in a group one observes "the character of a regression": Emotions are usually intensified and intellect is inhibited. The group, Freud pointed out, is held together by the members' erotic feelings toward one another, and when an individual gives up his distinctiveness in a group and lets its members influence him, "he does it because he feels the need of being in harmony with them rather than in opposition to them" (Freud, 1922, p. 40).

Freud viewed the role of the leader of the group as crucial, because he is experienced as a father figure who induces the members to give up much of their narcissism. Group members make the leader their ego ideal and identify with him, and it is because of the emotional tie with the leader who cares about the group members that the individuals in the group can identify with each other. A group was defined by Freud as "a number of individuals who have put one and the same object in the place of their ego ideal and have consequently identified themselves with one another in their ego" (1922, p. 61).

Although individuals in a group are frequently freer to love and be constructive because of their emotional tie to the parental figure in whom they have invested much libidinal energy, rarely is their allegiance to the leader unconflicted. Some ambivalence is usually present. This may take the form of group defenses or group resistances, as when "members of a group, in subtle ways, share a common reluctance to verbalize ideas and experiences; unconsciously they may virtually make a pact with each other to hold back." (Ormont, 1976, p. 286).

Therapeutic experience has expanded the psychoanalytic view of group processes. S. R. Slavson, the founder of psychoanalytic group therapy, pointed out in 1964 (p. 27): "It has been shown that the group serves *in loco maternis*. The leader usually represents symbolically the father figure, while the group represents the complementarity of the mother." Similarly, Foulkes said that "on different levels the group can symbolize a variety of objects or persons, e.g. the body . . . the inside of the mother, the womb. It frequently, possibly universally, represents the 'Image of the Mother'" (1964, p. 115). Scheidlinger's paper "On the Concept of the 'Mother Group'" (1976) concluded that one of the major dynamics in a group is the members' unconscious wish to restore an earlier state of unconflicted union with the mother. There is in each member, according to Scheidlinger, a regressive pull to move toward a "need-gratifying relationship" with the mother.

As psychoanalytically oriented group therapists have studied group phenomena they have been able to pinpoint those variables that endanger group cohesion, such as the uninhibited expression of sexual and/or aggressive drives, marked egocentricity in individual members, extreme competitiveness and jealousy, excessive negative transference reactions, and excessive frustration originating from the leader or the group code (Rosenthal, 1971).

The major contribution psychoanalysis can make to the assessment of group behavior is its understanding of unconscious transference and resistance phenomena as they become manifest in the group.

When the teacher of a group of ten-year-olds approached the school social worker for help in better understanding the behavior of a pupil named Samuel, the worker's grasp of the dynamics involved in transference and resistance enabled her to be of much assistance to the teacher. As the social worker reviewed Samuel's bullying behavior and his need to place other youngsters, particularly boys, in a tormented position, she was able to relate this to his position in his own family. Samuel was the youngest of three brothers, and his two older brothers continually berated and scapegoated him. Feeling helpless and unable to assert himself, Samuel handled his anxiety by placing his peers at school in the same subordinate position that he was in at home.

As we discussed earlier, the personality of the leader is crucial to the successful outcome of a group experience. If the leader is experienced as one who loves the members, the members usually identify with the leader and become quite constructive with each other. However, because the leader is experienced transferentially he is often accused of favoring one member over the other, and sibling rivalry and other forms of destructive behavior ensue.

In a parents' counseling group, Mrs. Victor, aged thirty, consistently insisted that the leader ignored her comments, praised others more, and "probably would like to get rid of me." Reassurances from the social worker did not help Mrs. Victor feel accepted. As the worker reassessed Mrs. Victor's behavior in the group and reviewed her childhood experiences in her own family, it became quite clear that Mrs. Victor had an unconscious wish to feel deprived by a parental figure. As long as she felt deprived, she could collect injustices. Her complaining defended her from acknowledging the emotional truth, which was a strong wish to be superior to her siblings and be more loved and admired by her parents than they were.

Because most group situations, particularly therapeutic groups, often induce aggression, the leader and group members often become the target of a member's infantile fantasies. A very frequent transference fantasy is that the leader is an omnipotent parental figure. The members, because of this shared belief, can then place all kinds of demands on the leader. If the leader gratifies requests for advice and environmental manipulation he

can reaffirm the members' fantasies; if he frustrates their requests, he may be experienced as cruel and rejecting.

In a group of mental patients who were planning to leave the hospital, the members handled a great deal of their separation anxiety and fear of the unknown by placing many demands on the social worker. Requests for legal, financial, and other forms of environmental manipulation filled the sessions. Because the leader had been so helpful in the past, he was experienced as a giving parent by the members. The patients exaggerated his powers in their minds; they needed a great deal of help to understand how they wanted to remain in a regressed, dependent position in relation to him, and how, by thinking that he "had all the answers," they were depreciating themselves.

When the social worker utilizes principles of metapsychology in assessing group phenomena, he or she is often in a position to determine why a client cannot utilize a group experience. To interact in a group requires the ability to listen, empathize, exercise frustration tolerance, and handle other ego functions without too much conflict. Many clients' problems are at a pre-Oedipal level of development; consequently, as with small children, their narcissism and grandiosity are too strong, and their reason, judgment, and ability to identify with others are too weak. When a client is not mature enough to handle a group experience, it is obvious that group counseling, group therapy, or recreational groups are contraindicated.

ASSESSMENT OF ORGANIZATIONS AND COMMUNITIES

When we move from assessment of the individual to larger units like the family, the group, and the community, psychoanalysis has a lesser role to play. As the units of diagnostic attention are enlarged, accessibility to the individuals' unconscious wishes, fantasies, and defenses is diminished, and this obviously limits the potential of a psychoanalytic perspective. As Van den Haag has stated: "The trouble with interpreting the behavior of groups or absent persons is that they do not respond with reactions that can be utilized to narrow the interpretive range" (1963), pp. 184–85).

The first attempt to apply psychoanalytic understanding to community life was in Freud's *Civilization and Its Discontents* (1930). Here Freud described how the individual is in constant conflict between the urge to gratify his instinctual impulses, on the one hand, and the desire to conform to the imperatives of authorities such as parents, school, church, or state.

> A great part of the struggle of mankind centers around the single task of finding some expedient solution between these individual claims and those of the civilized community; it is one of the problems of man's fate whether this solution can be arrived at in some particular form of culture or whether the conflict will prove irreconcilable. (p. 136)

As Freud pondered the state of civilized man, he voiced a certain pessimism about his fate. He questioned the ability of the authority structure in Western society to help individuals renounce their tendency toward "unbridled aggression" and "egoistic self-satisfaction." He felt that the "passions of instinct" are stronger than "reasoned interests" and that the quality of leadership available in society's institutions might never be strong or competent enough to "erect barriers against the instincts of men and hold their manifestations in check."

In examining community life, Freud pointed out that the researcher always should take into account two trends in the individual—one toward personal happiness and the other toward unity with the rest of humanity. In describing the logic behind his view that renunciation is essential to civilized society, he said:

> Human life in common is only made possible when a majority comes together which is stronger than any separate individual and which remains united against all separate individuals. . . . This replacement of the power of the individual by the power of the community constitutes the decisive step of civilization. The essence of it lies in the fact that the members of the community

restrict themselves in their possibilities of satisfaction, whereas the individual knew no such restrictions. (1930, p. 95)

Although Freud was always preoccupied with finding a means to make life more civilized and happier, he was equally adamant in condemning particular institutions—e.g., church, school, army—as too restrictive. In Freud's writings there is an ambivalence toward societal restrictions. He realized that coercion can stunt personalities but nonetheless is the instrument that made civilization possible (Roazen, 1968).

Freud's notion that the well-analyzed individual can oppose conventional restrictions without feeling guilty and that psychoanalytic treatment should involve much more than successful "adjustment" to society has been reaffirmed by his followers. There have been several pronouncements by analysts that "psychoanalysts should never make themselves puppets of society and accept superficial behavior patterns as indices of psychic reality" (Eissler, 1947). As Devereux pointed out, "Adjustment and conformity have very little to do with reality acceptance" (1939), and Money-Kyrle (1944) defined mental health as "optimum freedom from distortion in unconscious fantasy." Eisler (1947) maintained that "the resistance a person can put up against the onslaught of strong mass sentiments is an index of the degree of personality integration."

As psychoanalysts have been more influenced by ego psychologists, particularly by the work of Erikson and Hartmann, they have begun to view social institutions not only as expressing man's destructive tendencies but also as capable of lightening conflicts by confirming people's identities. Many analysts have taken the position that rules need not have only a psychologically inhibiting effect; they also provide individuals with the facilities to accomplish ends that would be impossible without social life (Roazen, 1968). Erikson has pointed out (1968) that society guides and narrows the individual's choices, as it confirms members in "the right life plan," and that the development of a child's positive identity depends on support from significant social groups. Erikson disagrees somewhat with Freud's outlook on society: "Instead of emphasizing what social organization denies the child, we wish to clarify what it may first grant to the infant, as it keeps him alive and as, in administering to his needs in a specific way, it seduces him to its particular life style" (1959, pp. 20–21).

As ego psychologists have stressed the urgency of adapting the social environment to fit human needs, there has been a growing psychoanalytic literature in the past ten to fifteen years that reflects this perspective. Starting with the work of Erikson (1950) who has attempted to examine how different cultures foster or retard psychosexual growth, communities have been intensively studied (Bensman and Vidich, 1957), political leaders have been assessed (Erikson, 1968), and the unconscious mechanisms in voting habits have been exposed (Dorn and Sigall, 1977). Harold Laswell was the first American to apply psychoanalytic insights and techniques to the study of politics. His now-famous formula, P = pdr—"political behavior" equals "private motives" becoming "displaced" to public causes and "rationalized in the public interest"—developed from his contacts with Freud's works and his studies in ego psychology (Laswell, 1930). He demonstrated that the latent potential for political behavior can be discovered through dream analysis and free association.

SOCIAL WORK AND THE "AVERAGE EXPECTABLE ENVIRONMENT"

The major means by which the psychoanalytically oriented social worker can assess community life and organizational milieu is through practice experience with individuals, families, and groups. As the worker notes how the environment is interfering with people's psychosocial functioning, he or she recommends, petitions, or collaborates with the appropriate personnel in behalf of change. For example, when practice experience demonstrates that pregnant women have predictable anxieties, the worker can show how a prenatal counseling center has much merit in a given community. Similarly, he or she can advocate modifying the organization of schools, neighborhoods, and hospitals when they are overcrowded, understaffed, or not providing the necessary services (Kahn, 1973; Meyer, 1976).

Social workers utilizing the insights of psychoanalysis have been successful in helping to establish day-care centers, social utilities for the poor, parents' guidance groups, and recreational activities for the aged (Riessman et al., 1964). They have also demonstrated how bureaucracies like county welfare departments hurt rather than help interpersonal and intrapsychic functioning (Strean, 1978).

The dynamically oriented social worker can be particularly effective in working with key leaders in a community or organization.

When it was observed by the school social worker that a number of students were involved in truancy, vandalism, arson, and drug abuse, she assessed the situation carefully. One of the major factors contributing to the students' impulsive and rebellious activities was the principal's punitive and authoritarian behavior. The teachers unconsciously identified with his attitude and were quite sadistic with many of the students. The social worker correctly reasoned that if the principal had an opportunity to discharge some of his resentment in a supportive and understanding relationship, he might eventually become more understanding himself.

When the social worker can integrate a metapsychological understanding of the individual and his knowledge of system theory, role theory, and ego psychology, he or she is in an excellent position to assess the psychosocial conflicts of communities, groups, families, dyads, and individuals (Wasserman, 1974).

Chapter 5

Using Psychoanalysis in Social Work Intervention

As was mentioned in Chapter 4, because social work is essentially eclectic, the sophisticated and skilled clinician will rely on some combination of system theory, organizational theory, learning theory, role theory, psychoanalytic theory, and ego psychology as he works on a short- or long-term basis with individuals, dyads, families, groups, and organizations.

Not only does the social work clinician combine psychoanalysis with other theoretical approaches, but he may draw on the psychoanalytic arsenal for uses that many orthodox psychoanalysts eschew, such as work with large units like groups and communities. For example, unlike many psychoanalysts, social workers relate to the "multiple transferences" of a group, a family's "defensive maneuvers," or an organization's "latent resistance to libidinal expression"—i.e., the fantasies that group members have about each other, the way a whole family unites to protect itself against danger, and the way an organization sets up barriers to showing concern for its members.

In this chapter we will consider how psychoanalysis can assist the social worker in conceptualizing his interventive role-set with client systems and in determining the appropriateness (or inappropriateness) of certain treatment interventions such as family therapy and group therapy. Case illustrations will demonstrate how such psychoanalytic treatment concepts as transference, countertransference, and resistance can be applied to one-to-one social work treatment, marital counseling, and parent-child problems, as well as family, group, and community work.

The Social Worker's Role-Set

The complexity of the person-situation constellations that confront the social worker requires him to enact many roles as part of his interventive repertoire. In a single case situation, he may at times be an advocate, a social broker, a persuader, a father or mother figure, a group leader, and a community organizer. Consequently, it is important for the practitioner to decide not only where, when, and with whom he will intervene, but also to determine how active or passive he will be, how firm or permissive, how verbal or nonverbal, and how gratifying or frustrating.

In planning the quality and quantity of their activities, many social workers have used notions from the work of Erik Erikson (1950), particularly his concept that maturational conflicts are "life tasks," which the individual's "radius of significant others" should help him resolve.

Most individuals who visit social workers are having difficulty with one or more life tasks (trust vs. mistrust, autonomy vs. shame and doubt, initiative vs. guilt, industry vs. inferiority, identity vs. identity diffusion, intimacy vs. isolation, generativity vs. stagnation, and ego integrity vs. despair). Either they have regressed or are fixated at a certain early state, and thus they are having difficulty coping with a current life task. The social worker, therefore, can conceive of his role in the interventive plan as that of a key "significant other" who through his attitudes and activities helps the client move up the psychosocial ladder and resolve his life task or tasks.

Not only does the social worker see himself as an important

significant-other who must enact a certain role or roles in accordance with the client's biological, social, economic, and psychological needs, but he is also the catalyst who helps significant others in the client's environment enact their roles with more maturity so that everyone's functioning can be improved.*

Life Tasks

TRUST VS. MISTRUST

While all individuals manifest signs of conflict and some resolution of conflict at all of the life stages, many clients show a heavy ratio of mistrust to trust. Clients of public welfare agencies who are or have been psychologically, socially, and/or physically neglected, battered, or improperly nourished belong in this category. Individuals with trust-mistrust problems may be people who find parenthood burdensome and therefore regress to dependent, helpless, and sometimes abusive behavior. In this category too, are many economically impoverished clients, whose environments are extremely deficient and malnourishing. Here are also clients who have suffered from environmental or situational crises like tornadoes, job layoffs, or the death of a loved one.

The client who is coping with trust-mistrust conflicts is reminiscent of an abandoned, unloved child, needing the protection of a parental surrogate who will listen to his angry outbursts, some of which may even be directed at the surrogate. The social worker in the role of parent first helps the client verbalize his anger and distrust and later provides the necessary food, safety, and other physical and emotional nutrients that will fill physical, emotional, and social voids. This enables the client to accept, to

*Parts of the following section are based on "Assessment and the Social Worker's Role in Intervention," Chapter 5 of H. Strean, *Clinical Social Work* (New York: Free Press, 1978).

some extent, the social worker as a trustworthy person, and as a byproduct of the social worker–client relationship the client learns to trust himself a little more.

The treatment of choice for the client who has problems at the trust-mistrust level is one-to-one therapy. The distrustful client cannot easily share with others and therefore needs a mothering person all to himself.

Because the client at the trust-mistrust level often feels like a fragile child, he needs help in his environment as well. After the client has voiced some of his anger at those who he feels have deprived him (including the worker), he usually begins to trust the worker more. Once some trust has been established, the worker can assume the role of advocate and social broker in the client's environment.

AUTONOMY VS. SHAME AND DOUBT

There are two subgroups of clients who fall into this category. The first consists of clients who have little confidence in their own capacities and limited faith in their environmental resources because they feel under strong pressure to be productive. These clients are or have been expected to do too much on their own and tend to be perfectionistic. In the second subgroup are clients who are or have been insufficiently encouraged to perform with some independence and autonomy.

Clients who hold high and exacting standards and/or are exposed to such standards in their social orbits feel like failures much of the time. They feel ashamed of themselves and harbor much self-hatred; they are the masochistic spouse, parent or child, the self-punishing employee, or the very compulsive student. Unable to assume much independence, they constantly fear failure. These clients are often depressed and keep themselves socially isolated.

For the individual who is reacting to imposed high standards, the significant other should be an individual or group that will permit and encourage the relaxation of controls and a lessening of perfectionistic standards. When the significant other accepts the client as he is, the client can come to accept himself as he is and his resources as they are. This often means that the client needs help in accepting failure and imperfection as an inherent part of everyone's life. As long as the therapeutic modality provides an atmosphere that will reduce the client's self-hatred and offer him encouragement to enjoy himself as he is, the modality can be either a small group or individual treatment.

Clients in the second subgroup are reluctant to assume automony and independence because they have been or are overindulged by their environment. Such clients might be the over-demanding spouse, parent or child, the rebellious student or employee, or the person with a "manipulating behavior disorder" who throws temper tantrums when he is called upon to assume responsibility.

The therapeutic atmosphere for the client who has been indulged will give him needed controls, prohibitions, and encouragement to negotiate by himself in his environment. Because the indulged client may be likened to a child who needs to be toilet-trained, the treatment of chioce would appear to be one-to-one therapy, unless the therapeutic small group can be consistently limiting and disciplining. In one-to-one treatment the client, like a child being trained, can be limited when he acts impulsively, rewarded and praised when he controls himself, and reinforced when he assumes autonomy and independence.

INITIATIVE VS. GUILT

Clients who have difficulties accepting and enjoying their sexual roles, but concomitantly have several strengths, have conflicts with initiative vs. guilt. Such clients might include a husband or wife who has anxiety about his or her sexual assertiveness and spontaneity. Also in this category may be a parent who finds it difficult to cope with a sexually maturing child's amorous advances and/or the child's competition with him or her. The client may also be one who fears success because in his mind this is equivalent to something destructive; the client who fails on the job or at school may belong in this category. Sometimes this client may appear seductive, charming, and sexually aggressive on the first meeting, but sooner or later problems with initiative and anxiety about sexual role become exposed.

When clients are having difficulty coping with initiative, the worker encourages the expression of sexual wishes and accepts the wish to gratify sexual desires as universal. He also helps the client's significant others to encourage and accept the universality of sexual wishes and fantasies. Often marital pairs and family members have a shared difficulty in assuming initiative in their respective roles. Consequently, in work with parent-child units, marital dyads, or families, a statement by the social worker to one member of the dyad or family is often experienced as a directive to all of the family members. For example, when Mr. Doe is encouraged by the worker to assume some initiative and take the family bowling, in all probability the rest of the Doe family will experience these remarks as a suggestion to go out and enjoy bowling.

The worker encourages the client with initiative-related problems to be more active not only in his marriage and family life but in other situations as well. He asks, for example, "Why can't you ask the boss for a raise?" "Why don't you allow yourself to enjoy dancing?" "What's wrong with winning at tennis, golf, or bowling?"

Industry vs. Inferiority

Clients who are too tied to the narrow radius of their primary families and fear engaging in other interpersonal endeavors are having difficulty coping with the life task of industry vs. inferiority. Here we have the "school phobic" child whose parents fear releasing him and who fears leaving them for too long. In general, clients who have interpersonal difficulties in small-group situations such as a job, recreational group, or friendship group fall into this category. Hindered by significant others in the past and/or present, these clients tend repeatedly to seek the protection of parental figures and cannot share satisfactorily with peers. Although the client with problems involving industry is capable in many areas of living and has many ego functions intact, he often experiences transactions with peers as overwhelming.

Because this client has been or is overprotected by parental figures, the modality of choice for him is a social or therapy group in which strong dependency on the social worker is not permitted. When the client attempts to induce the worker to take over (by answering questions or giving advice) he is encouraged to seek the answers within himself and to use his peers to help him. This process helps the client feel more industrious and less inferior. As he is forced to interact with peers in a social or therapeutic group rather than depend exclusively on a parental figure, he acquires new social and interpersonal skills and feels less inferior.

IDENTITY VS. IDENTITY DIFFUSION

When individuals have difficulty in knowing who they are—knowing their values, strengths, skills, roles, limitations, and so on—they are experiencing the conflict of identity vs. identity diffusion. In this category are the ambivalent teen-ager who is not sure whether he is adult or child, the housewife who feels unwanted because her children are off at school or have left home, and the employee in a new job who feels unsure of his new status and role-set. Other clients who experience identity conflicts are the victim of a job layoff, the divorcee or widow, and the newcomer to a community. All of these individuals wonder to some extent who they are and what can or should be expected from them.

Because clients in this category are often confused about social norms and subcultural expectations, a group of individuals who share these uncertainties can offer considerable support to them. As the adolescent or adult observes the role behavior of others, as he sees his adaptive and maladaptive behavior reflected back to him by the group, and as the leader helps him see his own strengths in his group encounters, the client can begin to form the rudiments of a stable identity with which he can experiment away from the group.

Sometimes the adolescent or adult can utilize the leader as a role model. As the client observes that the social worker is not always loved but is not devastated by it, can feel and act assertively without being overly rebellious, and can acknowledge failure and vulnerabilities without feeling destroyed, the client can identify with the worker, try to curb his own childish fantasies, and assume a more realistic identity.

INTIMACY VS. ISOLATION

Clients who have anxieties when involved in relationships with others, particularly members of the opposite sex, are having difficulties with the life task of intimacy vs. isolation. They may be gregarious people who have many ego strengths but fail repeatedly in marriages, switch from lover to lover, and for long periods of time isolate themselves entirely from intimate relationships. Not only do these clients find loving a member of the opposite sex difficult, but any close relationship such as a friendship poses difficulties for them. Unconsciously, they experience closeness as engulfment, entrapment, and control; that is why isolation seems like a useful defense.

The most appropriate treatment modality for clients struggling with intimacy vs. isolation is one-to-one therapy. Since the major task to be mastered is one of intimacy with a member of the opposite sex, it is helpful if the therapist is a member of that sex. Warmth and admiration, when appropriate, are expressed by the social worker, and the client's reactions to receiving these intimate expressions are explored. If the client is unable to express similar sentiments to the worker, this resistance is also investigated in treatment.

As the client becomes aware of his unrealistic fears in the intimate relationship of the social worker–client transaction, he will begin to see how he provokes rejection and/or rejects the social worker. As the social worker encourages intimacy and helps the client face his apprehensions, the client is better equipped to confront the life task of intimacy vs. isolation.

GENERATIVITY VS. STAGNATION

Clients who are bitter, frightened, angry, or anxious when they are with their own children or other members of the younger generation are in the midst of a struggle between generativity and stagnation. In this category are the angry boss, the frightened or angry parent, the threatened supervisor or teacher. Essentially, clients in this category fear taking on the responsibilities and role-set of parental figure and/or figure of authority. As long as the individual remains in a nonparental role, he is reasonably secure; in a parental role, he becomes very anxious.

If a parent, the client can usually derive benefit from family treatment as he examines his role difficulties in the here-and-now (Ackerman, 1958). He can also profit from a small-group modality—provided, of course, that his resistances to taking leadership in the group are the focus of his treatment. His relationship with the group leader can be a useful one as he observes a role model who can assume a parental role, give to others, and enjoy it. Often groups for individuals who have similar role conflicts can be helpful; groups for prospective parents, teachers, supervisors, and so on can help the members examine and cope with the anxieties and confusions that their new role-sets engender.

EGO INTEGRITY VS. DESPAIR

The retired man or woman who is quite depressed is frequently trying to cope with the conflict between ego integrity and despair.

Often feeling unproductive, he or she harbors a great deal of self-hate. Such a client questions the contributions he has made to the world and usually belittles them. Intensifying his despair, he is often shunned by his family and extended family; sometimes he has been placed in a home for the aged and is never visited.

Because the client in this category often needs to talk a great deal about himself and to be cared for, a one-to-one relationship is usually the intervention of choice. The client can reflect on the past and recall his strengths while he is with a social worker who truly values him. This work can be supplemented by helping the client find appropriate activities in the community such as political campaigning or recreation. As the aged person is helped to recognize that he has talents and skills and an identity that can be valued by himself and others, he becomes less desperate.

It should be reemphasized that the notion of the life task is only one of several concepts that guide the social worker in planning his or her role repertoire. Clients who share the same life task may differ markedly in the availability of ego resources and other internal strengths.

It should also be remembered that clients may have several life tasks unresolved. The social worker has to decide which tasks are most amenable to confrontation, which tasks the client and his significant others wish to face, and to which they assign priority.

Erikson's transactional picture of the individual facing specific life tasks not only provides a means for the social worker to conceptualize his role and attitude toward his clients as he intervenes for and with them; it also provides a means of "locating services where people are at the time that the services are needed" (Meyer, 1976). For example, individuals who are struggling with trust vs. mistrust frequently need mothering and care, and may also need to learn verbal and conceptual skills. In addition to a corrective emotional relationship with the social worker, these clients may need income-maintenance programs, prenatal care centers, hospitals, well-baby stations, homemakers or foster care. Similarly—to take one more of many possible examples—the client who has to resolve the task of identity vs. identity diffusion will need services such as vocational counseling, correctional services, and youth services like "hotlines."

Social Work Intervention with Different Units of Attention

THE INDIVIDUAL

One-to-one treatment, the form of intervention that psychoanalysis usually uses, is the treatment of choice for many social work clients. As we have already stated, it is most appropriate for clients who mistrust others and themselves. Dealing with more than one person (as in family therapy or group therapy) only strengthens their paranoid mechanisms and fragments their anger. However, if a mistrustful client can have an experience with one worker who tolerates his hostility, encourages examination of his suspicions, and does not withdraw when tested, he can usually learn to relate to others with more equanimity.

Clients who need help in becoming more autonomous and who need controls, limits, structure, firmness, and appropriate frustration from a consistent parental figure in most instances also need one-to-one treatment; however, if a group provides structure and controls, then increased autonomy and independence, can develop through peer interaction.

When ego functions are relatively intact and the client has the capacity to observe interpersonal transactions with some objectivity, he is less in need of one-to-one treatment. Yet even the more mature client sometimes has aggressive and sexual fantasies that he feels can be shared only in a one-to-one relationship. If he desires one-to-one contact, the clinic or agency should make it available.

One-to-one long-term treatment is usually necessary when the client's symptoms, maladaptive defenses, and character traits are maintained by repressions that need intensive exploration. When unconscious id impulses that generate a phobia, a sexual inhibition, or a job failure are strong and frightening to the client, one-to-one treatment seems indicated.

A psychoanalytic perspective recognizes that one-to-one treatment does not necessarily have to be long-term. It is now clear that critical events like school entry, mourning, physical illness, pregnancy, or divorce can induce a period of overwhelming anxiety, but many clients who suffer from the effects of these events can respond to help rather quickly and return to their former state of equilibrium in a short period of time (Rapaport, 1963; Parad, 1965; MacLeod, 1963; Golan, 1978).

The definition of "critical event" implies that the hazardous event appears quite different from "life as usual" (Rapaport, 1963). When maladaptive behavior is not usually characteristic of the client but emerges during such a crisis, the social worker can reasonably infer that a good state of ego functioning has existed in the client until now.

Crisis intervention and implicit short-term treatment appear to be the modality of choice when the client has the ego and environmental resources to cope with the "disruption of a steady state" (Rapaport, 1963). Therefore, in selecting short-term intervention for crises an important criterion is how the client or client system has been functioning previously. A steady state often implies that the client can remobilize himself rather quickly. However, some clients have limited personal and environmental resources, and for these clients it is often unreasonable to assume that after many years of malfunctioning they can respond quickly to short-term work.

Before deciding on crisis intervention and/or short-term work, the social worker also has to assess the client's defensive patterns. There are some clients who find the idea of sustained help burdensome, threatening, even overwhelming. These clients may find it quite comforting to know in advance that their defenses will not be attacked but supported (Wasserman, 1974), and that contact with the social worker and social agency can terminate in a short period of time. They may use whatever help they wish to use during the short period and return at a later point for a more prolonged relationship or for intermittent short dosages of help.

In sum, when the client can identify—with or without the social worker's help—what tasks have to be accomplished, and when he sees his stressful state as temporary and has sufficient personal and situational resources to cope with it, short-term help seems indicated (Reid and Epstein, 1972). It may also be utilized when the notion of long-term intervention is too anxiety-provoking or threatening to the client's psychological equilibrium.

A CASE EXAMPLE

A client who frequently perplexes the social worker is the individual who seems to possess many internal and external resources but is nonetheless unable to be very autonomous or independent. Frequently he is depressed, feels alone and unloved, and induces enormous sympathy in the social worker. When the worker attempts to gratify this client's wishes, after an initial period of elation and better functioning the client regresses to his depressed and needy position and eventually causes the worker to feel irritated and ineffectual.

A review of the history of this client's interpersonal relationships tends to reveal that significant others feel guilty and ambivalent when they had to say "no" to his requests. Consequently, the client is not able to cope with frustration, but instead has developed skills in exploiting people's generosities and vulnerabilities. As an adult, the client continues to seek childish gratifications in the form of constant admiration and attention. When he does not get what he wants he alternates between temper tantrums, crying fits, and depression. The client tends to favor a depressed, helpless position because through it he can gratify his wishes to be a passive baby. He often appears convinced that he is a victim of injustices and that others should be ministering to him with more kindness.

The client's behavior and dynamics demonstrate a conflict between autonomy and self-doubt. He doubts himself because he has never had the experience of testing his own capacities. Consequently, the corrective emotional experience that this client needs is weaning (Austin, 1948). The process of weaning implies that the therapist does not withdraw his or her symbolic breast abruptly; instead, the therapist listens to the client's demands, is attentive to his angry outbursts and does not retaliate against personal attacks, but stays with the client, firmly withholding temptations to gratify the client's infantile demands. When, for example, the client makes inappropriate requests or appears very depressed, the worker acknowledges his neediness and depression, but rather than directing or advising him, helps him explore the motives for making his requests. While anger and sullenness inevitably follow when the client does not receive what he demands, he slowly welcomes the worker's approach when he realizes that the worker cannot be seduced or manipulated easily. Because this client is swamped by insatiable id wishes that create enormous inner tension, he is relieved when he begins to sense that some of his demands are unrealistic. This form of psychological weaning slowly helps the client to use his energy for more constructive pursuits.

Nineteen-year-old Jack Amber sought therapeutic assistance because he wanted to avoid being drafted into the army. He was also failing in college, daydreamed incessantly, and was very depressed. His relationships with people consisted of a weekly chat with his father (who gave him a handsome allowance) and some contacts with call girls and prostitutes. Jack mentioned early in his treatment with the social worker that he had been the teacher's pet in grammar school and high school, but now that he was in a large metropolitan university where he was not receiving much individual attention he had little desire to study. Indeed, Jack's history indicated that he had succeeded in becoming "the apple of everybody's eye" throughout his childhood and adolescence. Since he could not manipulate college or army personnel very easily, he was feeling depressed and victimized. Hence he was attempting to persuade the worker to get him out of the army, despite the fact that he was physically fit.

The worker responded to this request with "How shall I do that?" After several moments of hesitation Jack mildly demanded, "Write me a letter!" When the worker asked what he should write, Jack became very angry: "I'm not the professional, how the hell should I know?" After a long silence, during which Jack appeared to recognize that his demands and temper tantrums were not getting him very far, he told the worker to write the army that "Jack Amber is a very disturbed person." Asked to describe his disturbances, Jack could only joke about "my schizophrenia." As each of Jack's requests for a letter to the army was subjected to examination, Jack either became more demanding and depressed or threatened to quit treatment. Because the worker did not appear flustered and could not be manipulated by Jack's infantile demands, he eventually abandoned his request for a letter.

However, Jack's resistance to autonomy was strong, his dependency wishes were intense, and his wish for a symbiotic transference relationship with the worker persisted. Consequently, Jack proposed, "Maybe you could write to my teachers at college to raise my marks or plead my case that I not be flunked out." Again, the worker subjected these requests to examination and Jack responded with sadness and anger, saying that the worker did not feel sufficient sympathy for him. The worker replied that this was a possibility, but since Jack claimed he could not study like other students unless he was the teacher's pet, it looked as though he would be flunked out of college and have to go into the army.

Jack threatened to leave treatment and tried to get the worker to feel guilty. "You are supposed to help people!" he bellowed one day. The worker replied, "I am trying to help you by showing you that neither you nor I can run a college or the army by ourselves." Gradually Jack began to pay somewhat more attention to his studies, but he told the worker, "You want to make me suffer!" The worker responded, "All people suffer when they have to give up unrealistic pleasures."

After Jack brought his grades up to A's and B's and received a student deferment, he asked the worker to help him find "beautiful and sexy women." Again, the worker subjected his client's requests to examination, and once more the client was furious because he did not receive instant gratification. Nonetheless, as the worker encouraged Jack to spell out his fantasies of the "beautiful women," Jack could slowly perceive what he called the "craziness" of his feminine ideal. Now the worker could point out that like a little boy, Jack was yearning for a perfect mother.

After a year of treatment Jack acknowledged that the reason he could only befriend prostitutes was because he was sure they would not reject him. "I have always had an image of having to be perfect for the woman, and since I secretly know I have problems like everybody else, I can't stand anything but a whore. Anybody else might reject me and I can't tolerate that. I've had to be king and never be rejected by anybody," he remarked insightfully. Jack, in effect, was slowly realizing that his wish to be worshipped was unrealistic, and with this understanding he began to feel a little more confident with girls and to relate to the world with less arrogance.

The case of Jack Amber is a good example of how one-to-one psychoanalytically oriented treatment can be effective in a social work setting. The worker, realizing that Jack's difficulties were at the autonomy vs. self-doubt stage, elected to enact the role of weaning parent. Because Jack's significant others had indulged him, it was important for the worker to frustrate Jack's infantile cravings, show Jack reality as it was, and not become guilty or ambivalent when he refused to let Jack go beyond certain limits. Jack, for his part, tried to effect a transference by forming a dependent, clinging, symbiotic relationship with the worker. His major resistance was his id wish to maintain his infantile omnipotence and grandiosity. The worker, by exploring requests rather than immediately gratifying or denying them, helped Jack diminish his infantile dependence and strengthen such ego functions as frustration tolerance, judgment, and success in interpersonal relations.

The Treatment of One Client by Two Workers

A client who frequently sees a social worker is the child or adult who lives or has lived with only one parent. The impact of the loss of a parent is usually quite severe. Investigations by Bowlby (1951), Glaser and Eisenberg (1955), and Anna Freud (1951) "demonstrate the inexorability with which the infant requires instinctual satisfaction through one consistent empathetic mother, and how failing this through separation from the mother in the first year of life, his future may be threatened by vegetative dysfunctioning [and] disturbances in object relations and ego structure" (Neubauer, 1960, p. 287).

While psychoanalytic studies describing treatment of fatherless children are sparse, there have been a few contributions to the literature. In 1905 Freud, in his *Three Essays on the Theory of Sexuality,* reported the results of his investigations on patients with hysteria. He stated that "the early loss of one of their parents, whether by death, divorce, or separation, with the result that the remaining parent absorbs the whole of the child's love, determines the sex of the person who is later to be chosen as a sexual object and may thus open the way to permanent inversion." In his study of Leonardo da Vinci, whose illegitimate birth deprived him of a father's influence until perhaps his fifth year and "left him open to the tender seductions of a mother whose only solace he was," Freud described a type of male homosexuality in which the etiological factors were the maternal seduction of a son because of the libidinal shift from husband to child and the absence of a paternal influence on the child's development (Freud, 1953). Ferenczi (1950) and Fenichel (1945) also concluded that a major etiological factor in male homosexuality was the absent father.

Neubauer, in "The One-Parent Child and His Oedipal Development" (1960), demonstrated how conflicts in sexual identification and superego formation evolve in one-parent children.

Until the 1960s most investigators reported poor results in treating the child or adult with one parent (Wylie and Delgado, 1959). However, increased understanding of ego functions such as object relations and defenses made it clear that the one-parent child or adult would do better in treatment if the therapeutic plan utilized "the average expectable environment," i.e., the environment structured to meet the client's maturational needs (Hartmann, 1958), and the "life tasks" (Erikson, 1950) as its paradigms. A three-year study concluded that when the one-parent child was treated by having "two parental figures working together in his behalf and the treatment was structured so that he had continuous access to a male and female who respected each other," treatment results became more positive in many instances (Strean, 1970, p. 95).

For many years the treatment of the "unmarried mother" was not very successful. Not until social workers began to realize that her conflicted sexual identity was not just a product of a tempestuous mother-daughter relationship but also an expression of girlhood conflicts with a seductive and frequently absent father did treatment become more successful. When the client was treated by a female worker dealing with her current crisis and regressive needs for mothering and a male worker dealing with her sexual conflicts, she was better able to resolve her problems (Strean, 1970). Many unmarried mothers have responded positively to a treatment approach that utilizes notions of the corrective emotional experience (Austin, 1948), life tasks, and the average expectable environment.

Miss Brewer, a black woman of thirty-one, had five illegitimate children. Living in a housing project and on welfare, she was frequently drunk or depressed, and managed her home and children with limited care and discipline. The management of the project sent a female case aide to "see what could be done" before processing an eviction.

The worker found Miss Brewer's house extremely untidy, her children poorly cared for, and the client in her third month of pregnancy. She told Miss Brewer that she had come at the suggestion of the management of the project, but before she could finish her opening remarks the client bellowed, "They want to throw me out because they don't like the way I keep the house!" The worker looked around the house and said calmly, "I'm sure things are very difficult for you. You must have it very rough." The client spent the next half-hour talking about how her children were a burden to her, how impossible it was to meet their physical needs, and how difficult it was to make ends meet financially—the only pleasure she got once in a while was "a little sex and a little drink." The worker remarked that she understood that sex and drinking were her few pleasures, but wondered if there was anything that she, the worker, could do to bring more pleasure into her life. Miss Brewer pointed to the children's clothes and her poor furniture and mentioned that she had limited time for herself. The worker responded, "I'll get in touch with a few places and people and see what can be done."

Although Miss Brewer initially was reluctant to accept the worker's tangible help, she eventually accepted clothes for the children, mattresses and beds, and a volunteer for some baby-sitting. Then she began to talk about her current pregnancy and previous ones. She told the worker that "I don't appeal to men" and that all of her sexual affairs were one-night stands. She tearfully reported how she remembered as a young girl wishing that a boyfriend of her mother's who intermittently visited the house "could be my father." She then spent some time talking about her wish for a father who "would have really cared about me."

As Miss Brewer continued to talk about her feelings of deprivation with regard to a father, the worker gradually introduced the subject of a male worker who was part of the same social service department of the housing project. The client did not ask for any explanation but seemed to sense the rationale behind his introduction and said, "Great!"

In contrast to the manner in which Miss Brewer usually cared for the house, the male worker at his first interview found it to be extremely tidy and the children and Miss Brewer well groomed. This was also true at subsequent visits. While the client continued to see her female worker about plans for the baby and dealt with the situation quite responsibly, with the male worker she brought up the possibility of getting a job. When he suggested that they explore this together, it became apparent that Miss Brewer was trying to please him much as she tried to ingratiate herself with men in general. The worker interpreted the transference reaction for her, stating that just as she did on dates with men, she was trying to please him—in regard to working—rather than see what was pleasurable for herself. Miss Brewer then spent some time talking about how guilty she felt when she wanted something from a man, and the worker was able to help her examine her rivalry for a man with her mother. As worker and client discussed Miss Brewer's competition with her mother, they learned that Miss Brewer's pregnancies in many ways were unconscious attempts to spite her mother, and that was why she felt so guilty about them.

As both workers continued to see Miss Brewer during the course of a year, she was able to take a job, date mature men, and like herself more.

The treatment of Miss Brewer helped her move up the psychosocial ladder. As the female worker helped her discharge her anger and mistrust without counterattacking or judging her, the client's self-respect improved. As she was able to trust a mother figure with her anxieties, she became more autonomous and began to focus on her relationships with men. The mother figure (female social worker) gave her permission, in effect, to relate to a father figure who was caring and consistent. Miss Brewer, after exploring her self-hate and her "father transference" with the male worker, could eventually relate more maturely to men. She recognized that because she had been acting out spite toward men and feeling guilty about it, she had only felt entitled to be used by them.

THE TREATMENT OF MARITAL CONFLICTS

Social work treatment of marital problems is usually based on psychosocial understanding of the individual members of the couple and of their interaction, which functions as a "third force." Each of the partners possesses personality traits and defensive patterns that contribute to the marital interaction, and the degree of marital equilibrium is not necessarily based on the degree of emotional health of the individual partners (Beatman, 1956).

Psychoanalytic theory has enhanced the social work treatment of marital problems in several ways. It has demonstrated that because many individuals with marital conflicts are too threatened to confront them, clients often present problems other than their conflicted marriages when they first seek out a social worker. If the social worker respects the clients' resistances and begins where the clients psychologically are, the clients may eventually feel safe enough to reveal their marital conflicts to the worker.

Conversely, the initial presentation of marital problems may serve as a defense against the exposure of other conflicts that are experienced as more painful—e.g., a parent-child relationship or problems with in-laws.

Psychoanalysis has taught social work that the most important consideration in treatment is the person with the problem, not the problem itself. If the practitioner begins where the client is and studies with him how he experiences his person-situation constellation, the worker will eventually be able to assess the client's conflicts, anxieties, fantasies, ego strengths, adaptive and maladaptive defenses, and so on. When the worker has assessed the client, the assessment will provide guidelines for treatment. Consequently, the social worker who treats marital problems will choose the preferred therapeutic modality on the basis of his metapsychological understanding of the couple as individuals and his understanding of their interaction. Sometimes the worker's assessment of the couple will make him opt for one-to-one treatment for each member of the marital pair. On other occasions, depending on his diagnostic thinking, he will choose joint counseling, or some other modality such as a married-couples group.

Again, the level of the client's psychosocial maturation should be a prime consideration in structuring the treatment. For example, when marital couples relate to each other symbiotically but can tolerate an exploration of the dynamic meaning of their symbiosis, one-to-one treatment for each of the partners is usually the treatment of choice. If each member of the marital dyad has a separate worker, there will be an opportunity to help each one deal with the fears of autonomy and individuality that will be activated in treatment. As husband and wife learn that each can have private thoughts without hurting the other and without experiencing or inflicting great loss, their marriage can be improved.

When Jack and Barbara Counts, a couple in their mid-thirties, sought marital counseling, their complaints about each other were quite similar. Each felt very neglected by the other; Barbara complained that Jack recently had bought a suit without consulting her, and Jack retaliated by pointing out that Barbara did not always tell him with whom she spoke on the telephone. When the worker pointed out that each was very jealous of the other's activities and relationships, both Jack and Barbara acknowledged fears of being abandoned and displaced.

Because Barbara and Jack were able to talk about their clinging symbiotic relationship, the worker felt that they could have different therapists. Initially both of them complained bitterly about being separated in therapy and felt that the worker was cruel. When the worker interpreted their resistance to autonomy by telling them that to be alone was experienced by each of them as being maimed, the Counts slowly began to explore some of their fears about being more independent of each other. Eventually they agreed to try one-to-one treatment with different workers, although they continued to voice reluctance.

A great deal of the treatment for both Jack and Barbara consisted of an examination of their mutual wish to find out what was going on in the other's treatment. When one asked his or her own therapist about an issue in the other's treatment, the therapist would answer with "Let's see why you need to know." Jack and Barbara then became furious, helpless, and frightened. They recalled memories of feeling lonely as children, but upon further examination of these memories it became clear that both of them had felt quite omnipotent as children and both of them were interested in maintaining this position as adults.

Jack and Barbara sometimes volunteered information to each other about what was going in their respective treatments. When this was examined with them by their workers, inevitably each would confess, "If I tell him (her), he'll (she'll) tell me what's going on with him (her)." Slowly Jack and Barbara recognized that their symbiotic behavior was a regressive device to defend against autonomy. As this issue was pursued in depth, it became clear that each experienced independence as a hostile assault on the other and feared subsequent punishment by being abandoned.

The treatment of marital partners who are overattached to each other must, of course, take into consideration how being autonomous can bring pleasure. In the treatment of the Counts, when this notion was introduced by both of their workers, Jack and Barbara reacted the same way. Both were surprised to hear that independence and separateness could bring something besides pain.

In a different type of situation, when marital partners isolate themselves from each other, fear intimacy, and resist communicating, the treatment of choice would appear to be joint counseling. This mode of treatment places the partners in their "phobic situation"; they have the opportunity to study in the here-and-now of therapy what activates the anxiety that forces them to use defenses like isolation and alienation.

Sam, aged forty-two, and Jean David, aged thirty-one, came to a family agency to adopt a child. When this request was explored, what emerged was that each of them felt unloved, isolated, and misunderstood by the other. In addition, each was frightened of his angry feelings toward the other, and each constantly anticipated that the other was going to launch an attack.

The worker soon realized that the Davids' wish to adopt a child was a disguised cry for help with their marriage, an attempt to bring something pleasurable to their relationship that they could not otherwise achieve. This hypothesis tended to be confirmed when fertility tests yielded negative findings, i.e., the couple was physically capable of having a child. It was decided that the Davids could best be helped if they were seen together in treatment so that their resistances to communication could be studied jointly.

Meeting Sam and Jean where they were, the worker asked each of them what a baby would do for them. Jean said she would have a friend who would compensate for her loneliness, and Sam said "I want a buddy, too!" On the worker's sharing her observation that each felt lonely and needy, Jean began to weep and talked about how unappreciated and unloved she felt. Sam appeared astonished when he heard this and attempted to reassure Jean immediately. He followed this up by saying how slighted he felt because Jean had never shared these feelings with him. The worker then asked Sam and Jean how much they did communicate their feelings to each other, and both acknowledged the fear that if they tried to communicate a bitter argument would ensue. When the worker asked what was so frightening about an argument, Sam and Jean talked about how they would hurt each other psychologically and maybe even physically.

It became clear that the Davids needed help to feel less afraid of their mutual angers, and as the worker encouraged both of them during several interviews to vent their complaints, they realized that their angers were not quite as dangerous as they fantasied.

After the Davids were able to ventilate their angers, share their self-doubts in front of the social worker, and reassure each other, they reported that their sexual life had improved. As often occurs when latent resentment is discharged and more libidinal satisfaction is achieved, the couple were able to have their own child.

In the treatment of the Counts and the Davids, the therapists took into consideration where the couples were maturationally and what could be done to enhance their functioning. As the individuals matured, so did their marriages. However, this is not always the result. Sometimes individuals improve their self-esteem, alter their self-images, and improve other parts of ego functioning, yet their marriages deteriorate because the neurotic complementarity of the relationship is weakened.

Stanley and Ethel Efram, a couple in their early twenties, met as high school students. They married six months later because "we both hated our parents and needed to run away from home," said Stanley, with Ethel concurring. Like two siblings joined together in a common rebellion, the Eframs spent their first year of marriage discussing how much they hated their parents.

As occurs in many marriages, the couple began to use each other as symbolic parents and engaged in defiant power struggles. In their treatment, which was held jointly, they examined some of their rebelliousness and sadism. However, as they focused more on their own individual needs and could take some psychological distance from their parents, their real differences became more apparent. Ethel had a very strong need to study, engage in community activity, and lead as much of an autonomous existence as possible. Stanley, on the other hand, liked home, TV, and closeness, and shunned intellectual pursuits.

Neither of the Eframs had much interest in modifying their life-styles, and they divorced.

This case should not be considered a failure. In psychoanalytically oriented marital counseling it is the worker's task to help the partners come to understand themselves and each other. Only as distortions are unraveled can more adaptive and mature functioning evolve. In many instances, when a husband and wife experience less anxiety the marriage does become more enjoyable for both. However, one or both partners may find that as they learn about themselves and each other, possibilities other than the current marriage become more attractive. The social worker who sees his function as that of a catalyst in self-understanding and maturation does not usually set continuation of the marriage as a treatment goal because he recognizes that mature behavior and a sustained marriage do not always go hand in hand.

TREATING PARENT-CHILD CONFLICTS

WORKING WITH THE PARENTS

As we discussed in Chapter 4, whatever the parent's reasons for coming for help with a child's difficulties, sooner or later it becomes apparent that the parent, too, is emotionally disturbed now or was disturbed as a child, and that his or her difficulties are very similar to the child's (Feldman, 1958). Consequently, in helping a parent resolve difficulties in interaction with a child, it is important to ascertain which life tasks the parent needs help with and then offer the corrective emotional experience he or she needs to overcome maturational hurdles. A parent's treatment, in effect, is very similar to a child's, because usually both require similar attitudes on the part of the social worker, who functions in the role of parent.

Early in the child-guidance movement there was a notion, still somewhat prevalent today, that if parents were simply told what they were doing that interfered with a child's mature functioning, they would behave differently. Psychoanalysis helped social workers realize that if a parent's own wishes, anxieties, defenses, and history were not taken into consideration and related to therapeutically, the parent could not alter attitudes or behavior in relation to the child.

It is naive to assume that telling a seductive parent to stop seducing a child means that she or he will do so, or that advising parents to stop rejecting a child means that they will accept the advice and modify their behavior. Clients can modify their maladaptive behavior only when they experience less anxiety, and usually this can be achieved only through a corrective relationship that motivates them to become more mature.

A psychoanalytic orientation to the treatment of parents is predicated on the notion that parents who are unequipped to meet their children's particular maturational needs have not received appropriate parenting themselves. For example, parents who cannot offer sufficient autonomy to a child probably did not receive sufficient help in accepting themselves and their own failures; parents who cannot offer consistent limits or provide appropriate sex information were probably deprived of these important nutrients by their own parents.

It is the therapist's task to give parents psychologically what they did not receive in their past. The therapist, in effect, becomes the symbolic parent that the parent never had.

Mr. Field, aged forty-five, did not seek therapeutic help directly. Unknown to him at first, and later against his wishes, his wife applied to the clinic for guidance in relation to their only son, Morton. Twelve-year-old Morton was a neurotic child who had fears of the dark and strong feelings of inferiority, could not tolerate competition or aggression, and was extremely passive and overly compliant.

Mrs. Field and Morton were involved in treatment for more than six months when Mr. Field became threatened by Morton's increased assertiveness. On the telephone he said to the social worker, "I am coming down to bawl you out. You don't know what you are doing!"

Mr. Field arrived ten minutes late for his appointment, and on entering the office took the therapist's seat and announced, "I'm going to tell you a thing or two." He remarked that he knew all about this "social work stuff" and that "there are many things wrong with the way social workers run their business." The worker told Mr. Field he was eager to learn about his mistakes, whereupon Mr. Field vented a great deal of anger. He pointed out that Morton had to be dealt with very firmly or else "he would not be kept in line." He further remarked that "permissiveness" is a lot of hokum and "nobody should be mollycoddled. That's what you do to my son!" With encouragement from the social worker, Mr. Field offered several suggestions on how young boys should be treated.

At the end of the first interview the worker told Mr. Field that he welcomed the conversation, and he invited him back to the clinic.

Mr. Field arrived on time for the second interview a week later. He proceeded to vilify the worker, the clinic, and the profession once more. He suggested to the worker that he "get out of the field and learn how to make money." In succeeding interviews, but with a more subdued tone, Mr. Field continued to give advice on the treatment of people in general and the approach to Morton in particular.

By the sixth session Mr. Field told the worker that he could have his seat back, and he thanked him for "taking all my advice and guff." He went on to say that a big change had come over Morton recently. "*I started to listen to his point of view and it works like magic!*" Mr. Field followed this up with a request to join a fathers' therapy group that the worker was leading. "Maybe," concluded Mr. Field, "I can learn from and teach the other fathers!"*

Unconsciously, Mr, Field was recapitulating with the worker what Morton was doing at his stage of treatment—acting out hostility toward a parental figure. As the worker demonstrated a method of dealing with Mr. Field's infantile demands and fantasies, Morton eventually became the recipient of a new mode of parental responsiveness. Because the worker appeared unthreatened by Mr. Field's barrages, Mr. Field identified with him and endeavored to emulate this behavior with Morton. Mr. Field observed that the therapist was seeking advice and learning; eventually he could do the same with Morton.

Prior to his visit to the agency, Mr. Field had to suppress Morton's assertiveness and aggression because of his inability to cope with his own assertiveness and aggression. When he had an

*Part of this case illustration appeared in "The Use of the Patient as Consultant," in *New Approaches in Child Guidance,* ed. H. Strean (Metuchen, N.J.: Scarecrow Press, 1970).

experience with a father figure who encouraged his aggressive expressions, he became less fearful of both his own assertiveness and Morton's. The social worker recognized that because Morton could not feel free to be himself with his father and offer his own opinions and feelings, this freedom was the experience that Mr. Field needed from a father figure.

When a parent receives the appropriate corrective experience in therapy, he usually recalls with affect those features of his own history that created anxiety for him. As Mr. Field's treatment continued, it became clear that he had introjected an image of a tough, intimidating father that compelled him to act the same way with Morton. Otherwise, he would have hated himself for being a "softy." When the social worker was not defensive about his own gentleness and permissiveness, Mr. Field could permit himself to be softer with Morton.

Although many parents need a permissive worker to help them be less constricting with their own children, parents who overindulge their children need a relationship with a therapist who offers firm limits and structure. As the parent learns to cope better with his own childish demands, he can help his youngster do the same.

Mrs. Gold, aged forty, sought help for her twelve-year-old daughter, Sandra, who, she claimed, was "always making unreasonable demands, nags me too much, is very selfish, can't accept 'no' for an answer, and is altogether too childish." Mrs. Gold felt it was necessary for Sandra to "learn some discipline," but regardless of her strenuous attempts "to help Sandra grow up," Sandra was unresponsive.

When Mrs. Gold was asked early in her treatment contact to describe a typical day of Sandra's, it became clear how the mother was helping the child's infantile pattern continue. Sandra was frequently bathed and dressed by her mother, who also helped her excessively with her schoolwork. Because Mrs. Gold's extreme overindulgence was so blatant and seemed destructive to the child's mental health, she was advised by the therapist not to dress and bathe her daughter. Mrs. Gold strongly objected. "She is my daughter and I should give her everything that is within my power. I refuse to be unkind to her."

Not only did Mrs. Gold balk at any advice given by the therapist, but she defended her position strongly and made it clear that she would defeat any plan that entailed modifying her overprotective habits. She continued, as a matter of fact, to complain that Sandra was getting worse, and attributed this to her own efforts to follow the therapist's poor advice.

Mrs. Gold said that she was "nice" to Sandra because "I always wanted my mother to take care of me better." She gave numerous examples of how she had felt deprived of "pretty clothes," "proper friends," and "recreation" by her own parents.

As Mrs. Gold gave examples to attest to her "deprived" background, she subtly began to ask the therapist to indulge her. She ordered him to "go to the school and see what you can do with Sandra's teacher" and to "get Sandra to camp for two trips instead of one—it's not enough." She also stated, "Your fee is too high; I can't afford to pay you that much."

The therapist did not immediately gratify Mrs. Gold's requests. Instead he asked how his visit to the school would help her to understand her relationship with Sandra better, what two trips to camp would accomplish, and why she felt she wasn't getting her money's worth in treatment. Mrs. Gold raged, bellowed, and further nagged the therapist with repeated phone calls: "You're only interested in my money. Why don't you think of me?" Despite many attempts on Mrs. Gold's part to manipulate the therapist, he remained firm in his insistence that her requests be subjected to examination rather than immediately gratified.

During Mrs. Gold's twentieth session, after several unsuccessful attempts to once again manipulate the therapist, she tearfully stated with much affect, "I make a big pest of myself but I'm glad you don't spoil me. I know what Sandra meant when she said last week, 'Mommy, you're getting stricter and I wish you'd decided to be that way a long time ago. It's good for me.' "*

Mrs. Gold was initially able to induce the worker to meet her demands: He gave her advice almost immediately. This paralleled her own relationship with her daughter, in which she gratified all Sandra's requests immediately. However, when the

---

*Part of this case illustration appeared in "Treating Parents of Emotionally Disturbed Children Through Role Playing," in *Crucial Issues in Psychotherapy*, ed. H. Strean (Metuchen, N.J.: Scarecrow Press, 1976).

worker became frustrated in his attempts to gratify Mrs. Gold's requests for advice (again, paralleling Mrs. Gold's reaction to her daughter's demands) and began to alter his approach with her by *examining the requests,* Mrs. Gold slowly did the same with Sandra. As the worker began to wean Mrs. Gold and absorb her anger when he frustrated her, Mrs. Gold could do likewise with Sandra.

The work with Mrs. Gold illustrates how the social worker's offer of educational guidance in childrearing can easily be defeated by the parent. Only when Mrs. Gold experienced a weaning experience herself could she be firmer with her daughter.

Just as many children seek to be indulged by their parents, many parents can induce a similar interchange with their social worker. However, just as a child can lose respect for an overgiving parent, a parent-client can do likewise. When parents are overprotective, they have infantile demands of their own that they are vicariously gratifying through their children. If parents are helped to tolerate frustration in the social worker–client relationship, they can eventually help their children to do the same.

TREATING THE CHILD

The social worker is called upon to treat psychosocial dysfunctions of children in many settings—in school, in child-guidance and mental health clinics, in hospitals, and in other institutions.

A psychoanalytically oriented child therapist's first consideration is to determine where difficulties have transpired in the child's psychosocial development. For example, if the child has not been given sufficient loving care in the early oral period and is depressed, a feeding, nourishing relationship should be established. If, on the other hand, the child has too strong a symbiosis with either parent, the therapist will attempt to offer limited gratification and appropriate controls so that the separation-individuation process can be effected (Neubauer, 1972).

Henry, aged five, was a depressed boy whose mother suffered from schizophrenia. She was unable to offer consistent warmth or concern, and Henry often sat by himself for hours. In the treatment, Henry's therapist supplied milk and candy, took his hand when he offered it, and let Henry call her on the phone in between appointments when he needed to do so. He was permitted to leave the playroom when he felt like it, but the therapist always reminded him that she would miss him.

In the case of a child like Henry, the worker should offer a nurturing role and provide some of the mothering the child never received. This stimulates the child to trust the adult, and he can then begin to mature.

Ida, aged seven, clung to the worker and wanted every toy in sight. She also wanted to sit on the worker's lap and crawl on her legs. In almost everything she did with the worker, she was extremely infantile. In contrast to Henry's therapist, who gratified his requests, Ida's therapist made interpretations. She told Ida that she wanted to be a baby like her little sister and was angry that she couldn't be her sister. When Ida would pout and sulk, the worker pointed out her infantile provocativeness. When Ida tried to hit or kick her, the worker stopped her. Ida, in contrast to Henry, had been indulged. Therefore, the therapist attempted to supply limits and controls.

One of the features of treatment with children is the use of play. In play the child releases tensions and expresses forbidden wishes. He assigns to dolls and other play figures some of the fears he has and demonstrates his fantasies. The social worker, by permitting certain play when it is called for, by interpreting content when it is clear, and by prohibiting certain play when it fosters unnecessary regression, helps the child reduce his anxiety so that he can grow within the corrective therapeutic relationship (Despert, 1965; Hamilton, 1947; Knoepfmacher, 1942).

When Joe, a constricted and inhibited eight-year-old, flirted with the fingerpaints the worker encouraged him to use them, since dirtying, soiling, and the expression of aggression were very frightening to him. Joe recoiled and said he would "get dirty," and the worker replied, "Sometimes it's fun to get dirty." Joe smiled and said, "You're not supposed to do that!" He then turned to the boy doll, yelled at him

"Bad boy, bad boy, you got dooty on the floor!" and added "He likes to get his mommy angry." Now the worker was able to say, "I think the boy's mommy made him do his dooty perfectly and didn't realize that all children have 'accidents,' and he's angry at her." Joe was visibly relieved, and continued to relive his harsh training by talking about the boy doll and how angry he felt.

When Joe arranged for the mother doll to punish the boy doll, the worker was able to help him see that he felt deserving of punishment for his legitimate anger. As Joe ventilated rage without being punished for it, his inhibited demeanor diminished.

Sometimes children use play repetitively as a defense against exposing conflicts. The worker often has to respect the child's defense and permit the play to continue until the child feels secure enough in the therapeutic relationship to expose his or her conflicts (Hamilton, 1947).

Ingrid, aged twelve, repetitively played checkers with the worker, offering few comments about her life or about her feelings toward the worker. She was a shy, frightened, phobic girl and distrustful of relationships. The worker, by respecting the youngster's wish to just play checkers week after week, was in effect not demanding anything but offering herself as a patient and accepting parental figure. Feeling more accepted and more trusting after three months of being with the worker, Ingrid was able to talk about hating to lose. When the worker mentioned that few, if any, youngsters like to lose, Ingrid looked surprised but went on to discharge a great deal of anger about being the youngest member of her family; almost every day one of her siblings "showed me up."

When Ingrid had the repeated opportunity with the worker to discharge her dissatisfaction, she was gradually able to look at the reality of her situation with less anxiety.

FAMILY THERAPY

As social workers began to recognize that modifications in one family member's adaptation have an impact on other family members, family therapy was greeted by many of them with much enthusiasm. Those who championed family therapy (treating the family unit with all of its members present) have demonstrated that the use of this modality can help locate the family's "most burdensome problem," distribute and "share blame" (Pollak, 1956), enhance communication, increase mutual understanding, and clarify role discomplementarities (Ackerman, 1958).

Psychoanalysis can contribute to the theory and practice of family therapy by demonstrating when it is indicated or contraindicated, and by refining some of the therapeutic techniques of family treatment. When notions that we have been considering in this text, such as "life tasks," "unconscious wishes," "resistances," "transferences," and "countertransferences," are utilized by the family therapist, the treatment can be more objectively administered.

To determine whether family therapy is the treatment of choice, one of the important questions that should be asked is: "Is the family at a level of psychosocial maturation so that its members can recognize a common problem to which all contribute?" An affirmative answer implies that most of the family members have the capacity to identify with each other, empathize, expose anxiety and imperfections, and tolerate listening to other family members complain about them. Many individuals in families who come to social agencies do not have these ego functions available. They project blame, cannot empathize, and have limited impulse control and frustration tolerance. Functioning at a psychosocial level of one- or two-year-old children, these individuals need the support, understanding, and structure that only a one-to-one relationship can provide.

An assessment of a family's defensive patterns and strengths will also help the worker decide whether family therapy is the treatment of choice. For example, if the worker observes that a strong symbiotic network is present, seeing the family together would tend to intensify the members' regressive behavior, and family therapy would be contraindicated. However, sometimes the ties that bind the family members may be so strong, albeit maladaptive, that the family may have to be seen as a unit because separating the members would create too much anxiety for them and they would flee from treatment.

Although family therapy is designed to help family members communicate better, some families are terrified of doing this; their resistance should be respected. After the members have had one-to-one treatment for a while they may feel strong enough to share problems in family treatment.

When the interpersonal difficulties of family members are manifestations of deeply repressed infantile wishes, strong defenses, and buried anxiety, one-to-one therapy would seem to be the treatment of choice.

From a psychoanalytic point of view, family therapy seems indicated in the following instances: when the family's resistances to individuation and autonomy are so great that one-to-one treatment is too threatening; when the family strongly desires family therapy and is not ready to consider other alternatives; and when the family members' ego functions are strong enough so that they can empathize with each other about shared problems they all want to resolve.

Frequently family members unconsciously cooperate to repress certain wishes and fantasies connected with sex or aggression. This hinders interpersonal pleasure, diminishes communication, and promotes alienation. Family therapy can frequently be of help here.

The Orrs sought family therapy because "everybody was bickering with everybody." Mr. and Mrs. Orr, eleven-year-old Jack, and nine-year-old Barbara all agreed that this was a mutual problem. As the family members discussed their complaints with each other and the therapist each week, a theme emerged. Just when the Orrs would come to some agreement on an issue, one member would squelch the warm feeling that was emerging. the worker realized that all of the family members had a resistance to expressions and feelings of love, and she shared this observation with the family. There was a long silence, which Mr. Orr broke by saying with a smile, "I guess the silence is significant!"

Eventually Mrs. Orr, Jack, and Barbara were able to agree that expressing and feeling warmth was a problem. Jack and Barbara talked about being "shy." Mr. Orr felt showing warmth was "sissified," and Mrs. Orr said it was "a sign of weakness." As the Orrs discussed their negative feelings about communicating love, what emerged was a shared conviction that they would all appear as weak infants if they gave and received love. Actually, each member of the Orr family was afraid of his or her wishes to depend on the others and be infantilized. When the worker told the Orrs that they were all fighting their mutual dependence rather than enjoying it, this helped them investigate their inhibitions about laughing and talking warmly with each other.

Family therapy, as the Orr case demonstrates, exposes a family resistance, helps the family members see what they fear, and helps them communicate feelings that have been repressed. Family therapy can also help the members realize that arguments about such issues as TV watching, the use of the car, and mutual responsibilities are a function of unexpressed fears or anxieties and unacceptable impulses.

Although family therapy is a relatively new modality in social work, it has become a popular one. Further research is necessary to determine with more certainty which families can best profit from it and which cannot. One of its most useful precepts is that the individual client cannot be totally understood unless viewed as part of a dynamic social context, which influences him and which he influences (Pollak, 1956; Ackerman, 1958). As we suggested in chapter 4, and earlier in this chapter, family therapy when viewed psychoanalytically seems to be a useful modality for those families whose members have capacities to communicate, can empathize with each other, and can assume responsibility in interpersonal difficulties. For families that cling symbiotically to each other and are threatened by any member's autonomy, family therapy is a useful medium to use as a beginning form of treatment.

WORK WITH SMALL GROUPS

Although clients of social workers have been seen in small groups for decades and for myriad reasons—recreation, therapy, social action, political purposes—group workers have too frequently failed to consider whether or not clients' levels of psychosocial functioning and defensive makeups are such that group work is the intervention of choice.

A psychoanalytic understanding of the client that addresses itself to the client's ego functions, particularly his interpersonal patterns, will help the group worker decide who should and who should not be in a group. It will also help the worker plan and execute his interventions. For example, a group may be very enriching and serve as a stimulant for maturer psychosocial functioning in children and adults who are too dependent on parental figures but possess some degree of interpersonal relatedness and impulse control. Activity-group therapy for children has been best utilized by those who fear being autonomous in a social or educational setting but who can, in interaction with peers under the social worker's direction, emerge as less socially anxious (Slavson, 1943). The same criterion should be considered in work with adults; if capacities for social relatedness are very weak and the client has never experienced a consistent and positive trusting relationship with at least one parent or parental figure, the group will, in all probability, be overwhelming for him.

Rosenthal (1977, p. 194) has stated:

> Proper selection involves choice of those patients who possess that degree of ego strength essential to constructive group membership. Fundamental to this process is the recognition that the group setting involves certain stresses and imposes certain demands that are not inherent aspects of the dyadic treatment relation: the ever-present possibility of exposure to sibling hostility, the unavoidable necessity of sharing therapist time, and the much greater degree of emotional stimulation. Thus, basic to the composition of a therapeutic group is the therapist's awareness that the client's capacity to enter and assimilate the world of multiple relations is based upon that which happens or does not happen in his first crucial group, i.e., his family.

The establishment of group viability is also predicated upon a therapeutic equilibrium among the diverse personalities of the group, particularly with respect to how each member handles aggression (Slavson, 1948; Rosenthal, 1977). Slavson (1948, p. 318) has said:

> The ability of any given group to withstand or absorb hostility and aggression has definite limits. Each individual and each aggregate of people has its own capacity to tolerate aggression or hostility. . . . When these limits are exceeded in groups, tension and anxiety set in which are expressed in hyperactivity or wanton destructiveness.

One of the serious limitations of group work as practiced by social workers is an insufficient understanding of psychodynamics. For example, if a prospective group member is a withdrawn and guarded child or adult, should he be invited by the group worker to participate and express himself? Would this invitation be gratefully received and enhance his self-image, or would it be perceived as a demand for achievement? If the client enters the meeting room silently with averted eyes, is he hoping for a warmly inviting greeting from the group leader or is he asking that his hostility be accepted without comment? The answers to these questions depend on a knowledge of the client's history, psychic structure, dynamics, and so on (Rosenthal, 1977).

If the worker has an understanding of the group members' dynamics, he varies his interventions according to where the members are psychosocially and according to the state of their transferences and resistance patterns.

Psychoanalytically oriented group treatment has been helpful for certain clients with marital problems. When husband and wife observe that other couples have conflicts similar to theirs, anxiety is reduced. Furthermore, when a couple observes how others resolve a conflict, they can identify with them and thereby increase their own problem-solving repertoire (Sherman, 1956; Hulse, 1956).

Margaret and Harry Rose, a couple in their mid-thirties, were in a marital-couples group. Margaret, according to Harry, was too involved with her mother, and this made him indignant. Margaret acknowledged that she spent a lot of time with her mother but felt that Harry should be more understanding. When Margaret and Harry observed that several other married couples in the group had a similar conflict, they visibly relaxed and began to share their anxieties with the group and the leader.

As other members acknowledged jealousy, Harry for the first time could be open with Margaret; he tearfully spoke of his feeling of rejection. This helped Margaret to say, "You really care about me! I always doubted it. Maybe I don't have to use my mother as a back-up so much anymore!"

Transferences emerge in a group as they do in individual therapy and in all therapies. In a group they are multiple: An individual can be experienced as a mother by one member, as a father by another, and as a sibling by still another. Similarly, that individual often "finds" parents and siblings in the group. Usually the leader is experienced as a mother or father. As the individual sees how he distorts perceptions in the group, he can begin to appreciate how he distorts other interpersonal relationships.

In a therapy group of college students, Arthur, aged twenty-one, was extremely critical of the group therapist, a woman. When several other men and women in the group became irritated with Arthur because "you are always collecting injustices," Arthur argued with them and said, "You are trying to force me to love her." When the therapist said, "Perhaps you are afraid to love me as you were afraid to love your mother," Arthur, with the group's help, could begin to realize that by being provocative he was defending against sexual feelings toward the therapist that scared him.

In sum, from a psychoanalytic perspective the use of groups seems to be best indicated for clients whose difficulties lie in their social and interpersonal relationships. In a group they can examine their interactions with peers and locate which forms of interaction lead to conflictful or estranged relationships. The psychoanalytically oriented group therapist studies clients' ego capacities to ascertain whether a group will be a constructive experience for them. With his knowledge of the members' histories, unconscious fantasies, and psychic structures, the group leader can help to stimulate the kind of interaction that will enable the members to unravel neurotic distortions and unresolved transferences.

INTERVENTION IN COMMUNITIES AND ORGANIZATIONS

One of the unfortunate schisms in social work that has not been resolved is the ongoing debate that engages social planners and clinicians. The clinician is often perceived by community-oriented workers as one who relates exclusively to his or her client's unconscious and is not concerned with environmental conditions that have an important role in the client's distress. Just as this is a distortion of the clinician's role, many direct-service practitioners have obfuscated the orientations of social planners and pejoratively charged that they are unconcerned with clients' inner feelings.

While psychoanalysis has always propounded the notion that people change, learn, and mature as a result of their interpersonal and social relationships, for many years this insight was almost exclusively applied to the two-person system of psychotherapy. However, the use of the total environment is a deliberate attempt to include all realtionships for the benefit of the client is a logical extension of this orientation (Kraft, 1966).

Sullivan (1949) and Menninger (1936) were among the first psychoanalytically oriented practitioners to move in the direction of using the patient's environment as part of the therapy. In mental hospitals, both of them created a favorable array of interpersonal relationships for each patient by prescribing attitudes for the staff to adopt. For example, the prescription of "kind firmness" by the doctor as an attitude for all staff to assume in their interactions with a depressed patient involved manipulation of the patient's interpersonal and social environment.

In many hospitals, children's residential treatment centers, and schools it has increasingly become the practice to use aspects of the environment, including the talents of staff, to enrich the client's or patient's interpersonal life. Occupational therapy, group discussions, and patient and student councils are all examples of attempts to create a favorable milieu for the client or patient.

In the 1950s Maxwell Jones (1953) originated the term "therapeutic community" to designate the involvement of the total social structure of the treatment unit in the helping process. His notion became very popular; and educational institutions (Farnsworth, 1966), day hospitals (Zwerling, 1966), and clinics and social agencies (Tannenbaum, 1966) became increasingly concerned with the social and interpersonal mechanisms that enhanced or interfered with treatment.

Whether he is connected with a treatment institution or not, the psychoanalytically oriented social worker can make an important contribution to an organization's manifest purposes. In a school or college he can expose some of the dynamics in staff conflicts and in conflicts between instructors and students. As he calls attention to the psychological needs of the students, he can demonstrate how certain institutional facilities such as dormitories, libraries, or cafeterias may or may not be helping them.

A psychoanalytically oriented social worker in a public welfare program can help the staff better understand the psychological problems of economically deprived clients—e.g., their trust-mistrust problems, their terror in assuming autonomy or taking initiative. With his knowledge of what individuals need to resolve life tasks, he can also be instrumental in exposing the deleterious effects of poor housing and slum neighborhoods. Finally, he can be instrumental in stimulating counseling and therapeutic programs—so dreadfully lacking in public welfare.

Whether in a school system or a public welfare program, the psychoanalytically oriented social worker can be helpful in effecting system change in a number of ways:

In Stevenson High School, which was in a depressed area of the community, there were gang fights, truancy, vandalism, and a host of other social and interpersonal problems. The morale of the staff was low; the teachers' absentee record was almost as poor as the students'. The principal of the school often appeared helpless, or else he would frequently handle the school's problems by behaving sadistically with parents, students, and teachers.

The worker assigned to Stevenson decided first of all to meet with the principal and help him ventilate his anger. As he did so, the worker acknowledged the legitimacy of the anger, and concomitantly praised and supported some of the principal's professional strengths. After a rise in the principal's self-esteem the worker suggested that both of them meet with groups of teachers.

A similar process occurred with the teachers. Their angers were discharged, their helplessness was responded to with empathy, and their strengths as teachers were supported. Eventually they could begin to identify with the angers and feelings of deprivation the students experienced.

The students were helped by the principal and teachers to take some responsibility in the governance of the school. They were helped to form a council, start a school newspaper, have parties at the school, and create liaison committees with the principal, the parents, and the community.

A PTA was organized and parents were invited to be student aides and tutors. Merchants gave contributions to improve facilities, and over a two-year period the school's morale improved greatly. Delinquent acts of students declined, the principal began to enjoy his job, and staff apathy was virtually eradicated.

Psychoanalysis as a therapy has limited possibitilies in intervention with communities, particularly when the communities consist of people who are more action-oriented than verbal. However, as a science that describes and explains behavior it can contribute toward increased understanding of problems in morale (as at the Stevenson School), tense interpersonal relations, and the malfunction of an authority structure.

In recent years social work has placed increasing emphasis on the worker's responsibility in intervening in the client's environment—schools, legal aid offices, hospitals, and so on—and roles like social broker and advocate have become popular. Where psychoanalysis can be useful is in helping the worker decide whether or not being the client's advocate will advance the client maturationally. Will it foster dependence, which will result in the client losing self-esteem, or will it eventually help the mistrustful client to trust? Answering questions like these helps the worker to manipulate the client's environment more scientifically.

While psychoanalysis makes its best contribution to the understanding and treatment of the individual, together with other perspectives like system theory, role theory, and ego psychology it can be of assistance to the social worker who is involved in parent-child guidance, marital counseling, family therapy, and work with groups and communities.

Chapter 6

Psychoanalysis and Research

Results of Psychoanalytically Oriented
Psychotherapy

Modern psychotherapy traces its beginnings to the pioneering work of Sigmund Freud. It is a tribute to his genius that he was able to discern from his patients' accounts a meaning, continuity, and logic that had escaped the attention of his predecessors. In many ways the past seventy years have been devoted to the verification and elaboration of Freud's hypotheses (Strupp, Fox, and Lesser, 1969).

Although psychoanalytically oriented psychotherapy has been subjected to evaluation on numerous occasions, and although the classical studies in the literature report that between 50 and 70 percent of the patient have terminated treatment markedly improved (Fenichel, 1930; Jones, 1936; Alexander, 1937; Knight, 1941; Ferenczi, 1955; Feldman, 1968), these research results have been questioned. Because of the absence of control groups and the possible bias of the investigators, who, because of their psychoanalytic orientation, may have wanted to prove that the treatment is effective, many clinicians and researchers have challenged the results of psychoanalytic research (Eysenck, 1965; Briar and Miller, 1971; Fischer, 1976).

Jerome Frank has pointed out that the analytically oriented therapist has considerable emotional involvement in his methods: "His self-esteem, status, and financial security are linked to its effectiveness. Under these circumstances he can hardly be expected to be an impartial student of his own method, and any data he reports cannot escape the suspicion of bias" (1961, p. 226).

Eysenck (1965) has been the most vociferous proponent of the thesis that psychotherapy, particularly psychoanalytic psychotherapy, is totally ineffective. He has even said that in certain cases, psychoanalytic therapy is harmful to the patient. Eysenck's work, even though it purports to have a scientific bent, reveals his own predilections in favor of behavior-modification therapy, and his findings have been questioned by a number of authors (Kubie, 1965; Zetzel, 1965).

Problems in Clinical Research

Although it is frequently averred by psychoanalysts, social workers, and other clinicians that every therapist should become a good "consumer of research" and a firm believer in its necessity and value (Wallerstein, 1971; Rosenblatt, 1968; Briar and Miller, 1971) there are many problems in performing effective clinical research.

The first problem in doing research on treatment begins with deciding what ails the client or patient. Because it is so difficult to accurately describe the nature of maladaptive behavior, it is a difficult task to collect a group of clients with similar problems so that the influence of a given treatment can be scientifically evaluated. A second problem is in defining the exact nature of the intervention utilized (the independent variable). Finally, the researcher is frustrated by the reluctance of many therapists to have their results examined. Some therapists assert, often correctly, that such an examination interferes with the confidentiality of the patient-therapist relationship (Halleck, 1977).

A logic-tight, comprehensive, and objective demonstration of the therapeutic results of psychoanalytic treatment or psychoanalytically oriented psychotherapy is probably impossible. The number of variables involved inevitably present an onerous and virtually impossible task for the scientific statistician (Hendrick, 1963).

Chassan (1967) has pointed out that the problems of documentation in psychoanalysis "appear more formidable than in less sophisticated approaches" in which the observation of manifest affect and behavior represent the main foci of investigation and in which dynamic interpretations and inferences of a theoretical nature play a minimal role.

> For example, when the patient expresses hostility toward the therapist, there are presumably much more direct and specific behavioral manifestations than when he evinces phallic strivings. The latter must be inferred from trends in the patient's free associations and the total context of impulse and defense constellations. (Bellak, Salk, and Rosehan, 1961, p. 371)

Strupp has pointed out that in any evaluation of psychotherapy there are "multiple perspectives to be considered." At least three interested parties are concerned with the outcome of psychotherapy: (1) society (significant persons in the patient's life); (2) the individual patient; and (3) the mental health professional (Strupp, 1977). These parties define mental health "in terms of certain unique purposes" and will evaluate the outcome of therapy in terms of their predilections.

Nor are assessments by patients of their own therapy always reliable. During the course of treatment they are apt to evaluate it in terms of their current transference position, which is usually in a state of flux. The retrospective conviction of the patient that his treatment was successful is a more valuable criterion, but not to be advanced as final. Having invested a considerable amount of time, energy, and often money in a treatment program, many patients have to insist that the experience was worthwhile.

Although patients' intimate friends and family are in a position to observe changes that accrue from psychoanalysis and psychotherapy, their opinions are not always reliable either. The alteration of some aspects of a personality that were previously pleasing to friends and family may produce a markedly negative evaluation of the therapy. For example, a tightly knit group of women may severely criticize the "change" in an analyzed friend who has become less responsive to their enthusiasms and hobbies since heterosexual life and the prospects of a happy marriage and motherhood have come to dominate her conscious attitudes. A husband who enjoyed controlling his wife's activities may miss this pleasure and declare his wife worse after therapy, oblivious to the fact that the happiness he derives from her increased tenderness and consideration is also the result of her therapy.

While we have suggested that analysts and other therapists have as natural an inclination as other human beings to overesteem their own work, several writers have contended that psychoanalytically oriented therapists can evaluate the work of colleagues with great objectivity (Fine, 1971; Strupp, 1977; Hendrick, 1963). Hendrick has said that analytic colleagues "are in a position to appraise all aspects of therapy as no other critics are. They [can evaluate] the details of each patient's previous experience, even those which he has most scrupulously concealed from his intimates. The analyst does not need to compare the lives of the patients with some personal theory of what [a person] should be, for he can compare the actual lives of a series of patients before and after analysis in every detail" (1963, p. 37).

When one applies the rules of scientific observation to clinical research, the problems once again seem manifold. Scientific observation is usually characterized by three properties:

1. It is *systematic*. While haphazard and chance observations happen in science and important discoveries have occurred this way (e.g., penicillin), they are rare. In science, systematic observations are guided by a specific hypothesis, which organizes observations and links them to specific concerns.

2. It is *recorded*. Systematic observations must be recorded and not left to the fallibility of human memory.

3. It is *controlled*. Various checks are applied to observations with respect to precision, objectivity, reliability, and validity so that the question "Does the specific intervention cause the change in the client or would it have occurred without the intervention?" can be answered with some confidence.

Let us now look at the standard clinical situation and discuss the problems of systematizing, recording, and controlling.

SYSTEMATIZING

What should be observed in the clinical situation? The scientist would like to reply "everything," but as we discussed earlier in this chapter, it is impossible to observe everything. In psychotherapeutic research we must *select* variables relevant to a hypothesis concerning the problem under study. Suppose our hypothesis postulates something about the patient's anxiety in interviews. Since anxiety is an affect directly observable only to the person experiencing it, how can the observer be sure when he sees it or does not see it? He may assign units of motor, verbal, affective, and autonomic behaviors which indicate the presence of anxiety, but the observer may be noting the presence of something else besides anxiety when he uses these referents and the validity of the experiment is then doubtful. Also, it is virtually impossible to measure anxiety quantitatively and problems of reliability then emerge.

RECORDING

It is well known by psychoanalysts and other therapists that note taking during the time of treatment harms the therapy: The therapist must withdraw some of his attention, and the patient inevitably assumes that the notes are more important to the therapist than what he or she is feeling and thinking.

Yet it has been long recognized that there is always a considerable amount of distortion even when a therapist reports his observations and activity minutes after the session has been terminated (Fine, 1971). Some researchers feel that tape or television recordings obviate the problems of retrospective falsification that occur in reporting. However, being on TV or tape certainly does influence the productions of both therapist and patient, and this dimension of the therapeutic interaction cannot be rejected as a variable that influences the outcome of the therapy.

CONTROLLING

We said initially that observation begins with a selection based on a tentative hypothesis. The research hypothesis determining our selection operates to *exclude* as well as to include observable features or properties. However, such exclusions may constitute a serious distorting bias. Observations may be collected in a way that favor only one alternative hypothesis. Colby gives an excellent example of this in his book *Psychoanalytic Research* (1960, p. 30).

> Consider the early days of psychosomatic research when some of us were trying to correlate oral dependency with peptic ulcer. In every case of peptic ulcer we looked for oral dependency, neglecting other observations . . . and limited ourselves to the overly simple transitive equation, oral cravings = food craving = gastric hyperactivity. Today we know the problem is more complex, that oral dependency is not a single entity, and that there are no one-to-one correlations between a specific psychic wish and a specific organ activity.

It is important in all research to scrutinize our activity to make sure that we are counting negative as well as positive instances of our hypotheses. One check on self-scrutiny consists of having multiple independent observers. The assumption underlying the use of independent observers is that they are capable of truly independent judgments about reality. However, as several writers have observed (Strupp, 1977; Colby, 1960), and as we have also suggested earlier in the chapter, observers might agree only because they share the same conceptual biases and not because of what exists in external reality.

Besides flaws of distortion in recording, controlling, and systematizing psychotherapeutic events, there are flaws of omission. Often so many events occur with such split-second rapidity that an analyst or therapist cannot note them all, especially when he is under pressure to make some therapeutic response. Also, at these moments he is too close to the events to judge their relative long-run significance, so that his selection may result in serious omissions (Colby, 1963).

THE MEASUREMENT PROBLEM

One of the most difficult dimensions of research in social work and psychotherapy is the problem of measurement. If one looks solely at external behavior, there is little problem. For example, Briar and Miller (1971), behaviorists in social work, have stated that goals and objectives should be "symptom-oriented" and posed in such a manner that their attainment is measurable. Thus they contend:

> A youngster who, for whatever reasons, is judged to be a problem because he will not attend school can be thought of as successfully treated when his school attendance becomes reasonably frequent. A child who suffers from enuresis is "cured" when he no longer wets himself. The case of an impotent man can be closed when he experiences erections. An unemployed father is satisfactorily treated when he obtains and holds gainful employment. (pp. 168–69)

For those social workers who view the human being as a more complex biological, psychological, and social organism, measurement poses considerable problems. If the social worker-researcher believes that hopes, dreams, emotions, fantasies, and other internal states are important data, then his research activities must take these phenomena into account.

In order to appraise social work activity scientifically, particularly the dynamic nature of human change, the internal environment must be considered to be an "intervening variable." Some social workers and other professionals, particularly those of a behavioristic orientation, feel very squeamish about such a notion. MacCorquodale and Meehl (1948) have stated that one often observes "tough minded" practitioners using terms such as "unobservable" and "hypothetical" in an essentially derogatory manner, and "an almost compulsive fear" of passing beyond the directly observable data.

In a sense, once we start dealing with intervening variables, the whole fabric of behaviorism becomes radically altered.

> If we must rely on inference again, why should we eliminate introspective data? Introspection after all leads to another series of inferences, which can then be collated with behavioral data. But then the original argument of behaviorism, that we should only deal with observables, obviously collapses.... Thus behaviorism when pushed to its conclusion, as has been done, leads to an inherent logical contradiction. If we confine ourselves to purely objective data, we cannot explain them. And if we try to explain them we get away from pure objectivity.... The behavioristic position rests upon certain essential misconceptions of scientific theory and scientific method. The crucial role of inner psychological data cannot be denied. (Fine, 1960, p. 93)

The difficulty with much research on human beings, and with social work research in particular, is that it must take full account of introspective data. If one human being asks another a question, the answer is a variable one. It depends on the question, the relationship between the questioner and questionee, and many other factors. If a person introspects, the nature and meaning of his findings are variable, and these two empirical observations of variability, easily subject to confirmation, form the heart of the measurement problem.

Few theories, with the exception of psychoanalytic theory, take into full account the measurement problem. As has been demonstrated in previous chapters, this perspective allows for internal motives and recognizes that what a subject tells the experimenter in an experiment (whether the experiment be written questionnaires or oral interviews) depends on the relationship between the two—i.e., transference and countertransference reactions.

Unless motivation of the subjects is taken into account in research experiments, the observations will be contaminated. The fact that certain types of behavior can be enumerated while motives cannot does not mean that solid research should dispense with such as important dimension of the human being.

Because so many examinations of social work practice have failed to include an appraisal of the client's internal evaluation of his own transference to the agency and the social worker, and an appraisal of the relationship between the subject of the research and the investigator (e.g., H. Meyer, 1965; Brown, 1968), the results from the research have to be questioned. This does not necessarily mean that the social work activity that was judged ineffective should be declared effective or vice versa; but much of the research done in social work has not taken into sufficient account pertinent intervening variables that effect outcome and the client's perception of it.

CLINICAL SKILLS AND RESEARCH

In effective psychotherapy and social work treatment the client achieves gains that are subjective and usually, if not always, defy quantification. Such gains include interpersonal competence, mastery of life situations, and concomitant increments in self-esteem (Strupp, 1972). Furthermore, when patients or clients report that they have been helped, they experience qualities in their therapists that cannot be statistically analyzed with confidence—nonpossessive warmth, genuineness, and empathy that convey the message "I am with you" (Truax, 1973).

It would appear that the only effective method of evaluating the results of psychoanalytic therapy (and perhaps any therapy) is to interview the client. In this follow-up, the interviewer and the client study the client's reactions to the interviewer as well as to the therapist who helped him. When the client is helped to examine in detail modifications in his circumstances, internally and externally, then change (for better or worse) can be trusted with some confidence.

Fine, in concluding that the only way to evaluate the results of psychotherapy is a clinical one, has stated:

> At the present time no available statistical technique can provide a substitute for clinical judgment. Even the American Psychoanalytic Association, which organized a gigantic fact-finding undertaking in 1952, pursuing a routine statistical course with diagnosis, outcomes, and so on, was faced with the increased meaninglessness of its results. The committee was so embarrassed by its work that it waited more than ten years to publish even a preliminary report. (1971, p. 274)

A psychoanalytic orientation to research that seeks to understand the most individual features of the person and that "shuns the statistical handling of human beings" (Alexander, 1960) has been receiving support from a variety of psychotherapy and social science researchers. For example, Labov and Fanshel have noted: "There is now good precedent for an intense scrutiny of a single case, both within the history of therapy and in the history of science in general. We believe that such microanalysis is a necessary prelude to useful generalizations" (1977, p. 8).

Allen Bergin, a well-known researcher in psychotherapy, has stated:

> Experimental designs and inferential statistics have little relevance to the study of clinical problems in the currently primitive state of therapeutic technologies. Most of the methodological sophistication I learned as a graduate student and postdoctoral fellow and which is constantly reinforced by the criteria of major journal editors is too precise, too demanding of controls, too far advanced for most studies of clinical intervention. I am convinced by experience that... the experimental case study, the intensive analysis of a limited range of phenomena, is correct and appropriate for the field in its present stage of evolution. Most of our studies of clinical phenomena suffer from weak results dictated by overly heterogeneous samples, a divergent aggregate of interven-

tions and measurements too imprecise to keep the margin of error in our definitions of syndromes and of change within reasonable limits. (Bergin and Strupp, 1972, pp. 452–53)

In a paper, "A Procedure for Evaluating the Results of Psychoanalysis," Pfeffer (1959) describes a procedure that consists essentially of follow-up interviews with an analyzed patient by a second analyst several years after the termination of the analysis. The interviews take place once a week for about six weeks. According to Pfeffer, this procedure appears to elicit the necessary information for an adequate evaluation of the results of an analysis. The treating analyst provides the interviewing analyst with information about the patient according to a questionnaire concerning the initial and emerging problems, the course of the analysis, the formulation of the patient's central problems, what was achieved analytically and therapeutically, and predictions as to what the patient's status in regard to these various problems will be at the time of the follow-up study. The information from the treating analyst is not read by the follow-up analyst until just before the final follow-up interview, thus adding to the opportunity for an unbiased point of view.

Another elaborate research program has been set up by Robert Wallerstein (1963) at the Menninger Clinic. The number of cases studied has been small, but each one has been studied intensively and meticulously. Strupp et al. (1969), in their book *Patients View Their Psychotherapy*, intensively studied two sizable samples of patients who were treated by psychoanalytically oriented therapists at the psychiatric outpatient clinic of a major university. As in most studies of psychoanalytically oriented therapy, about two-thirds of the patients, according to the patients' own accounts, improved substantially in many areas of functioning.

Social Work, Psychoanalysis, and Research

It would appear that follow-up interviews with clients by a second social worker attuned to and knowledgeable about psychosocial functioning, interpersonal and intrapsychic dynamics, and transference and resistance phenomena can produce valuable research results. This procedure when tried in social work appears to elicit the necessary information for an adequate evaluation of the effects of social work intervention (Hollis, 1976; Weissman and Paykel, 1974; Beck and Jones, 1973).

Many of the therapeutic modalities that have been discussed in this text could be subjected to research investigation by conducting follow-up interviews. For example, instead of having clients fill out forms after they have received short-term treatment, crisis intervention, or task-oriented casework, in which they focus on a narrow range of changes in "target complaints," intensive follow-up interviews could be conducted with them. Many of the questionnaires that focus on target complaints fail to provide a complete assessment of the impact of the therapy on the totality of the client's life (Strupp, 1977).

Inasmuch as social work is a form of intervention that deals with the person-in-the-situation, it would also be useful to conduct follow-up interviews not only with the client but with significant others and with the treating social worker. To achieve a more scientific orientation to social work research it would also be helpful to interview clients, significant others, and workers before, during, and after the interventions.

Since one-third of social work applicants leave the agency prematurely, usually after the first or second interview (Perlman, 1960), it would be of enormous assistance to practitioners to conduct in-depth follow-up interviews with these clients. Follow-up interviews with the social workers involved—focusing on transference and countertransference reactions, and resistance and counter-resistance phenomena—might also be helpful.

Frequently in social work research there has been a failure to establish goals against which change can be measured. It is a well-known principle of research that if one is trying to examine the effects of a given procedure one must first ascertain that the given procedure has actually been employed in the cases being studied (Hollis, 1972). Here a psychoanalytic orientation can be helpful. Which ego functions will be strengthened and through which procedures? Will certain id wishes be made conscious and through which kinds of intervention? If the environment will be manipulated, how will this affect the transference?

Social work research is still at the stage of generalized studies in which only a small proportion of the individuals studied along a given dimension have actually been offered the type of treatment presumably being studied. Researchers often fail to design their studies so that the worker can identify specific goals against which progress can be measured (Hollis, 1972).

THE INEFFECTIVENESS OF SOCIAL WORK INTERVENTION

When social work treatment has been found to be ineffective, critics have frequently alleged that the major variable accounting for treatment failure is the worker's psychoanalytic orientation (Fischer, 1976; Mahoney and Mahoney, 1974; Briar and Miller, 1971; Ackerman, 1958). As was suggested in Chapter 1, psychoanalysis as described in this text has frequently been incompletely mastered and misused by social workers. Many social workers fail to comprehend the complex metapsychology and therapeutic implications of writers like Sigmund and Anna Freud, Hartmann, and Erikson. Notions like psychosocial and psychosexual development, transference, resistance, and the corrective emotional experience are frequently half-understood and abused.

An example of a misapplication of psychoanalytic theory is the many economically poor and psychologically depressed clients who are gratified and indulged, i.e., patronized in the manner of the friendly visitor of Mary Richmond's day. A full grasp of the client's psychodynamics would prompt the worker to try to resolve the client's resistances against expressing aggression toward everything he distrusts, including his social worker and the profession of social work.

Because many social workers have unresolved countertransference problems and therefore frequently desire to have "love and be loved" relationships with their clients, they cannot provide many of the depressed, angry, and impoverished clients with what they frequently need—an opportunity to express distrust and hatred and actively test the worker for long periods of time. Only after such an opportunity can the very suspicious and angry client learn to love and be productive.

Social work intervention that understands the client-in-the-situation, that relates to the client's pressures and stresses, that notes and helps the client with maturational tasks, and that provides a controlled treatment relationship with full respect given to the client's fixations, regressions, and transference responses can and does enrich psychosocial functioning.

While psychoanalysis has its limitations, it is already clear that a psychoanalytically oriented psychotherapy is effective. Despite the fact that most people come to a therapist only when they have become desperate, and that both the selection and the training of therapists leave much to be desired, there is evidence that individuals who undergo psychoanalytic therapy move toward what Fine (1971) has called the "analytic ideal": They can love more genuinely, seek pleasure in life, have sexual gratification, express their emotions yet be guided by reason, have a role in the family, have a sense of identity, be constructive, be able to work, be creative, have a role in the social order, be able to communicate, and be free of symptoms.

The social worker should have much of the knowledge of the psychoanalyst and something else besides. He or she not only needs to know the details of the client's environment but is also called upon to meet a much wider range of problems than the analyst. It is necessary to treat people afflicted with everything from severe character disorders to psychoses, many of whom would founder on the analyst's couch. Furthermore, the social worker frequently has to work in an atmosphere of immediacy; it is often impossible to wait days or weeks for verification of data. In the face-to-face therapy that the social worker conducts, it is not easy to rely on the defense of anonymity as a shield. The social worker must be "for real" as well as for fantasy, and the demands made upon him or her are always great.

References

ACKERMAN, N. 1958. *The Psychodynamics of Family Life*. New York: Basic Books.

ALEXANDER, F. 1960. *The Western Mind in Transition*. New York: Random House.

_____. 1937. *Five-Year Report of the Chicago Institute for Psychoanalysis*. Chicago: Chicago Institute for Psychoanalysis.

AUSTIN, L. 1958. "Dynamics and Treatment of the Client with Anxiety Hysteria." In *Ego Psychology and Dynamic Casework,* ed. H. J. Parad. New York: Family Service Association of America.

_____. 1948. "Trends in Differential Treatment in Social Casework." *Social Casework,* vol. 29.

BANDLER, B. 1963. "The Concept of Ego-Supportive Psychotherapy." In *Ego-Oriented Casework,* ed. H. J. Parad and R. R. Miller. New York: Family Service Association of America.

BARBARA, D. 1958. *The Art of Listening*. Springfield, Ill.: Charles C Thomas, Publisher.

BATESON, G.; JACKSON, D.; HALEY, J.; WEAKLAND, J. 1956. "Toward a Theory of Schizophrenia." *Behavioral Science,* vol. 1.

BEATMAN, F. 1956. "Casework Treatment of Marital Problems: Evolution of Treatment Methods." In *Neurotic Interaction in Marriage,* ed. V. Eisenstein. New York: Basic Books.

BECK, D.; JONES, M. 1973. *Progress on Family Problems*. New York: Family Service Association of America.

BELLAK, L.; SALK, L.; ROSEHAN, D. 1961. "A Process Study of the Effects of Deprol on Depression." *Journal of Nervous and Mental Diseases,* vol. 132.

BENJAMIN, A. 1974. *The Helping Interview,* 2nd ed. Boston: Houghton Mifflin Co.

BENSMAN, J.; VIDICH, A. 1957. "The Future of Community Life: A Case Study and Reflections." In *Psychoanalysis and the Future,* ed. B. Nelson. New York: National Psychological Association for Psychoanalysis.

BERGIN, A.; STRUPP, H. 1972. *Changing Frontiers in the Science of Psychotherapy*. New York: Aldine Publishing Co.

BERNARD, V. 1953. "Application of Psychoanalytic Concepts to Adoption Agency Practice." In *Psychoanalysis and Social Work,* ed. M. Heiman. New York: International Universities Press.

BERRON, L. 1944. "Fathers as Clients of a Child Guidance Clinic." *Smith College Studies in Social Work,* vol. 14.

BERTHELSDORF, S. 1976. "Survey of the Successful Analysis of a Young Man Addicted to Heroin." In *The Psychoanalytic Study of the Child,* vol. 31, ed. R. Eissler. New Haven: Yale University Press.

BLANCK, R.; BLANCK, G. 1968. *Marriage and Personal Development*. New York: Columbia University Press.

BOLTON, C. 1961. "Mate Selection as the Development of a Relationship." *Marriage and Family Living,* vol. 23, no. 4.

BORENZWEIG, H. 1971. "Social Work and Psychoanalytic Theory" *Social Work,* vol. 16, no. 1.

BOWLBY, J. 1951. *Maternal Care and Mental Health*. Geneva: World Health Organization.

BRENNER, C. 1976. *Psychoanalytic Technique and Psychic Conflict*. New York: International Universities Press.

————. 1955. *An Elementary Textbook of Psychoanalysis*. New York: International Universities Press.

BREUER, J.; FREUD, S. 1936. *Three Contributions to the Theory of Sex*. New York: Nervous and Mental Disease Publishing Co.

BRIAR, S.; MILLER, H. 1971. *Problems and Issues in Social Casework*. New York: Columbia University Press.

BROWN, G. 1968. *The Multiproblem Dilemma.* Metuchen, N.J.: Scarecrow Press.

BURGUM, M. 1942. "The Father Gets Worse: A Child Guidance Problem." *American Journal of Orthopsychiatry,* vol. 12.

CAMERON, N. 1963. *Personality Development and Psychopathology.* New York: Houghton Mifflin Co.

CHASSAN, J. 1967. *Research Design in Clinical Psychology and Psychiatry.* New York: Appleton-Century-Crofts.

COLBY, K. 1960. *Psychoanalytic Research.* New York: Basic Books.

COLM, H. 1970. "Phobias in Children." In *New Approaches in Child Guidance,* ed. H. Strean. Metuchen, N.J.: Scarecrow Press.

DAVIDSON, P.; COSTELLO, C. 1969. *N = 1: Experimental Studies of Single Cases.* New York: Van Nostrand Reinhold Co.

DESPERT, J. 1965. *The Emotionally Disturbed Child—Then and Now.* New York: Robert Brunner.

DEUTSCH, F. 1953. "The Application of Psychoanalysis to Psychosomatic Aspects." In *Psychoanalysis and Social Work,* ed. M. Heiman. New York: International Universities Press.

DEVEREUX, G. 1939. "Maladjustment and Social Neurosis." *American Sociological Review,* vol. 4, no. 6.

DORN, R.; SIGALL, M. 1977. "Political Science and Psychoanalysis." *Psychoanalytic Review,* vol. 64, no. 2.

EIDELBERG, L. 1956. "Neurotic Choice of Mate." In *Neurotic Interaction in Marriage,* ed. V. Eisenstein. New York: Basic Books.

EISENSTEIN, V. 1956. "Sexual Problems in Marriage." In *Neurotic Interaction in Marriage,* ed. V. Eisenstein. New York: Basic Books.

EISSLER, K. 1965. *Medical Orthodoxy and the Future of Psychoanalysis.* New York: International Universities Press.

————. 1947. "Objective Criteria of Recovery from Neuropsychiatric Disorders." *Journal of Nervous and Mental Disease,* vol. 106, no. 5.

EKSTEIN, R. 1977. "Normality and Pathology in Marriage." *Modern Psychoanalysis,* vol. 2, no. 1.

ENGLISH, O. B.; PEARSON, G. H. 1945. *Emotional Problems of Living.* New York: W. W. Norton & Co.

ERIKSON, E. 1968. *Idnetity: Youth and Crisis.* New York: W. W. Norton & Co.

_____. 1964. *Insight and Responsibility*. New York: W. W. Norton & Co.

_____. 1959. *Identity and the Life Cycle*. New York: International Universities Press.

_____. 1950. *Childhood and Society*, 1st ed. New York: W. W. Norton & Co.

EYSENECK, H. 1965. "The Effects of Psychotherapy." *International Journal of Psychiatry*, vol. 1.

FALCK, H. 1977. "Interdisciplinary Education and Implications for Social Work Practice." *Journal of Education for Social Work*, vol. 13, no. 2.

FARNSWORTH, D. 1966. "Educational Psychiatry." In *American Handbook of Psychiatry*, vol. 3, ed. S. Arieti. New York: Basic Books.

FEDERN, P. 1952. *Ego Psychology and the Psychoses*. New York: Basic Books.

FELDMAN, F. 1968. "Results of Psychoanalysis." *Journal of the American Psychoanalytic Association*, vol. 16.

FELDMAN, Y. 1958. "A Casework Approach Toward Understanding Parents of Emotionally Disturbed Children," *Social Work*, vol. III.

FENICHEL, O. 1945. *The Psychoanalytic Theory of Neuroses*. New York: W. W. Norton & Co.

_____. 1930. *Zehn Jahre Berliner Psychoanalytisches Institute*. Berlin: Berlin Psychoanalytic Institute.

FERENCZI, S. 1955. "The Problem of the Termination of the Analysis." In *Final Contributions to the Problems and Methods of Psychoanalysis*. New York: Basic Books.

_____. 1950. *Sex in Psychoanalysis*, vol. 1. New York: Basic Books.

FINE, R. 1975. *Psychoanalytic Psychology*. New York: Jason Aronson.

_____. 1973. "Psychoanalysis." In *Current Psychotherapies*, ed. R. Corsini. Itasca, Ill.: F. E. Peacock, Publishers.

_____. 1971. *The Healing of the Mind*, New York: David McKay.

_____. 1968. "Interpretation: The Patient's Response." In *Uses of Interpretation in Treatment: Technique and Art*, ed. E. Hammer. New York: Grune & Stratton.

_____. 1960. "The Measurement Problem." *The Psychoanalytic Review*, vol. 47, no. 3.

FISCHER, J. 1976. *The Effectiveness of Social Casework*. Springfield, Ill.: Charles C Thomas, Publisher.

FOULKES, S. 1964. *Therapeutic Group Analysis*. New York: International Universities Press.

FRANK, J. 1961. *Persuasion and Healing*. Baltimore: Johns Hopkins Press.

FREED, A. O. 1977. "Social Casework: More Than a Modality." *Social Casework,* vol. 58, no. 4.

FREUD, A. 1965. *Normality and Pathology in Childhood*. New York: International Universities Press.

_____. 1951. "Observations of Child Development." *The Psychoanalytic Study of the Child,* vol. 6. New York: International Universities Press.

_____. 1937. *The Ego and the Mechanisms of Defense*. London: Hogarth Press.

FREUD, S. 1959. "Psychoanalytic Notes on an Autobiographical Account of a Case of Paranoia." In *Collected Papers of Sigmund Freud,* vol. 3. New York: Basic Books.

_____. 1953. "On Narcissism." Vol. 14, *Standard Edition*. London: Hogarth Press.

_____. 1950. *The Question of Lay Analysis*. New York: W. W. Norton & Co.

_____. 1949. "Further Recommendations in the Technique of Psychoanalysis." In *Collected Papers of Sigmund Freud,* vol. 2. London: Hogarth Press.

_____. 1948. "Instincts and Their Vicissistudes." In *Collected Papers of Sigmund Freud,* vol. 4. London: Hogarth Press.

_____. 1939 (1953). *An Outline of Psychoanalysis*. Vol. 23, *Standard Edition*. London: Hogarth Press.

_____. 1938. *The Basic Writings of Sigmund Freud*. New York: Random House (Modern Library).

_____. 1937. *Constructions in Analysis*. Vol. 23, *Standard Edition*. London: Hogarth Press.

_____. 1933. *New Introductory Lectures on Psychoanalysis*. Vol. 22, *Standard Edition*. London: Hogarth Press.

_____. 1930. *Civilization and Its Discontents*. London: Hogarth Press.

————. 1926. *Inhibitions, Symptoms, and Anxiety.* Vol. 20, *Standard Edition.* London: Hogarth Press.

————. 1925. *An Autobiographical Study.* Vol. 20, *Standard Edition.* London: Hogarth Press.

————. 1923. *The Ego and the Id.* Vol. 19, *Standard Edition.* London: Hogarth Press.

————. 1922. *Group Psychology and the Analysis of the Ego.* New York: Liveright Publishing Corp.

————. 1914a. "Introduction to Narcissism." Vol. 12, *Standard Edition.* London: Hogarth Press.

————. 1914b. "Remembering, Repeating, and Working Through," *Standard Edition,* Vol. 12. London: Hogarth Press.

————. 1913a. *The Disposition to Obsessional Neurosis.* Vol. 12, *Standard Edition.* London: Hogarth Press.

————. 1913b. *Totem and Taboo.* Vol. 12, *Standard Edition.* London: Hogarth Press.

————. 1912. *The Dynamics of Transference.* Vol. 12, *Standard Edition.* London: Hogarth Press.

————. 1910. "The Future Prospects of Psychoanalytic Therapy." Vol. 11, *Standard Edition.* London: Hogarth Press.

————. 1909. "Analysis of a Phobia in a Five-Year-Old Boy." Vol. 10, *Standard Edition.* London: Hogarth Press.

————. 1905. *Three Essays on the Theory of Sexuality.* Vol. 7, *Standard Edition.* London: Hogarth Press.

————. 1904. *Freud's Psychoanalytic Procedure.* Vol. 7, *Standard Edition.* London: Hogarth Press.

————. 1900. *The Interpretation of Dreams.* Vol. 4, *Standard Edition.* London: Hogarth Press.

GARRETT, A. 1958. "Modern Casework: The Contribution of Ego Psychology." In *Ego Psychology and Dynamic Casework,* ed. H. J. Parad. New York: Family Service Association of America.

————. 1940. "Contributions of Freud to Casework." *The Family,* vol. 20, no. 1.

GLASER, K.; EISENBERG, L. 1955. "Maternal Deprivation." *Pediatrics,* vol. 18, no. 2.

GLOVER, E. 1958. "Ego Distortion." *International Journal of Psychoanalysis,* vol. 39.

_____. 1955. *The Technique of Psychoanalysis.* New York: International Universities Press.

_____. 1949. *Psychoanalysis.* London: Staples Press.

GOLAN, N. 1978. *Treatment in Crisis Situations.* New York: Free Press.

GREENHILL, M. 1976. "Fifty Years of American Psychiatry." *Research Communications in Psychology, Psychiatry and Behavior,* vol. 1, no. 2.

GREENSON, R. 1967. *The Technique and Practice of Psychoanalysis.* New York: International Universities Press.

GRUNEBAUM, H. 1962. "Group Psychotherapy of Fathers: Problems of Technnique." *British Journal of Medical Psychology,* vol. 35.

_____; STREAN, H. 1970. "Some Considerations on the Therapeutic Neglect of Fathers in Child Guidance." In *New Approaches in Guidance,* ed. H. Strean. Metuchen, N.J.: Scarecrow Press.

HALLECK, S. 1977. "Can We Fit the Treatment to the Patient? Current Methodological and Theoretical Problems." *Bulletin of the Menninger Clinic,* vol. 41, no. 4.

HAMILTON, G. 1958. "A Theory of Personality: Freud's Contribution to Social Work." In *Ego Psychology and Dynamic Casework,* ed. H. Parad. New York: The Family Services Association of America.

_____. 1951. *Theory and Practice of Social Work.* New York: Columbia University Press.

_____. 1947. *Psychotherapy in Child Guidance.* New York: Columbia University Press.

HARTMANN, H. 1964. *Essays on Ego Psychology.* New York: International Universities Press.

_____. 1951. *Ego Psychology and the Problem of Adaptation.* New York: International Universities Press.

HEIMAN, M. 1956. "The Problem of Family Diagnosis." In *Neurotic Interaction in Marriage,* ed. V. Eisenstein. New York: Basic Books.

HELLENBRAND, S. C. 1972. "Freud's Influence on Social Casework." *Bulletin of the Menninger Clinic,* vol. 36, no. 4.

HENDRICK, I. 1963. "Therapeutic Results of Psychoanalysis." In *A Handbook of Psychoanalysis,* ed. H. Herma. New York: World Publishing Co.

HERMA, J. 1968. "The Therapeutic Act." In *Use of Interpretation in*

Treatment: Technique and Art, ed. E. Hammer. New York: Grune & Stratton.

HOBBS, N. 1968. "Sources of Gain in Psychotherapy." In *Use of Interpretation in Treatment: Technique and Art,* ed. E. Hammer. New York: Grune & Stratton.

HOLLIS, F. 1976. "Evaluation: Clinical Results and Research Methodology." *Clinical Social Work,* vol. 4, no. 3.

––––––. 1972. *Casework: A Psychosocial Therapy,* 2nd ed. New York: Random House.

––––––. 1964. *Casework: A Psychosocial Therapy,* 1st ed. New York: Random House.

HULSE, W. 1956. "Group Psychotherapy." In *Neurotic Interaction in Marraige,* ed. V. Eisenstein. New York: Basic Books.

JACKSON, D. 1957. "The Question of Family Homeostasis." *Psychiatric Quarterly,* vol. 31.

JONES, E. 1936. *Decennial Report of the London Clinic of Psychoanalysis.* London: London Clinic of Psychoanalysis.

JONES, M. 1953. *The Therapeutic Community: A New Treatment Method in Psychiatry.* New York: Basic Books.

JOSSELYN, I. M. 1948. *Psychosocial Development of Children.* New York: Family Service Association of America.

KADUSHIN, A. 1972. *The Social Work Interview.* New York: Columbia University Press.

KAHN, A. 1973. *Shaping the New Social Work.* New York: Columbia University Press.

KALINKOWITZ, B. 1971. "An Ideal Training Program for Psychotherapists: Contributions from Clinical Psychology." In *New Horizon for Psychotherapy,* ed. R. Holt. New York: International Universities Press.

KAPLAN, L. 1953. "Foster Home Placement." In *Psychoanalysis and Social Work,* ed. M. Heiman. New York: International Universities Press.

KARDINER, A. 1945. *The Psychological Frontiers of Society.* New York: Columbia University Press.

––––––. 1939. *The Individual and His Society.* New York: Columbia University Press.

KAUFMAN, I. 1958. "Therapeutic Considerations of the Borderline Personality Structure." In *Ego Psychology and Dynamic Casework*, ed. H. J. Parad. New York: Family Service Association of America.

KNIGHT, R. P. 1953. "Borderline States." *Bulletin of the Menninger Clinic*, vol. 17, no. 1.

_____. 1952. "An Evaluation of Psychotherapeutic Techniques." In *Psychoanalytic Psychiatry and Psychology*, ed. R. Knight and C. Friedman. New York: International Universities Press.

_____. 1941. "Evaluation of the Results of Psychoanalytic Therapy." *American Journal of Psychiatry*, vol. 94.

KNOEPFMACHER, L. 1942. "The Use of Play in Diagnosis and Therapy in a Child Guidance Clinic." *Smith College Studies in Social Work*, vol. 12.

KRAFT, A. 1966. "The Therapeutic Community." In *The American Handbook of Psychiatry*, vol. 3, ed. S. Arieti. New York: Basic Books.

KUBIE, L. 1965. "Discussion of Eysenck Paper." *International Journal of Psychiatry*, vol. 1.

_____. 1956. "Psychoanalysis and Marriage: Practical and Theoretical Issues." In *Neurotic Interaction in Marriage*, ed. V. Eisenstein. New York: International Universities Press.

LABOV, W.; FANSHEL, D. 1977. *Therapeutic Discourse: Psychotherapy as Conversation*. New York: Academic Press.

LANGS, R. 1976. *Theapeutic Interaction*, vol. 1. New York: Jason Aronson.

LASSWELL, H. 1930. *Psychopathology and Politics*. Chicago: University of Chicago Press.

LITTLE, M. 1960. "Countertransference." *British Journal of Medical Psychology*, vol. 33.

LOVE, S.; MAYER, H. 1970. "Going Along with Defenses in Resistive Families." In *New Approaches in Child Guidance*, ed. H. Strean. Metuchen, N.J.: Scarecrow Press.

LUTZ, W. 1964. "Marital Incompatibility." In *Social Work and Social Problems*, ed. N. Cohen. New York: National Association of Social Workers.

LYNCH, J. J. 1977. *The Broken Heart*. New York: Basic Books.

MACCORQUODALE, K.; MEEHL, P. 1948. "Hypothetical Constructs and Intervening Variables." *Psychological Review,* vol. 55.

MACLEOD, J. 1963. "Some Criteria for the Modification of Treatment Arrangements." In *Ego-Oriented Casework,* ed. H. Parad and R. Miller. New York: Family Service Association of America.

MAHONEY, K.; MAHONEY, M. 1974. "Psychoanalytic Guidelines for Child Placement." *Social Work,* vol. 19, no. 6.

MARCUS, K.; FRANCIS, J. 1975. *Masturbation from Infancy to Senescence.* New York: International Universities Press.

MENNINGER, K. 1958. *Theory of Psychoanalytic Technique.* New York: Basic Books.

MENNINGER, W. 1936. "Psychiatric Hospital Therapy Designed to Meet Unconscious Needs." *American Journal of Psychiatry,* vol. 93.

MEYER, C. 1976. *Social Work Practice: The Changing Landscape.* New York: Free Press.

MEYER, H. 1965. *Girls at Vocational High.* New York: Russell Sage Foundation.

MITTELMANN, B. 1956. "Analysis of Reciprocal Neurotic Patterns in Family Relationships." In *Neurotic Interaction in Marriage,* ed. V. Eisenstein. New York: Basic Books.

MILLER, S. 1963. "Poverty and Inequality in America." *Child Welfare,* vol. 42, no. 9.

MONEY-KRYLE, R. 1956. "Normal Countertransference and Some of Its Deviations." *International Journal of Psychoanalysis,* vol. 37.

———. 1944. "Some Aspects of Political Ethics from the Psychoanalytic Point of View." *International Journal of Psychoanalysis,* vol. 25.

MONTAGU, A. 1956. "Marriage: A Cultural Perspective." In *Neurotic Interaction in Marriage,* ed. V. Eisenstein. New York: Basic Books.

NEUBAUER, P. 1972. "Psychoanalysis of the Preschool Child." In *Handbook of Child Psychoanalysis,* ed. B. Wolman. New York: Van Nostrand Reinhold Co.

———. 1960. "The One-Parent Child and His Oedipal Development." In *The Psychoanalytic Study of the Child,* vol. 15. New York: International Universities Press.

———. 1953. "The Psychoanalyst's Contribution to the Family

Agency." In *Psychoanalysis and Social Work,* ed. M. Heiman. New York: International Universities Press.

ORMONT, L. 1976. "Group Resistance and the Therapeutic Contract." In *From Group Dynamics to Group Psychoanalysis,* ed. M. Kissen. New York: Halsted Press.

PARAD, H. 1965. *Crisis Intervention.* New York: Family Service Association of America.

PERLMAN, H. 1970. "Casework and 'the Diminished Man.'" *Social Casework,* vol. 22.

_____. 1968. *Persona: Social Role and Personality.* Chicago: University of Chicago Press.

_____. 1960. "Intake and Some Role Considerations." *Social Casework,* vol. 41.

_____. 1957. *Social Casework: A Problem Solving Process.* Chicago: University of Chicago Press.

PERRY, S. 1958. "The Conscious Use of Relationship with the Neurotic Client." In *Ego Psychology and Dynamic Casework,* ed., H. J. Parad. New York: Family Service Association of America.

PFEFFER, A. 1959. "A Procedure for Evaluating the Results of Psychoanalysis." *Journal of the American Psychoanalytic Association,* vol. 7.

PINCUS, A.; MINAHAN, A. 1973. *Social Work Practice: Model and Method.* Itasca, Ill.: F. E. Peacock Publishers.

POLLAK, O. 1956. *Integrating Sociological and Psychoanalytic Concepts.* New York: Russell Sage Foundation.

PUMPHREY, M. 1956. "Mary Richmond and the Rise of Professional Social Work in Baltimore: The Foundations of a Creative Career." Ph.D. diss., Columbia University School of Social Work.

RAPAPORT, D. 1951. *The Organization and Pathology of Thought.* New York: Columbia University Press.

RAPAPORT, R., 1963. "Normal Crisis, Family Structure, and Mental Health." *Family Process,* vol. 2, no. 1.

REICH, A. 1951. "On Countertransference." *International Journal of Psychoanalysis,* vol. 32.

REID, W.; EPSTEIN, L. 1972. *Task-Oriented Casework.* New York: Columbia University Press.

RENNE, D. 1977. "The Infertility Problem." *Child Welfare,* vol. 56, no. 7.

RICHMOND, M. 1917. *Social Diagnosis.* New York: Russell Sage Foundation.

RIESMAN, D. 1958. *Constraint and Variety in American Education.* New York: Doubleday & Co. (Anchor Books).

RIESSMAN, F.; COHEN, J.; PEARL, A. 1964. *The Mental Health of the Poor.* New York: Free Press.

ROAZEN, P. 1976. *Erik H. Erikson: The Power and Limits of a Vision.* New York: Free Press.

———. 1968. *Freud: Political and Social Thought.* New York: Alfred A. Knopf.

ROGERS, C. 1951. *Client-Centered Therapy.* Boston: Houghton Mifflin Co.

ROSEN, V. 1956. "Changes in Family Equilibrium Through Psychoanalytic Treatment." In *Neurotic Interaction in Marriage,* ed. V. Eisenstein. New York: Basic Books.

ROSENBLATT, A. 1968. "The Practitioner's Use and Evaluation of Research." *Social Work,* vol. 13, no. 1.

———. 1962. "The Application of Role Concepts to the Intake Process." *Social Casework,* vol. 43.

ROSENTHAL, L. 1977. "Qualifications and Tasks of the Therapist in Group Therapy with Children." *Clinical Social Work,* vol. 5, no. 3.

———. 1971. "Application of Small Groups to Casework Practice and Theory." In *Social Casework: Theories in Action,* ed. H. Strean. Metuchen. N.J.: Scarecrow Press.

SANDLER, J; DARE, C.; HOLDER, A. 1973. *The Patient and the Analyst.* New York: International Universities Press.

SCHAFER, R. 1977. "The Interpretation of Transference and the Conditions for Loving." *Journal of the American Psychoanalytic Association,* vol. 25, no. 7.

SCHEIDLINGER, S. 1976. "On the Concept of the 'Mother Group.'" In *From Group Dynamics to Group Psychoanalysis,* ed. M. Kissen. New York: Halsted Press.

SEARLES, H. 1965. *Collected Papers on Schizophrenia and Related Subjects.* New York: International Universities Press.

SHAPIRO, S. 1976. *Moment of Insight.* New York: International Universities Press.

SHARPE, E. 1947. "The Psychoanalyst." In *Collected Papers on Psychoanalysis.* London: Hogarth Press.

SHERMAN, S. 1956. "Group Counseling." In *Neurotic Interaction in Marriage,* ed. V. Eisenstein. New York: Basic Books.

SHYNE, A. 1957. "What Research Tells Us About Short-Term Cases in Family Agencies." *Social Casework,* vol. 38.

SIPORIN, M. 1975. *Introduction to Social Work Practice.* New York: Macmillan Co.

SLAVSON, S. 1964. *A Textbook in Analytic Group Psychotherapy.* New York: International Universities Press.

————. 1950. *Analytic Group Psychotherapy.* New York: Columbia University Press.

————. 1948. "Play Group Therapy for Young Children." *The Nervous Child,* vol. 7.

————. 1943. *An Introduction to Group Therapy.* New York: Commonwealth Fund.

SOBEL, R. 1953. "The Contribution of Psychoanalysis to the Residential Treatment of Adolescents." In *Psychoanalysis and Social Work,* ed. M. Heiman. New York: International Universities Press.

SPITZ, R. 1965. *The First Year of Life.* New York: International Universities Press.

SPOTNITZ, H. 1969. *Modern Psychoanalysis of the Schizophrenic Patient.* New York: Grune & Stratton.

STAMM, I. 1972. "Family Therapy." In *Casework: A Psychosocial Therapy,* vol. 2, ed. F. Hollis. New York: Random House.

————. 1959. "Ego Psychology in the Emerging Theoretical Base of Casework." In *Issues in American Social Work,* ed. A. J. Kahn. New York: Columbia University Press.

STARK, F. 1959. "Barriers to Client-Worker Communication at Intake." *Social Casework,* vol. 40, no. 4.

STEIN, H.; CLOWARD, R. 1958. *Social Perspectives on Behavior.* Glencoe, Ill.: Free Press.

STERNBACH, O. 1947. "Arrested Ego Development and Its Treatment in Conduct Disorders and Neuroses of Childhood." *The Nervous Child,* vol. 6.

Strean, H. 1978. *Clinical Social Work, Theory and Practice.* New York: Free Press.

————, ed. 1976. *Crucial Issues in Psychotherapy.* Metuchen, N.J.: Scarecrow Press.

Strean, H. 1976a. "A Note on the Treatment of the Schizophrenic Patient." In *Crucial Issues in Psychotherapy,* ed. H. Strean. Metuchen, N.J.: Scarecrow Press.

————. 1976b. "Some Psychological Problems in Psychoanalytic Training." In *Crucial Issues in Psychotherapy,* ed. H. Strean. Metuchen, N.J.: Scarecrow Press.

————. 1976c. "Is the Psychoanalytic Model Obsolete?" In *The Effectiveness of Social Casework,* ed. J. Fischer. Springfield, Ill.: Charles C Thomas, Publisher.

————. 1974. *The Social Worker as Psychotherapist.* Metuchen, N.J.: Scarecrow Press.

————. 1970. *New Approaches in Child Guidance,* Metuchen, N.J.

Strupp, H. 1977. *Psychotherapy for Better or Worse: The Problem of Negative Effects.* New York: Jason Aronson.

————. 1972. "Ferment in Psychoanalysis and Psychotherapy." In *Success and Failure in Psychoanalysis and Psychotherapy,* ed. B. Wolman. New York: Macmillan Co.

————; Fox, R.; and Lesser, K. 1969. *Patients View Their Psychotherapy.* Baltimore: The Johns Hopkins Press.

Sullivan, H. 1953. *The Interpersonal Theory of Psychiatry.* New York: W. W. Norton & Co.

————. 1949. "Psychiatry: An Introduction to the Study of Interpersonal Relations." In *A Study of Interpersonal Relations.* New York: Hermitage Press.

Szurek, S.; Berlin, I. 1973. *Clinical Studies in Childhood Psychoses.* New York: Brunner/Mazell.

Tannenbaum, G. 1966. "The Walk-In Clinic." In *The American Handbook of Psychiatry,* vol. 3. New York: Basic Books.

————; Fox, Ronald E.; Lessler, Ken. 1969. *Patients View Their Psychotherapy.* Baltimore: Johns Hopkins Press.

THOMAS, E. 1977. *Marital Communication and Decision Making: Analysis, Assessment and Change.* New York: Free Press.

TRAUX, C. 1973. "Effective Ingredients in Psychotherapy." In *Creative Developments in Psychotherapy,* ed. A. Mahrer and L. Pearson. New York: Jason Aronson.

TURNER, S. M. 1963. "A Group Approach to Clients with Ego Defects." In *Ego-Oriented Casework,* ed. H. J. Parad and R. R. Miller. New York: Family Service Association of America.

VAN DEN HAAG, E. 1963. *Passion and Social Constraint.* New York: Stein & Day.

VINTER, R. 1965. "Social Group Work." In *Encyclopedia of Social Work.* New York: National Association of Social Workers.

WAELDER, R. 1941. "The Scientific Approach to Casework with Special Emphasis on Psychoanalysis. *Journal of Social Casework,* vol. 22.

WALLERSTEIN, R. 1971. "The Role of Research Training: How Much, What Kind, How?" In *New Horizon for Psychotherapy.* New York: International Universities Press.

———. 1963. "The Problem of the Assessment of Change in Psychotherapy." *International Journal of Psychoanalysis,* vol. 44.

WASSERMAN, S. 1974. "Ego Psychology." In *Social Work Treatment,* ed. F. Turner. New York: Free Press.

WEINBERGER, J. L. 1958. "Basic Concepts in Diagnosis and Treatment of Borderline States." In *Ego Psychology and Dynamic Casework.* New York: Family Service Association of America.

WEISSMAN, M; PAYKEL, E. 1974. *The Depressed Woman.* Chicago: Univeristy of Chicago Press.

WINNICOTT, D. 1965. *The Family and Individual Development.* London: Tavistock Publications.

WITMER, H. 1942. *Social Work: An Analysis of a Social Institution.* New York: Rinehart and Co.

WOOD, K. 1971. "The Application of Psychoanalysis and Ego Psychology to Social Casework." In *Social Casework: Theories in Action,* ed. H. Strean. Metuchen, N.J.: Scarecrow Press.

WYLIE, H.; DELGADO, R. 1959. "A Pattern of Mother-Son Relationship Involving the Absence of the Father." *American Journal of Orthopsychiatry,* vol. 29, no. 3.

ZETZEL, E. 1965. "Discussion of Eysenck." *International Journal of Psychiatry*, vol. 1.

ZILBACH, J. 1968. "Family Development." In *Modern Psychoanalysis*, ed. J. Marmor. New York: Basic Books.

ZWERLING, I. 1966. "The Psychiatric Day Hospital." In *The American Handbook of Psychiatry*, vol. 3. New York: Basic Books.

Index

Index